Papers on Indian Writing In English

Papers on Indian Writing In English

Second Revised and Enlarged Edition

VOLUME 2 : FICTION

A.N. DWIVEDI

ATLANTIC

PUBLISHERS & DISTRIBUTORS (P) LTD

Published by
ATLANTIC
PUBLISHERS & DISTRIBUTORS (P) LTD
7/22, Ansari Road, Darya Ganj, New Delhi-110002
Phones : +91-11-40775252, 40775214, 23273880, 23275880
Fax: +91-11-23285873
Web: www.atlanticbooks.com
E-mail: orders@atlanticbooks.com

First Edition: 1991
Second Edition: 2002

Printed & bound in India by Atlantic Print Services

PREFACE TO THE SECOND EDITION

I feel immense pleasure in placing the second revised and enlarged edition of this book into the hands of the readers. Needless to add, this is a collection of critical essays and papers prepared by me over the years. But for the keen interest taken by my publishers, especially Dr. K.R. Gupta, Managing Director of M/s Atlantic Publishers and Distributors, New Delhi, this edition would not have seen the light of the day.

A.N. DWIVEDI

PREFACE TO THE FIRST EDITION

This is the second volume of my *Papers on Indian Writing in English,* comprising some thirty seven-papers of mine written over the years. As the first part was exclusively devoted to Indian Poetry in English (from its beginning to the present day), this second part deals with Indian English Fiction. Nowadays, Indian Writing in English has acquired a certain respectability and popularity both in India and abroad, and hence scholars and researchers in this area will find this book quite useful and rewarding.

The papers called herein are mostly author-based and text-based. Those which do not attempt a survey of a particular period or form concentrate on a certain author or text. Personally, I am of the firm view that critics and reviewers should now pay greater heed to non-major writers and virgin areas like Short Story and Literary Criticism (in Indian English). So many studies have already been made on 'the Big Three' or on major writers and popular areas. Temperamentally, I am damn against 'big bossism' in any form and in any area, — maybe, because of a newly awakened democratic consciousness. One good point of text-based studies is that they bring out the strengths or weaknesses of a particular text in a notable manner.

A.N. DWIVEDI

CONTENTS

1

INDIAN FICTION IN ENGLISH : RETROSPECT AND PROSPECT*

I. A BACKWARD GLANCE

Indian fiction in English, like other branches of Indo-English literature, originated and grew up under the tutelage of Britishers. The first Indian novel in English, Bankim Chandra Chatterjee's *Rajmohan's Wife*, appeared in 1864 and created a history whose roots have gone deep enough by this day. It was in 1792 that Charles Grant, one of the Directors of the East India Company, had pleaded to make the English language 'a vehicle for imparting Western ideas,' but Grant's plea could materialize only with the active support of Raja Ram Mohan Roy and Lord Macaulay. The monumental *Minute* of Macaulay prepared in 1833 provided for the adoption of English as the medium of instruction in schools and colleges, saying 'the English tongue is that which would be the most useful to our native subjects.' English was, as a result, introduced in educational institutions and important offices and judicial courts, dislodging the age-old customs and traditions of Sanskrit or Arabic study. It was supposed to open up fresh avenues of thought and culture, art and literature, science and technology, and hence was strongly backed by progressive thinkers like Thakur Dwarka Nath Tagore, Keshub Chandra Sen, Raja Ram Mohan Roy and the followers of the Brahmo Samaj. The announcement of Lord William Bentinck dated 7th March,

---

* First published in *Studies in Contemporary Indian Fiction in English*, ed. A.N. Dwivedi (Allahabad : Kitab Mahal, 1987), pp. 3-30.

1835, favouring 'English education alone' and 'a knowledge of English literature and science through the medium of the English language', sealed the fate of the native vernaculars and offered a fresh fillip to the growth and expansion of English in India. The exemplary work of the Christian missionaries — Carey, Ward and Marshman (the founders of the Serampore College, 1818), Lewis Rice, Cotter, Brown, F.E. Key, Nicol Macnicol and a host of others — proved decisive in channelising the course of education and literature in this renascent country. Of the three factors operating forcefully towards the crystallization of a perplexing and fluid situation, the perseverance of the Christian missionaries finds a merited description in one of Prof. K.R.S. Iyengar's critical works on Indo-English literature.[1] The Wood Dispatch of 1854 proclaimed the establishment of the Universities of Bombay, Calcutta and Madras and thereby rendered English accessible to a large number of students, professors, intellectuals, and administrators. The time was now ripe for "India's political and cultural renaissance", as Prof. Mehta puts it.[2]

In the wake of this 'renaissance', the floodgates of English were thrown open to the whole of India. The learning of English was thought to be a matter of proud privilege; it produced not only 'learners' and 'babus' (clerks) but also poets and creative writers. The latter could write it with ease and command, though they still looked to the West for their models — to Sir Walter Scott and Charles Dickens, to Balzac, Hugo and Dumas, in particular. Bengalis took lead in the matter and did the spadework for the origin and growth of Indian fiction in English in the late nineteenth and early twentieth centuries.

We have already mentioned Bankim's contribution to this *genre* — *Rajmohan's Wife*, which was a romantic story of domestic life set in a Bengal village, advocating the virtue of renunciation over self-love for the attainment of freedom from slavery. Bankim's ardent patriotism finds an articulate voice in his Bengali novels too — in his *Anandamath* (1882), *Kapalkundala* (1885), *Durgeshnandini* (1890) and *Krishnakantar*

Uyil (1895). Bankim (1838–1894) reigned supreme in his lifetime as "the literary dictator of renascent Bengal."[3]

Meanwhile, some other Bengalis also became active in writing novels. Raj Lakshmi Devi published her novel, *The Hindu Wife*, in 1876; Toru Dutt, an 'exotic blossom of song,' experimented with this form in Bianca, or *The Young Spanish Maiden* (1878); and Kali Krishna Lahiri's *Roshinara* came out in 1881; H. Dutt produced his *Bijoy Chand* in 1888; and Khetrapal Chakravarti's *Sarata* and *Hingana* appeared in 1895. All these novels, but for *Bianca*, have little literary merit in them.

The beginning of the twentieth century witnessed a gradual growth of the fictional form. One of the significant novelists of this time was Romesh Chunder Dutt (1848–1909), who adorned some important Government posts before retiring into the service of Baroda State as its Dewan for some time. He produced six novels in Bengali, two social and four historical ones, out of which he translated two into English : *The Lake of Palms*, 1902 (its Bengali title being *Sansar*), and *The Slave Girl of Agra*, 1909 (its Bengali heading being *Madhvi Kankan*). Of these two novels, *The Lake of Palms* is a tale of Indian domestic life wherein the author makes a spirited plea for the re-marriage of widows. Herein the hero, Sarat, ultimately succeeds in marrying a young widow, Sudha, but only after experiencing a considerable trouble and disappointment. *The Slave Girl of Agra*, a historical romance, paints the life of love, intrigue and jealousy during the Moghul period. Both the novels of Romesh published in London have admirably woven plots and depict their characters vividly.

Romesh left his mark on a number of writers who followed him, especially on T. Ramkrishna who wrote *The Dive for Death* and on Mrs. Swarna Kumari Ghoshal who wrote *The Fatal Garland*. Some others continued in their works the social reformist zeal of Romesh Chunder; for example, Krupabai Satthianandan in *Kamala, a Story of Hindu Life* (1894), Bal Krishna in *The Love of Kusuma* (1910), Sir Jogendra Singh in *Nasrin* (1915), Rajam Iyer in *Vasudeo Sastri* (1905), and A. Madhavan in

Thillai Gobindan (1916). These novelists and their works are merely historically valuable, and they display very little originality and authenticity. In his *Kamala* (1925) and *Kamini* (1931), Sir Jogendra Singh raises his powerful voice against the tabooed, custom-ridden Indian society. The first-named novel is actually a romance of a hill girl who was kidnapped by the agent of a king, but the second one is a quite serious work attempting to emphasise the evils of caste system in our country. Kamini's unrequited love for her Christian tutor finds release in her tragic death, and tutor-lover starts imparting education to women as a measure of expiration. The didactic note of the novel is so conspicuous in the story.

One distinguished name to be mentioned here is that of Rabindranath Tagore, a prolific writer with at least two hundred songs, several plays and numerous novels to his credit. This would be a mere repetition of a self-evident truth to state that Tagore, who hailed from an aristocratic and affluent Bengali family, wrote most of his works originally in Bengali, but some of his novels have since been rendered into English — *The Home and the World* (1919), *The Wreck* (1921) and *Gora* (1923), all of which are socially relevant and thought-provoking. Through these novels, Tagore has conjured up the vision of a modern India. The first one depicts the story of Nikhil, his wife Bimala, and his close friend Sandip, having the undercurrents of psychological portrayal and political consciousness. The second one, like the first, is again a social story highlighting in unequivocal terms the vexed problem of marriage. And the third one is a patriotic novel, a political novel articulating vigorously the hopes and aspirations of the resurgent India. *Gora* is definitely one of the most-liked, finished products of Tagore, and adds to his literary immortality like his celebrated *Gitanjali* (1913).

The tormenting problem of marriage is also articulated, though in a subdued tone, in *Indira Devi* (1931) of A. Subramanyam, — here the problem arising from the love of an Indian woman for an Englishman. The same problem in a different shape — the re-marriage of child-widows — is ventilated in Dewan

Sharar's *The Gong of Shiva* (1939). V.V. Chintamani's novel, *Vedantam : A Clash of Traditions* (1928), and Hari Singh Gaur's *His Only Love* (1930) also dwell on the hapless, helpless conditions of the younger generation plagued by the evils of conservative and arranged marriages. Another work focusing on this problem is K. Nagarajan's *Athwar House* (1939), which details the social changes wrought by the Indian renaissance. Kumara Guru's *Life Shadows* (in 2 Vols., 1938 & 1944) shows the gradually tightening grip of English education upon the Indian family life, shattering the age-old traditions of the joint family system. His second work, *A Daughter's Shadow* (1944), is no better than the first.

II. THE BIG THREE

The time was now ripe for the emergence of a few talented writers of Indo-English fiction, — of the writers who could lift this form to international status and universal recognition. The three names usually mentioned in literary circles in this context are : Mulk Raj Anand (1905), R.K. Narayan (1906), and Raja Rao (1909). They are known as 'The Big Three,' an epithet coined by the noted English critic, William Walsh.[4] The enthusiastic critic may be quoted at some length here :

> There is no doubt that there has always been a remarkable quality of first rate Indian work in English in scholarship, philosophy, autobiography, religion, and especially in politics. Gandhi and Nehru themselves were both in their different styles masters of an oratorical idiom. But it was not till the 1930s that a number of novelists began to write in English — genuine novelists that is, for whom fiction is an end in itself and not a means for communication of other kinds of truth. Some forty years later it is clear that this was the form peculiarly suited to the Indian sensibility, and the one to which Indian writers have made a distinct and significant contribution.[5]

Speaking of 'the Big Three,' Walsh writes :

> It is these three writers who defined the area in which the Indian novel was to operate. They established its assumptions, they sketched its main themes, freed the first models of its characters, and elaborated its peculiar logic. Each of them used an easy, natural idiom which was unaffected by the opacity of a British inheritance. Their language has been freed of the foggy taste of Britain and transferred to a wholly new setting of brutal heat and brilliant light. [6]

Of these three novelists, Mulk Raj Anand is wholeheartedly devoted to the simple life of villagers, whose poverty and caste-feeling touch him deeply. He is equally concerned with orphans, untouchables, and urban labourers, and in this he is not much different from Dickens and Wells. There is a strong touch of humanism in his writings; he comes out in them as a 'semi-Marxist' and a social reformist. Even politics and propaganda are not excluded. His Lalu trilogy consisting of *The Village* (1939), *Across the Black Waters* (1940) and *The Sword and the Sickle* (1942), and the most recent work, *The Seven Ages of Man* (still in the process of publication), display the man behind his writing, and in them we have unmistakable confessional strands and leanings. Anand has, by now, traversed a long course of journey in the realm of fiction (we know, he began his career with *Untouchable* in 1939), and has consolidated his position unshakably.

R.K. Narayan whose first novel, *Swami and Friends*, appeared in 1935 is the most unpretentious and unassuming novelist. He always creates a convincing situation to suit his characters who move about and live in the limited region of Malgudi, recalling immediately Thomas Hardy to our minds. This small South Indian town — "a blend of oriental and pre-1914 British" — imposes structural limits on Narayan's novels, but its also tends to provide them with textural cohesion and unity, leaving little space for digressions and ramblings. Narayan is the truest artist who does not bother about social or political doctrines, nor is he bothered about the contemporaneity of his subject-matter. Sex does not make an appealing theme to him. With the possible exception of *Mr. Sampath*, all his novels are invariably qualitative and well-executed. Narayan writes in a lucid and simple style and prefers easy and natural expressions to intricate and complex ones (in this he is essentially different from Raja Rao). In *Waiting for the Mahatma* (1955), he does accommodate the 'Quit India' movement, but elsewhere he does not concentrate on political affairs. *The Dark Room* (1938) deals with the miserable life of an Indian woman, Savitri, in the compassionless company of her husband, Ramani. *The Financial Expert* (1952) and *The Guide* (1958) are the two grand successes of Narayan as a novelist. Of the two, the first one graphically portrays the rise and fall of Margayya as the financial agent, while the second one depicts the romantic and dubious role of Raju as the guide of tourists like Professor Marco and his wife Rosie (later the beloved of Raju). Narayan's comic propensity stands him in good stead and saves him sufficiently from an undue interference in the affairs of his creations. It is this that renders him a detached observer of human life and activities. This also keeps him distinct and distinguished from other Indo-English novelists.

Raja Rao, whose fictional corpus is very meagre as compared to that of Mulk Raj Anand or R.K. Narayan, makes "a remarkable triad,"[7] as Prof. Iyenger puts it. He has produced just four novels and two collections of short stories to date : *Kanthapura* (1938), *The Serpent and the Rope* (1960), *The Cat and Shakespeare* (1995), and *Comrade Kirillov* (1976 — all novels), *The Cow of the Barricades* (1947) and *The Policeman & the Rose* (1978). Raja Rao is no committed writer like Mulk Raj Anand, nor is he a carefree, humorous talent like R.K. Narayan. He is rather 'poetic, metaphysical, Lawrentian.' His *Kanthapura* is located in the single South Indian village and told in the traditional way by a grandam. It depicts the impact of Gandhiji and his struggle for national freedom on the villagers led by Moorthy. *The Serpent and the Rope* is Raja Rao's most elaborate and most philosophical work. It has a strikingly individual tone, a curious mixture of 'Indian tenderness and French clarity.' The action, or still better the meditation, moves from India to France to England, and admits a few sharply realized characters, particularly the Southern Brahmin Ramaswamy and his wife Madeleine. *The Cat and Shakespeare* is almost free from the labyrinthine formlessness and metaphysical preponderateness of *The Serpent and the Rope*. It is a *novella* of mere 117 pages, abounding in racial and poetic wisdom. It is cast in the form of a fable, in which the cat-kitten analogy represents the idea of blind surrender to the divine care and Shakespeare stands for the ordinary life of joy and sorrow. The first signifies the ideal world, whereas the second denotes the real world of petty involvements and mysterious relationships. Ramakrishna (the protagonist) and Govindan Nair are the two dominant characters in this novel. The fourth and last novel, *Comrade Kirillov*, has Kirillov, an "Inverted Brahmin" (p. 119), as the central character. What the novelist suggests here is that Kirillov as a Marxist attaches greater importance to the material ends of life than to the spiritual ones as a caste Brahmin. He is all happy and contented until he is swept away by a foreign ideology (Marxism). The novel has, significantly enough, a sub-title — "A New Novel." But there is nothing particularly 'new' in it except the ample use of the structural device of irony which adds vigour and pungency to it.

Now something important about 'the Big Three.' In the first place, the title itself is somewhat pinching and painful, as this exalts a few Indian novelists over a score of others who are presently actively engaged in the production of Indo-English fiction. In the second, this smacks of the anti-India stance of the imperialistic Britishers who vehemently believed in the 'divide-and-rule' policy, which they unsparingly implemented till they were here in India. The most unfortunate thing is that some Indian scholars like Prof. C.D. Narasimhaiah and Prof. K.R. Srinivasa Iyengar also fell into this well-laid trap. I would like to know what tempted them to delimit the number of senior novelists to 'three' only? Why did they exclude Bhabani

Bhattacharya from this list if 'Chronology' was the measuring rod for them? And if the considerations were merit and recognition, why did they leave out a talented novelist like Kamala Markandaya? Why not to swell this number to 'four'? Of course, like 'the Four Wheels' of the English Novel. And if Prof. Narasimhaiah and Prof. M.K. Naik (with due regards to their scholarship) could be overwhelmed by the technical accomplishments of Raja Rao, what has hindered them from according a rightful position to Kamala Markandaya or to Bhabani Bhattacharya? I suggest, the number must be raised in order to properly accommodate these novelists too. Mark further : Raja Rao has painted the turbulent time in India's history, just one generation, in his *Kanthapura*, whereas Kamala Markandaya spans at least three generations of Indian history in her *The Golden Honeycomb* (1977). Why this treatment to her, then? Possibly because she is now an 'inside outsider.' But where does stand Raja Rao, after all?

III. THE OTHER MAIN PROPS

In point of chronology, Bhabani Bhattacharya (born 1906) comes next to those already considered. He has published six novels to this day : *So Many Hungers* (1947), *Music for Mohini* (1952), *He Who Rides a Tiger* (1954), *A Goddess Named Gold* (1960), *Shadow* from *Ladakh* (1966), and *A Dream in Hawii* (1978), and these form no mean achievement for the author.[8] The Sahitya Akademic award to him in 1967 was a befitting recognition of his merits. As a novelist, he deals with the social, economic and political problems of his people, but he also envisions a bright future for them. His attitude largely remains "rational tinged with idealism."[9] His first novel, *So Many Hungers*, highlights the reign of terror let loose by Britishers during pre-Independence days and the equally strong emotional upsurge of the Indian people for national freedom. The protagonist, Baruni Devata, wages a relentless war against famine and injustice, trickery and slavery, and when he is arrested, a young charming girl, Kajoli, took over the mantle of leadership, keeping at bay the hunger of the body. Here we have the noble ideals of self-sacrifice and renunciation for the liberation of the motherland. In *Music for Mohini*, the hero Jayadev, who hails from the Big House of Behula, is concerned with the evolution of a fresh culture for the people of India, — the culture that should bring about a perfect harmony between the old and the new, between the outworn and the living. The clash of values is represented by Mohini (the wife of Jayadev) and Jayadev's mother. In *He Who Rides a Tiger*, Bhattacharya takes us to a study of the misery of the poor and the cruelty of the rich. Kalo of Jharna town, a poor and honest worker, wants his daughter Lekha to settle down happily in life, but he has to encounter so many staggering hardships to realize his dream. The fourth novel, like the first one, attempts to record the importance of freedom, but that freedom which does not allow laziness and inactivity, arson and violence, profiteering and black-marketing. It should rather be the freedom of all from 'ignorance, superstition and poverty.' Mira, the central character, is the symbol of the soul of independent India, just as Atmaram is the symbol of the idealism of Mahatma Gandhi. The novel, *Shadow from Ladakh*, was written in the wake of the Chinese invasion of India in 1962. The novelist seems to suggest here that the Gandhian philosophy of peace and non-violence which suited in the British days was now outmoded due to the need of the hour. Satyajit is an embodiment of the purist Gandhian attitude, and Bhaskar is the epitome of the advancing forces of modernism and industrialism. The vision of Bhaskar saves the ideals of Satyajit without any harm to his own side. We, thus, see that Bhattacharya is a novelist gifted with insight and imagination, — the one who creates engrossing scenes and characters.

Kamala Markandaya (born 1924) is one of those Indo-English fictionists who have ever stuck to the ground. She is highly fecund and productive. The continuity and meritoriousness of her work guarantee her an immortal place among the Indian novelists of this day. And though she is married to Mr. Taylor, a British, she still writes in her maiden name. That definitely demonstrates her deep love of India and her people. She has produced ten novels to this day : *Nectar in a Sieve* (1954), *Some Inner Fury* (1955), *A Silence of Desire* (1960), *Possession* (1963), *A Handful of Rice* (1967), *The Coffer Dams* (1969), *The Nowhere Man* (1972), *Two Virgins* (1973), *The Golden Honeycomb* (1977), and *Pleasure City* (1982). The first three novels have women protagonists, who unfold the web of the narratives : Rukmani in the first, Mira in the second and Sarojini in the third. In the fourth Anasuya, the narrator, is other than the heroine (in it Caroline has that vital position). The central characters very often represent a clash of cultural views. There is not so much the clash of turbulent passions in them as the vehemence of cultural contradictions. The fourth novel, *Possession*, juxtaposes Caroline and the Swamy in their endeavours to have hold on Valmiki. The fifth novel studies the desperate yet heroic struggle of Ravi for his bare survival. His love for Nalini lands him in a disastrous existence, but he sticks to his gun thinking of his domestic responsibilities and moral commitments. *The Coffer Dams* exhibits the impact of science and technology over agrarian India. The spirit of India is embodied in Bashiam, whereas the ratiocination of the West (namely, the British) is signaled by the techno-experts like Clinton and Mackendrick. And the twain meet in the loveful, harmonious relationship of Helen and Bashiam. In *The Nowhere Man*, the sensitive writer throws light on the East-West contact and its harmful effects on the Indians living in England whose typical representative is Srinivas. The next novel, *Two Virgins*, is a contrastive study of the two sisters living in a village : Lalitha and Saroja. The first one is attracted by the glamours of the city, where she disappears in a mysterious fashion, while Saroja loves her village for its natural surroundings and shuns the city. *The Golden Honeycomb* is conceived and executed on a grand scale. Its action is placed in the monarchial State of Devapur. Here the novelist shows her unmistakable sense of History, depicting the life-story of Bawajiraj I, II, and III. She also shows the ascendancy of the commonalty into power whose representative Rabi, the son of an ordinary woman Mohini, is. In her latest novel, *Pleasure City*, Kamala Markandaya artistically portrays a pleasure resort called 'Shalimar' in an isolated fishing village in South India. The East-West theme once again becomes paramount herein, and this is remarkably reflected in the close relationship of Mr. Tully of AIDCORP (the company that undertakes the construction of the 'Pleasure City') and Rikhi, a young native fisher boy. The truth emerging from a study of these novels is that Kamala Markandaya has been one of the most dedicated and sustained writers of fiction. Writing of her distinctive place in contemporary Indo-English novel, S.C. Harrex remarks : "Kamala Markandaya's fiction is of particular interest within the context of the modern Indian novel because it crystallizes various literary directions that the quest for identity has taken since the Thirties."[10] And of these directions, the two dominant ones are : philosophical and sociological. The cross-cultural relationship also forms one of the significant directions in Markandaya's novels.

If Kamala Markandaya is an illustration of an 'inside outsider,' Ruth Prawer Jhabvala (born 1927) is a poignant example of an 'outside insider.' Jhabvala has written a fairly good number of novels: *To Whom She Will* (1955), *The Nature of Passion* (1956), *Esmond in India* (1958), *The Householder* (1960), *Get Ready for Battle* (1962), *A Backward Place* (1965), *A Stronger Climate* (1968), *A New Dominion* (1973), and *Heat and Dust* (1975). In all these novels, Jhabvala is concerned primarily with an analysis of "domestic friction"[11] with an "evaluation of the extent to which the Western culture has pervaded the life of Indians."[12] Throughout her mode of perception remains ironic and satiric, but she does not sacrifice her art at the altar of the tensions arising out of the peculiar situations of characters. She is ever subtle and deep in her writing. Though India attracts her for its 'immense pulse and power,' for its variegated colours of life, she seems to be ill at ease here, and in novel after novel (the locale of which is usually Delhi) she is driven to spotlighting the foibles and failures of this ancient seat of culture. Her characters, especially the Europeans, look upon India as the abode of 'heat and dust,' as the 'backward place,' not unlike the belligerent attitude of V.S. Naipaul, the well-known Caribbean author. Her characters are often drawn from the middle class and with considerable insight.

Among the expatriates, B. Rajan (born 1920) occupies a distinctive position as a creative writer. He is securely established as a critic of Milton, Eliot and Yeats, and has composed a volume of verse, *Damayanti*. His two novels, *The Dark Dancer* (1959) and *Too Long in the West* (1961), are partly autobiographical and partly elitistic. There is too much of Rajan, the refined critic, in them, and their sophistry is well reflected in the language and technique used. It appears, he can't allow his Eliot to have some rest. In his illuminating article, "Dancing in the Dark : Balachandra Rajan and T.S. Eliot."[13] S.C. Harrex has pinpointed the pervasive influence of T.S. Eliot upon this novelist. The charm of Rajan's novels, however, lies in their cross-cultural interaction and in their philosophical outlook upon life. Krishnan in the first and Nalini in the second novel are the central characters, whose main problem is the adjustment in the conservative Indian society after their long training and education, like the novelist's own, in the West.

Khaushwant Singh is another novelist of the fifties. His two novels, *Train to Pakistan* (1956 — published as *Mano Majra* in the U.S.A.) and *I Shall Not Hear The Nightingale* (1959), depict the tragic circumstances leading to India's partition in 1947. There is a thick layer of disenchantment and disillusionment, of bereavement and bewilderment, in them. The vision remains realistic throughout, and the 'communal barbarism' is depicted with a great deal of irony and satire. The style is tough and terse, concise and spare, in both the novels, and it is likely that Singh is influenced by Hemingway in this matter. In the words of Harrex, "Some of Singh's best stylistic effects depend upon vivid accuracy and immediacy of apprehension."[14] The first novel portrays the central characters Iqbal and Juggut with the consummate skill of an artist. Hukum Chand, the magistrate, fails in his duty, and continues to get his bribes and special favours. The time of Singh's second novel is a little earlier — the war years of 1942-43. In it the "failure of a young Westernized

Sikh to act heroically is recapitulated in the story of Sher Singh."[15] Though Sher Singh's father, the magistrate Buta Singh, is selfish and career-oriented, his mother, Sabhrai, is truly selfless and heroic. There are 'peaks of sexual and political excitement' in this novel. Khushwant Singh's down-to-earth realism has induced some scholars to characterize him as 'a novelist without vision' (Chirantan Kulshrestha). The noted critic, Stephen Ignatius Hemingway, remarks that it is better for Singh that he "minimizes his elaboration and dramatization of the nuances behind the facts."[16] And what is more demanding of him is the truth that he, as B. Rajan, should come forth with more novels to show to the literary world that his creative spring has not gone dry.

One of the greatly interesting novelists of modern India is Manohar Malgonkar (born 1913). He is 'interesting' because he does not lose his grip over Indian history and its impact on the resurgent nation. His lens are often fixed on socio-political problems. He has given us the following novels : *Distant Drum* (1960), *Combat of Shadows* (1962), *The Princes* (1963), *A Bend in the Ganges* (1964) and *The Devil's Wind* (1972). The other works, besides these, are either theatrical or espionage thrillers, and hence they do not belong to the domain of fiction proper. The favourite themes of Malgonkar are : Indian history, Indo-British conflict for freedom, native princes and the merger of their states into British empire, non-violence and its relevance in pre-Independent Bharat. Some other subsidiary themes to be had in his novels are : sex, adultery, hunting, military-life, war-operations, and sensational scenes. *Distant Drum* brings to the fore the cemented friendship of Kiran Garud and Abdul despite the unfortunate division of India. *Combat of Shadows* highlights the miserable life of the poor workers of tea plantations in Assam whose loved leader Jugal Kishore is. Though himself corrupt morally, Jugal always incites workers against the Tea Estate Manager, Mr. Henry Winton, who always leads a life of tension and uncertainty. In *The Princes*, the novelist take us to a study of the prince Abhayraj, his royal father, and their delicate relationship with the British. The prince and his father stand for aristocracy, while Kanakchand Gur, one of the proteges of the royal family, represents the advancing forces of nationalism and democracy. Abhay has to abdicate his throne eventually. *A Bend in the Ganges* is a very powerful novel, depicting the terrorist activities before India's independence and the horror, the bloodshed and the butchery of the partition days. Debi Dayal, the bold upright brother of Sundari, is a terror to the Empire; he is tried and deported to the Andamans along with the convict Gian Talwar. At this juncture, the story moves ahead with great sweep and suspense. Later, Debi is killed by the Muslims while returning to the Punjab, while Gian is seen escorting Sundari (and her father) to a safer place. Where is the room for non-violence in such a sad situation? In *The Devil's Wind*, subtitled as Nana Saheb's Story, the heroic activities and daredevilry of Nana Saheb have been presented in a striking fashion. The Britishers used to look upon him as the 'arch-villain,' the monster of Indian Mutiny of 1857-58, but the present generation esteems him as the beacon-light of national struggle for freedom. As a novelist, Malgonkar stands apart from others in his wonderful admixture of fact and fiction, history and imagination. No wonder, then, that *The Times Literary Supplement* of London paid him a deserving compliment, recording that "his novels are conceived on a large scale, they are full of action, they are exciting stories. They are also valuable documents." And Malgonkar always writes against an Indian background. "As a writer, Malgonkar does not suffer from an obsession with the heritage of Indianness, but he knows that to be authentic he has to write from within the Indian ethos and milieu."[17]

Another novelist who earned his immortal reputation through a single book and who adopted the course of humour throughout is G.V. Desani. His work, *All About H. Hatterr* (1948), is a class by itself, wherein the narrator-hero, Mr. Hatterr, half-European and half-Malayan, journeys through life, like James Joyce's creation Stephen Dedalus, beyond the confines of class, creed, profession and continent. In his journey he collects impressions and instructions and presumptions at different places from different people. The language and the narration remain lively everywhere, and they do not allow the reader to feel the tedium of a bulky novel; for example in : 'A man's choice (of words)...is conditioned by his experience... To one, M.P. stands for a Member of Parliament. To another, it might mean, major parasite. Depends on his experience.' There are free coinages and arbitrary uses of language in it. We only wish, the directions shown by Desani were continued in Indo-English fiction, though there is not much hope but for R.K. Narayan in a lesser degree. Commenting on the work of Desani, Prof. Iyengar rightly remarks : "Unquestionably *All About H. Hatterr is a tour de force*, an astonishing feat of verbal legerdemain."[18]

A few promising and talented writers of the fifties, sixties, seventies and eighties have still not figured in this chart : Nayantara Sahgal, Anita Desai, Arun Joshi, and Chaman Nahal in particular. Of these, Nayantara (born 1927), the daughter of well-known Vijaya Lakshmi Pandit and the niece of Pt. Jawaharla Nehru, entered the literary arena with her autobiographical *Prison and Chocolate Cake* (1954), which was followed by a few more : *A Time to Be Happy* (1958), *From Fear Set Free* (1962), *This Time of Morning* (1965), *Storm in Chandigarh* (1969), and *The Day in Shadow* (1971). All these works of Mrs. Sahgal (her husband's name is Gautam Sahgal who lives in Bombay along with the family) display her acute awareness of the political and social issues of India. The first novel narrates the childhood and adolescence of the author. The second tells us about the Gandhian movement of the forties. *From Fear Set Free* pictures the novelist's life after India's independence; its title comes from one of the famous remarks of Mahatma Gandhi. The fourth novel is different from the first three inasmuch as it does not become autobiographical in its content. The action of the novel covers the end of the fifties and the beginning of the sixties, and tends to be highly suggestive and mysterious. The Ministry of External Affairs decides all important matters 'during the morning haze.' The political and official circles are sharply focused, and the characters of Kalyan Singh, Nita Narang and Hari Mohan are graphically portrayed in it. *Storm in Chandigarh* immediately recalls to our minds the vexed and insoluble problem of the division of the Punjab — the problem which is yet a headache for the Government of India. Writing about Mrs. Sahgal, the Russian scholar Elena J. Kalinnikova comments somewhat inadvertently that "Tara which in Hindi means 'Star' entered the scene of Indian literature first with her autobiographical works."[19] The comment is correct in all respects, but it apparently misses to grasp the full meaning and significance of 'Nayantara' which is verily a Hindi word for 'the cynosure of the eye' (as the writer's parents would have liked to call her). *The Day in Shadow* is not different in content from the others.

Anita Desai (born 1937) is one of the established writers of Indo-English fiction. Besides short stories, she has published nine novels to this day : *Cry the Peacock* (1963*), Voices in the City* (1965), *Bye-Bye Blackbird* (1971), *Where Shall We Go This Summer*? (1975), *Fire on the Mountain* (1977), *Clear Light of Day* (1980), *The Village By The Sea* (1983), etc. She got the Sahitya Akademi Award in 1978 on her *Fire on the Mountain*, and was runner in the Booker Prize Award in 1981 for her Novel *Clear Light of Day* (the Award-winner being William Golding, the celebrated writer of the previously published work, *The Lord of the Flies*). Almost all her novels are poetic and lyrical in language, and existential in their treatment of human life. The air which the protagonists, who are mostly women, breathe in is hardly congenial and hygienic. Consequently, they are irresistibly driven from one condition of anxiety and restlessness to another. They seem to be alienated from their family and their surroundings, and prompt the reader to believe that there is a touch of morbidity, a leaven of unredeemable obsession, about them : such are Maya, Monisha, Sita, Nanda Kaul, Bim, etc. Even the male characters like Nirode and Dev and Adit are no better than them. From artistic view-point, *Clear Light of Day* should be thoroughly assessed *vis-a-vis* Golding's *Rites of Passage* (the Booker Prize Winner). *The Village by the Sea* is actually a *novella* with a rural backdrop.

Arun Joshi, like Anita Desai, represents the younger generation of Indo-English novelists. The writings of Joshi and Desai turn inward rather than outward in their analysis of persons, places and things. There is an indubitably existential approach manifest in them. Joshi has written merely four novels to date : *The Foreigner* (1963), *The Strange Case of Billy Biswas* (1971), *The Apprentice* (1974), and *The Last Labyrinth* (1981). His main concerns in them appear to be : hypocrisy, bribery, falsehood, drunkenness, womanizing, unjust distribution of money, and the problem of adjustment in a culturally degraded and dehumanized society. The protagonists in his novels, who are all males, are bitten deep down in their hearts and look completely disconsolate and dispirited in an unwholesome world around them. In *The Foreigner*, we have Sindi Oberoi, who 'belongs' to no place and to none, reminding us of Yank in O'Neill's play *The Hairy Ape*. *The Strange Case of Billy Biswas* studies minutely the unpredictable and psychic personality of Bimal Biswas, who is a Ph.D. holder from the New York University and who is married to Meena, an ever-demanding girl, and employed in the Delhi University as a teacher. During one of the trips to Central India (Madhya Pradesh), he disappears from the camp and joins the society of tribals for his peace of mind and happiness. Biswas's case is 'strange' as it deserves a thorough probe by a psycho-analyst. In the third novel, *The Apprentice*, the restlessness and the sense of frustration of Ratan Rathore is vividly portrayed. The last novel traces the erratic and erotic nature of Som Bhaskar, an industrialist of Bombay, who is dissatisfied with his own wife, Geeta (a dutiful and lovable lady), and runs after the glamorous yet obsolete Anuradha of Banaras. The protagonist here is caught in the mazes of the world, and finds no redemption from them.

Chaman Nahal is an academic turned novelist living and teaching in Delhi. He began his creative career in 1973 with the publication of *My True Faces*, which has been quickly followed by *Azadi* (The Sahitya Academi Award Winner, 1975), *Into Another Dawn* (1977), *The English Queens* (1979), and *The*

Crown and the Loin Cloth (1981). The first novel of Nahal is neither much impressive from the standpoint of story nor from that of language; in fact, the latter tends to be studied and banal, lacking the refinement and spontaneity of B. Rajan, another case of the same type. But Malti and Kamal are interesting characters in it. In *Azadi*, the novelist successfully evokes the vision of Indian independence and the painful partition of the country accompanied by mass killing and vast influx of refugees. Lala Kansi Ram, the true embodiment of love and compassion, is an uprooted person travelling from across the border to India, to its capital Delhi precisely. *Into Another Dawn* depicts the passionate union of Ravi and Irene, two highly sensitive individuals, cutting across the national, social and racial boundaries. Its theme of East-West encounter recalls Raja Rao's *The Serpent and the Rope and* B. Rajan's *The Dark Dancer* and Kamala Markandaya's *The Coffer Dams* and *Pleasure City*. The fourth novel, *The English Queens*, deals with the representatives of the Indians "bitten by the English bug,"[20] it relates neither to English nor to the queens of the language, but to the affected Indian Anglophiles, who are invariably women. The fifth and last novel, *The Crown and the Loin Cloth*, turns to Mahatma Gandhi for its treatment. Here Gandhi symbolizes the hopes and aspirations of millions of Indians striving ceaselessly for freedom from a mighty foreign power — the 'Crown.' It portrays the non-cooperation movement of the Indian nationalists against the British during 1920-22.

I know, I have not yet spoken of those novelists who fall beyond the purview of this selective anthology, and whose contribution must be taken into account in any exhaustive survey of the *genre*. One of the prominent writers of yester years is Sudhin N. Ghose, who has published four novels, all from London, which are : *And Gazelles Leaping* (1949), *Cradle of the Clouds* (1951), *The Vermilion Boat* (1953), and *The Flame of the Forest* (1955). His novels, as Meenakhi Mukherjee points out, deal with "the childhood, adolescence and youth of his central character,"[21] who is usually the first-person narrator of the story. Another fictionist of fame is Santha Rama Rau, who has written so many interesting travel books but merely two novels : *Remember the House* (1956) and *The Adventures* (1971), which are both born of the author's own experiences. If Kamala Markandaya is Mrs. Taylor now, Santha is Mrs. Bowers presently, — the two sensitive Indian women having married the Westerners. Another well-known woman novelist is Attia Hussain, who has written *Sunlight on a Broken Column* (1961). The author commanding some respect for his imaginative inventiveness and smooth tale-telling is K. Nagarajan with two novels to his credit : *Athawar House* (1939), *Chronicles of Kedaram* (1961). If the first novel is a kind of domestic document ending with the inter-caste marriage of Sona, a Marathi Brahmin girl, and Venkataramani, a Tamil *Smartha*, the second is decidedly cast on a larger canvas, covering the freedom movement and communal distensions. It is said that Nagarajan "attempts no style but seems to write straight on."[22] Two Mulsim writers — Ahmed Ali (born 1912) and Khawaja Ahmed Abbas — also deserve a special mention. The former has written *Twilight in Delhi* (1940) and *Ocean of Night* (1964), while the latter has authored the spirited *Inquilab* (1955) and *Mera Nam Joker* (1970 — now filmized). The distinguished names of pre-independent India must also be noted here — K.S. Venkataramani and Humayun Kabir. While Kabir has given us *Men and Rivers* (1945), which shows the intimate relationship between Man and Nature, Venkataramani has produced *Murugan the Tiller* (1927) and *Kandan the Patriot* (1934) which paint the peasantry and its deep sense of worship and the national upsurge of patriotic forces respectively.

Two well-known novelists having already won some recognition of their creative talent are : M.V. Rama Sarma and Romen Basu. Of these, Sarma, a Milton academic like his predecessor B. Rajan, has adorned his literary cap with four novels — *The Stream* (1956), *The Farewell Party* (1976), *Look Homeward* (1976), and *The Bliss of Life* (1979) — in which he presents the variegated pictures of Indian life. They are the articulations of a talented writer who tries to seek the true meaning of life on earth. The other novelist, Basu, is highly fertile, and has published about half a dozen works, beginning with *A House Full of People* (1968), to be followed in quick succession by *Your Life to Live* (1972), *A Gift of Love* (1975), *The Tamarind Tree* (1975), *Candles and Roses* (1978), etc. Set in rural Bengal, *The Tamarind Tree* is undoubtedly the best of Basu's novels. In other novels, he often turns to the West for his locale and treatment.

Others who deserve mention in passing are : Nergis Dalal (*Minari,* 1967, *The Sisters,* 1973, *The Inner Door,* 1975, and *The Girls from Overseas,* 1979), Ruskin Bond (*The Room on the Roof,* 1956, *An Axe for the Rani,* 1972, *Love is a Sad Song,* 1975), Michael Chako Daniels (*Anything Out of Place is Dirt, 1971,* and *That Damn Romantic Fool,* 1972 — both Writers Workshop products), Bharati Mukherjee (*The Tiger's Daughter,* 1973, and *Wife*, 1976), Sasthi Brata (*Confessions of an Indian Woman Eater,* 1971, *She and He*, and *A Search for Home*, 1975 — all novels; *The Sensuous Guru* — a fantasy, 1960; *My God Died Young*, 1976, an autobiography), Raji Narasimhan (*The Heart of Standing is You Cannot Fly*, 1973, and *Forever Free*, 1979), and Veena Painteal (*Roshini or Serenity in Storm*, 1967, *Link in the Broken Chain*, 1967, *An Autumn Leaf*, 1976, *Spring Returns*, 1977, and *Midnight Woman,* 1979). The last-named novel reminds us of Salman Rushdie's *Midnight Children* (published in England); in fact, Rushdie has written two more novels, and he merits a serious consideration (happily, *The Journal of Indian Writing in English*, edited by Dr. Balarama Gupta, is going to bring out a special issue on him). The dilettanti in fictional art, however, must be decried and discouraged to leave it alone. Shiv K. Kumar, Syed Amanuddin (since long in the U.S.A.), K.N. Daruwalla are really good poets, and they must discover the area of their talent.

IV. FICTIONAL THEMES, LANGUAGE, AND TECHNIQUES

The foregoing account of Indian fictionists in English is by no means intended to be exhaustive, and the left-outs might find place somewhere else (say, in a comprehensive critical work like

Prof. Iyengar's *Indian Writing in English*, latest edition 1982). The above account is, however, sufficient to throw light on the dominant themes and techniques of the recognized novelists. Here we will take a brief and succinct stock of these matters.

Obviously, the most dominant and pervasive theme used by the writers of Indo-English novel has been the focus on the burning problems of contemporary Indian life. No one of the stalwarts is free from this contagious theme, as literature reflects the life of its time. Related to this are the four thematic sub-groups, which have been brilliantly summarized in an article recently published by Prof. Dieter Riemenschneider.[23] The first sub-group consists of the novels depicting the social, economic, and political oppression of individuals. Most of the novels of Mulk Raj Anand, Raja Rao's *Kanthapura*, Kamala Markandaya's *Nectar in a Sieve* and *A Handful of Rice*, Bhabani Bhattacharya's *So Many Hungers*, Manohar Malgonkar's *The Princes* belong to this category. The second sub-group concentrates on an individual's search for identity, and this is to be seen in Anand's Lalu trilogy (1939–42), Markandaya's *Some Inner Fury*, B. Rajan's *The Dark Dancer* and *Too Long in the West*, Attia Hussain's *Sunlight on a Broken Column*, and Anita Desai's and Arun Joshi's most of the novels. In G.V. Desani's *All About H. Hatterr*, Markandaya's *Possession*, Raja Rao's *The Serpent and the Rope*, and Khushwant Singh's *Train to Pakistan*, we discover a slight variation of this theme. The third sub-group comprises those novels which are mainly concerned with man's "role and position in society" and not with his "autonomous character."[24] Such are the works of R.K. Narayan and Bhattacharya's *He Who Rides a Tiger*, Nayanatara Sahgal's *Storm in Chandigarh* and Arun Joshi's novels. The fourth sub-group is constituted of a very small number of novels where attempts are made to bridge the undesirable gulf between India and the West, such as in K. Nararajan's *Chronicles of Kedaram* and Bhattacharya's *Shadow from Ladakh* and Markandaya's *The Coffer Dams* and *Pleasure City*. Apart from these categories of novels remarkably discussed in the article by Riemenschneider, there is altogether a separate category of those works which subtly portray human nature in a psychological fashion. In this category, the protagonist is a victim of his own inner tensions and struggles. Such are *The Dark Dancer* by B. Rajan, *A Silence of Desire* by Markandaya, the novels of Anita Desai and Arun Joshi.

The problem of the language to be used by Indo-English novelist in particular, and by Indo-English writer in general, has raked the minds of thinkers and literatti. The use of English in the national context is thought by some to be non-patriotic. They argue that Indians write in English to seek the Western market and readership, and that they do so for earning a huge sum of royalty in dollars and sterling. But the truth remains that the choice of English or any other language is a prerogative of the writer, and that he should be allowed to employ the language he is at home in. In her poem "An Introduction," Kamala Das has expressed this idea beautifully. A writer's first obligation is to satisfy himself, to look to his needs and requirements. Accordingly, he can remake or mould it to suit his own design and purpose, such as in Desani's *All About H. Hatterr*, in Raja Rao's *Kanthapura* and *The Serpent and the Rope*, and in Arun Joshi's *The Strage Case of Billy Biswas*. In his book, *The King Emperor's English or the role of the English Language in Free India* (Bombay : Hind Kitabs, 1948), the noted Indo-English novelist Mulk Raj Anand pleads strongly for the adoption of an Indian style of writing English. Anand himself as a practitioner of fiction uses so many translations of the words and expressions in the Punjabi vernacular; *e.g.*, 'rape mother,' 'rape daughter,' 'eaters of monsters,' 'where have you died.' Such insertions are possibly necessary to introduce an air of realism in his art. But they are not needed when equivalent English words or phrases are readily available; *e.g.,* 'haspatal' for 'hospital' and 'dakter' for 'doctor.' C. Paul Verghese is not far from the truth when he remarks : "An Indian novelist in English should employ his skill in contriving a dialogue that is at once natural and lively, supple and functional. He may even catch the speech rhythms and the turns of phrases used by all kinds of people in the village and translate some of the abuses, curses, imprecations and proverbs to advantage."[25] But some Hindi words or vernacular phrases may be sparingly used when they are absolutely unavoidable. It may be that we do not find precise English equivalents of them; *e.g.*, 'neem,' 'swadeshi,' 'khaddar,' 'charkha,' etc. Though P. Lal's boast of having found in English the language of his emotional makeup as a poet is undoubtedly questionable and untenable, it is certainly the language of our intellectual make-up, as Raja Rao nicely puts it : "It is the language of our intellectual make-up like Sanskrit or Persian was before — but not of our emotional make-up."[26] This sharp writer further remarks : "We are all instinctively bilingual, many of us writing in our own language and in English. We cannot write like the English. We should not. We cannot write only as Indians. We have grown to look at the large world as part of us."[27] Speaking on behalf of his own brethren in Indo-English fiction, Manohar Malgonkar writes that "whether we speak the English language well or badly, we have come to feel much more at home in it than in our own tongues — otherwise we would not be doing our writing in it."[28] In his "The Writer and the Word," Raja Rao comes close to the Aurobindonian solution of the language controversy, and desires of us to 'recognize our inheritance" and be "an *upasaka* of the word."[29] And finally, a brilliant Indian scholar, Prof. V.Y. Kantak, in an illuminating article observes that to be able to present the truth as well as the superstitions, the writer has to free himself from jargons, cants, cliches and literariness (the bane of academic writers). Kantak rightly states that "The language has to be broken to it (truth or superstition), as it were, and made new."[30] This is surely a Coleridgean demand!

And now a few words about fictional techniques. English being a foreign tongue has created some problems for learners and writers. The main difficulty is that we are not much exposed to it; barring the class-rooms or occasionally the high offices we do not use it. But this does not apply to those writers who have attained international standards and universal acclaim. The appearance of notices about them and their works in *The Times Literary Supplement* dated 18th April, 1958, and 10th August, 1962, simply affirms the growing popularity and acceptability of Indian literature being written in English today. Indian English fiction, which has now come of age, has shown steady improvement in its bulk and quality due to bold stylistic experiments of its practitioners. Mulk Raj Anand, R.K. Narayan, Raja Rao, Kamala Markandaya, Bhabani Bhattacharya, Manohar Malgonkar, B. Rajan — all have experimented with it in their own ways. These experiments, as Mrs. Mukherjee points out, can be broadly classified under three heads : (1) experiment in diction (literal translation of idioms), (2) experiment in syntax (changing the structure of sentences) and (3) imagery.[31] The most significant feature of the first is noticeable in "the collocational deviations and compounding of words in Indian English."[32] Some of these have now become fixed collocations, for instance, 'high caste,' 'low caste,' 'sacred thread,' 'communal riots,' etc. But some others are constantly being formed in order to express fresh modes of life and thought, for example, 'touched man,' 'caste well,' 'English-aping,' 'hair-flower' (all from Anand), 'twice born,' 'salt givers,' 'camphor ceremony,' 'registration bribes' (all from Raja Rao), 'casteless girl,' 'caste restrictions,' 'horse gram' 'foreign-returned people,' 'permit-holder' (all from R.K. Narayan), 'bull calf,' 'buffalo pair,' 'dung-cake,' 'matrimonial game,' (all from Kamala Markandaya). The creative Indian writers have also used collocations and compounds through a process of hybridization, such as in 'kumkum mark,' 'marriage pandal' and 'lathi charge.' Occasionally, they have added English suffixes to Indian words, *e.g.*, 'sadhuhood,' 'upanishadic' and 'goondaism.' The instances of literal translation of idioms and expressions into English may be had in the following :

> 'As if rats were running about his belly' (*Untouchable*).
>
> 'Hello — Mr. Late Latif' (*Private Life of an Indian Prince*).
>
> '[Moorthy], had gone through life like a noble cow' (*Kanthapura*).

> 'My Professor will eat me up' (*Bachelor of Arts*).
> 'The unbeaten brat will remain unlearned' (*Nectar in a Sieve*).
> 'Stop thinking like stupid water buffaloes' (*A Handful of Rice*).

These examples clearly demonstrate the extent and scope of Indian English. Even the dialogues and narrations are occasionally tempered with 'Indianisms' in the works of Indo-English novelists. This they do in order to establish "a consistency between speech and character" and to preserve "an illusion of reality in fiction."[33]

Along with the problems of language, we also come across cases of syntactical peculiarities in Indo-English fiction. One of the traits, on a microscopic plane, is the extension of meaning of English words and phrases, *e.g.*, 'family' (extended to mean 'wife') and 'colony'. In changing the normal structure and rhythm of English, two writers — Raja Rao and Bhabani Bhattacharya — stand out. Here are some illustrations from Raja Rao : "He is so tender and fine-limbed, is my brother" (*The Serpent and the Rope*, p. 12), "the sorrow of woman be indeed the barrenness of man" (p. 27), and "They are so immoral, the English are" (p. 146). And a few more from Bhattacharya : "Kanu — he was safe?" (*So Many Hungers*, p. 204) and the clipped, tortuous sentence : "Who more proud than I on this day...." (*Music for Mohini* p. 88). Such illustrations are studied at some length in Mrs. Mukherjee's book, *The Twice Born Fiction* (1974).

The imagistic and pictorial details abound in Raja Rao and Anita Desai. These two novelists have been claimed to be 'poets' in prose. Their dialogues and descriptions tend be picturesque and arresting. Here is an example from Raja Rao's *The Serpent and the Rope* :

> Mother Ganga had her feet all yellowed with turmeric, and she carried the flowers of our evenings in her hair. The Himalaya was like Lord Shiva himself...He was like space made articulate, not before you but behind you... (p. 42).

And here is a perfectly monosyllabic sentence from Desai :

> At last a sigh went up and Ila Das let forth again with a sound that made the hoopoes on the bit of grass take off and flee the garden and the crickets draw in their heads and hide (*Fire on the Mountain*, pp. 115-116).

This kind of poetic passage full of concrete and visual details may also be seen in B. Rajan's *The Dark Dancer*.

Besides, a number of Indian novelists in English have beautifully employed the stylistic devices of irony, wit, and satire. These devices are amply witnessed in the works of R.K. Narayan, R.P. Jhabvala, and B. Rajan and Khushwant Singh. Even the Indian scriptures and mythologies have also been put to an excellent creative use, and Dr. K. Narayan and Raja Rao excel in their treatment of these sources. But one thing in which Indian fiction in English, like other Indo-English *genres*, is woefully lagging behind is the use of humour. It is rarely seen in R.K. Narayan and Khushwant Singh, but *never* in others.

V. PROSPECT

An overall account of the origin, growth and expansion of Indian fiction in English as given above convinces us that this brand of Indian literature has almost attained maturity and strength. It is, therefore, deplorable to find a few disgruntled, disparaging critics, at the head of whom stands Uma Parmeswaran with her ill-conceived notions and generalized formulations. Parmeswaran sets A.D. 2000 as the dirge-date for Indo-English literature,[34] but I may assure her of the continuity and enrichment of this literature in the days to come, and advise her to desist from such gloomy and pessimistic observations. A literature is an integral part of a culture, and the prevailing conditions (social, cultural, political, etc.) in India do not presage its destruction in any way. Another staunch critic of Indian writing in English is B. Rajan, but he appears to be more realistic in his approach than Parmeswaran when he concedes 'commitment and vitality' to it. A more objective and discerning judge of Indo-English fiction is

Khushwant Singh, who passes the following remarks about it :

> Nirad Chaudhuri's autobiography and *The Continent of Circe* are safe bets for 2,000 A.D. So also are G.V. Desani's *All About Hatterr*, R.K. Narayan's *The Financial Expert*, Ruth Jhabvala's *Get Ready for Battle* and Kamala Markandaya's *Nectar in a Sieve*. Malgonkar, who is more easily readable than any other Indian, may also survive with *A Bend in the Ganges*. I would not bet on any others.[35]

But this remark was made more than fifteen years ago, and the climate of situation has since changed to the better. I am sure, Khushwant Singh would have added a few more names to the list — such as Anita Desai, Arun Joshi, and Chaman Nahal with his *Azadi* — to revise and update it, had he made the remarks today. Things as they stand presently warrant that there is nothing to be gloomy or giddy about Indian novel in English, which like all other living and expanding organisms, has now become self-generating and self-diversifying. It has got some really talented and reputed practitioners to guide the course of its destiny. Why should it feel shy of itself in the present-day circumstances?—

After such knowledge, what forgiveness? (T.S. Eliot).

NOTES AND REFERENCES

1. K.R. Srinivasa Iyenger, *Indian Contribution to English Literature* (Bombay : Karnatak Publishing House, 1945), p. 3.
2. P.P. Mehta, *Indo-Anglian Fiction* : *An Assessment* (Bereilly : Prakash Book Depot, 1968), p. 6. Sri Aurobindo has also dwelt at length on this aspect of Indian awakening in his work, *The Renaissance in India* (Pondicherry: Sri Aurobindo Ashram, 1973).
3. K.R. Srinivasa Iyengar, *Indian Writing in English* (Bombay : Asia Publishing House, 1973), p. 315.
4. See William Walsh's article "The Big Three," *Indian Writing in English*, ed. Ramesh Mohan (Madras : Orient Longman Ltd., 1978), pp. 26-36.
5. *Ibid.*, p. 26.
6. *Ibid.*, p. 27.
7. Iyengar, *op. cit.*, at No. 3, p. 386.

8. Prof. K.R.S. Iyengar is also of the same view. *See* his work cited at No. 3, p. 412.
9. R.S. Singh, *Indian Novel in English* (New Delhi : Arnold-Heinemann, 1977), p. 96.
10. S.C. Harrex, *The Fire and the Offering*, Vol. I (Calcutta : Writers Workshop, 1977), p. 245.
11. William Walsh, *Commonwealth Literature* (London : O.U.P., 1973), p. 18.
12. Singh, *op. cit.*, p. 163.
13. Harrex, *op. cit.*, pp. 185–195.
14. *Ibid.,* p. 182.
15. Haydn Moore Williams, *Studies in Modern Indian Fiction in English*, Vol. II (Calcutta : Writers Workshop, 1973), p. 141.
16. Stephen Ignatius Hemenway, *The Novel of India*, Vol. 2 (Calcutta : Writers Workshop, 1975), p. 49.
17. G.S. Amur, *Manohar Malgonkar* (New Delhi : Arnold-Heinemann, 1973), p. 12.
18. Iyengar, *op. cit.* at No. 3, p. 489.
19. Elena J. Kalinnikova, *Indian English Literature : A Perspective* (Ghaziabad : Vimal Prakashan, 1982), p. 180.
20. Chaman Nahal, *The English Queens* (New Delhi : Vision Books, 1979), p. 34.
21. Meenakshi Mukherjee, *The Twice Born Fiction* (New Delhi : Arnold-Heinemann, 1974), pp. 135-136.
22. C. Paul Verghese, *Problems of the Indian Creative Writer in English* (Bombay : Somaiya Publications Pvt. Ltd., 1971), p. 122.
23. See Dieter Riemenschneider, "The Indo-English Novel," *Indian Literature*, XXVI, No. 5 (Sept.-Oct. 1983).
24. *Ibid.,* p. 29.
25. Verghese, *op. cit.*, p. 102.
26. Raja Rao, "Foreword", *Kanthapura* (Madras : O.U.P., 1947), p. 5.
27. *Idem.*
28. Manohar Malgonkar, "Purdah and Caste-Marks," *The Times Literary Supplement* (June 4, 1964), p. 491.
29. Raja Rao, "The Writer and the Word," *Critical Essays on Indian Writing in English*, eds. Naik, Desai & Amur (Dharwar : Karnatak University, 1972), p. 5.
30. V.Y. Kantak, "The Language of Indian Fiction in English", *op. cit.*, at No. 29, p. 211.

31. Mukherjee, *op. cit.*, p. 170.
32. Ramesh Mohan, "Some Aspects of Style and Language in Indian English Fiction," *Indian Writing in English*, ed. Ramesh Mohan, p. 195.
33. *Ibid.*, p. 198.
34. Uma Parmeswaran, *A Study of Representative Indo-English Novelists* (New Delhi : Vikas Publishing House, 1976), p. 6.
35. *See The Banasthali Patrika*, ed. Rameshwar Gupta (Jan., 1969), p. 9.

2

THE NARRATIVE TECHNIQUE OF KAMALA MARKANDAYA*

Kamala Markandaya's novels of contemporary Indian life stand out for their characteristic modes of expression and narration. Her skill as a novelist is vividly reflected in the remarkable handling of story and plot, in the pointedly relevant social commentary on events and characters, and in the deft arrangement of the raw material at hand. The slight yet subtle distinction between 'story' and 'plot,' as aptly pointed out by E.M. Forster, the noted English novelist, must be kept in mind while appreciating the technical art of Markandaya :

> We have defined a story as a narrative of events arranged in their item sequence. A plot is also a narrative of events, the emphasis falling on causality.
>
> 'The king died and then the queen died,' is a story.
>
> 'The king died and then the queen died of grief,' is a plot.[1]

Markandaya, who happens to be a conscious artist moving in her well-drawn circle with sure steps and perfect poise, is unquestionably aware of the subtle dividing line between 'story' and 'plot' and pays due attention to both (which we will examine hereafter as 'narration' and 'plot-construction'). She may not be

---

* Written in collaboration with Dr. Niroj Banerji. Included in the *Prof. Prabhakar Festschrifts* (Madras, 1991).

so profound in her art of characterisation as Anita Desai and Arun Joshi (who portray their characters with a wonderful psychological insight), her technique may not have the complexities of Raja Rao and G.V. Desani, and her outlook upon life may not be so sound and inclusive as that of Mulk Raj Anand and R.K. Narayan, but she has greatly succeeded in evolving her own mild-natured technique and vision of life and her novels tend to be an index of the current age in all its manifestations — sociological, political, economic, communal and cultural. Her single-minded devotion to the art of fiction-writing has earned to her worldwide recognition and reputation. Reviewing her novel, *Possession* (1963), Robert Payne once remarked about Indian-English novelists in general and Kamala Markandaya in particular as follows :

> They now write superbly, with a command of their unique rhythms and an understanding of the potentialities of the sentence that sometimes shame us. It is self-conscious writing, but they know what they are doing to a hair's breadth.[2]

Taking into account Markandaya's overall contribution to Indian novel in English, Uma Parmeswaran has rightly observed that —

> She has artistic instinct enough to know where the roots are but not the artistic care to keep in constant touch with her subject. Her chief merit lies in that she presents Indian ways of life without authorial commentary.[3]

True, Markandaya does not indulge in 'authorial commentary' but there are certain leading female characters like Mira and Anasuya who have a remarkable resemblance with their creator, and hence we do not find complete detachment in her fiction, especially in her earlier novels.

Mere description of scenes or situations is the work of a dilettante, but narration of events in sequential order is the task of an artist. In reality, we discover both description and narration in the novels of Markandaya. She is naive and idyllic when she writes such descriptive passages as the following :

> In the Valley sirens were blaring, modern muezzins announcing the end of the working day. The distant humming slackened, like a run-down dynamo. After the daily pounding, blasting and drilling the air seemed strangely still, the tremors that travelled up from the valley and were felt even here, finally subsided. In the mounting silence the purl of the river grew stronger (*The Coffer Dams*, pp. 57-8).

She, however, does not grow eloquent like Thomas Hardy in such descriptive passages, and very swiftly resorts to short, crisp and racy dialogues, as in the following :

> 'All alone, Lennie?'
> 'All alone, darling. Except for cook.'
> 'Can't stand the man. Where's Das, Das!' he shouted
> 'Millie's borrowed him', Helen said.
> 'What for?'
> 'The party.'
> 'What party?'
> 'Millie's.'
> 'My God,' he said, 'do we have to go?'
> 'Only if you want.'
>
> (*Ibid.*, p. 58)

This is the usual mode of her narration, which furthers the story step by step, sentence by sentence. The above-truncated conversation between Clinton and his wife Helen in *The Coffer Dams* reveals the truth that Millie has arranged for a party to which the Clintons must go. In Markandaya's novels, dialogues and conversations occupy larger space than scenic descriptions do, and she apparently adopts this mode of approach to effectively tell her tale, to further the plot of her novel, and to reveal the socially relevant situations and characters.

The narration in Markandaya's first novel, *Nectar in a Sieve* (1954), takes place through the mouth of its principal female character. Rukmani, and that too in the first person. Rukmani is seen here reminiscing her own past, since she was twelve, when she was married as a childbride to Nathan, a village boy. The novel is thus written in a reminiscential mood, and Markandaya's technique rises to meet its tensions and complexities. Rukmani's recollection of her life ends exactly where it begins, winding up the story in a circular shape. The story is straightforward and divided into two parts, — the first part telling us about Rukmani's unfortunate married life and the second one depicting the tortuous wanderings of the couple in search of a job in the city and their disappointment. Writing of the novel's technique, K.S. Narayan Rao has remarked as under :

> In a detached and yet not wholly unemotional manner, Rukmani recalls the events of her life in a chronological manner. The dream-like quality of her recollection is particularly impressive. Rukmani recaptures the tragic intonation of her life in a clear, lyrical manner. She misses nothing, not a detail. Divided into short chapters, which have a psychological advantage of keeping the reader's interest, the story purports to be a narrative of events in the life of narrator.[4]

The end of the novel is tragic, and it seems that the novelist cleverly contrived it in order to elicit the reader's sympathy for the poor and the destitute (as Rukmani is). The overall impression of the novel on the reader's mind is that the story is somewhat tampered with and that the plot has not been allowed to grow naturally. R.S. Singh has rightly drawn our attention to this fact when he comments thus :

> The writer has probably exaggerated the circumstantial pressures on the narrator to create tragic effects, but the fact remains that the novel is, on the whole, melodramatic. One gets the impression on going through the ordeals of Nathan and Rukmani that the whole thing is engineered, contrived a little too cleverly, rather than developed on chance events alone.[5]

In the novel under scrutiny, the narrative highlights Rukmani's reactions to the past events of her life and the action is subordinated to her thoughts and feelings alone. The opening of the tannery brings humming industry to the otherwise sleepy village, though it might have created miseries for Nathan and Rukmani. So, her reactions to the running of tannery are partly impressionistic because they do not constitute the whole truth.

Some Inner Fury (1955) is also a female-dominated novel where the narrator-heroine Mira recounts the tale once again in the first person. But Mira is a young, lovable woman, not a haggard like Rukmani. Mira, a westernised lady of the upper class society, opens her little silver-box one day and finds the scrap of material she had once torn from her lover Richard's shirt after the nationalists' mob had attacked him during the 'Quit India Movement' of 1942. She is at once transported into her past and recounts all the happenings of her life right from her first meeting with Richard to her separation from him for good. The story is quite gripping unto the very last and remarkably recaptures the tense moments of Indo-British relationship during the pre-Independence days. There are some fine autobiographical flashes in the work, and the reader is tempted to believe that Mira is no one else but the author herself. Prof. R.S. Singh has streamlined their points of resemblance in the following manner :

> Their dates of birth, interest in creative writing, birth in the Brahmin family and visits to England in connection with publications and their infatuation with some Englishman (Markandaya herself is married to Mr. Taylor, a Britisher) lead one to believe that they are one and the same.[6]

As in *Nectar in a Sieve,* the narrative pattern remains 'circular' here too. The plot is beautifully executed herein.

The next novel, *A Silence of Desire* (1960), takes to the method of third-person narration and in this makes a noticeable departure from Markandaya's previous two novels. Also, it presents Dandekar's point of view, and not that of a dominant female character. Dandekar is depicted as hovering between the twin pulls of his love for his wife Sarojini and children and his jealousy for the Swamy. The main interest of the novel lies in the revelation of the complex character of Dandekar as well as in the conflict between science and superstition represented by Dandekar and his wife respectively. There is a wealth of suggestion in this novel, as nicely pointed out by Prof. K.R. Srinivasa Iyengar : "Perhaps her most ambitious novel, *A Silence of Desire*, dares the invisible and the writing is competent enough to forge here and there coils of intricate suggestion that almost seem to bridge the chasm between matter and spirit, doubt and faith."[7]

In *Possession* (1963), the narrative is once again, as in the first two novels, managed by a sensitive woman, namely by Anasuya, who is a writer of stature and who frequently visits England in connection with the publication of her books. Anasuya can thus establish her contact with the developments of the story in England where Caroline, a possessive woman of wealth and influence, has whisked away Valmiki, the peasant-boy of India, in order to avoid his touch with his spiritual teacher, the Swamy. The scene keeps shifting here from India to England and America and back to India again. Prof. Iyengar sees "an extravagance"[8] in the shifting scene and situation. Unlike the first two novels, *Possession* does not have a central figure as the narrator of the story. Anasuya, like the author herself, remains largely detached and objective. Her detachment stands her in good stead as a narrator of events.

All the novels that follow — *A Handful of Rice* (1966), *The Coffer Dams* (1969), *The Nowhere Man* (1972), *Two Virgins* (1973), *The Golden Honeycomb* (1977) and *Pleasure City* (1982) — are third-person narratives. Barring *Two Virgins,* we do not find domineering women characters in any other novel, and even in *Two Virgins* everything seems to be messed up. Some scholars feel that the novelist should have presented here the narrative through the mouth of Lalitha, the elder sister of Saroja, whose viewpoint forms the real fabric of the work. There is no solid story or compact plot, and in this matter the novel resembles the first fictional flower of Markandaya's genius. In *A Handful of Rice,* the narrative thread is controlled by Ravi, the principal character in the story. Prema Nandakumar is of the opinion that this novel is clearly based on Bernard Malamud's *The Assistant* (1957), wherein Frank comes to steal from a Jewish grocer's store but stays on to assist the latter and wins his daughter's (Helen's) love. A very similar situation obtains in Markandaya's novel too. Ravi chased by the police enters a tailor's shop where he is beaten and bruised and yet he gets the love of Nalini, the tailor's daughter. Ravi assists the tailor and marries Nalini in due course and becomes the head of the family after the death of the tailor Apu.

The Coffer Dams is a moving narrative of "the East-West encounter or of the problems of industrialization," as Uma Parmeswaran puts it.[9] Herein we witness a profound "understanding of human motivations, and a bold experimentation in prose style."[10] The Clinton-Mackendrick engineering firm comes to India to construct dams across a South Indian river, and strives to complete the work before the onset of the monsoon. Indian engineers like Krishnan and local technicians extend their helping hand to the project. But the dreaded monsoon comes, creating a dramatic situation of deep suspense. The dying tribal headman, Bashiam, provides the clue for the safety of dams — 'when the ridges clear....' etc. The art of characterisation attains a new height here, and the novelist's technique succeeds in evoking a proper atmosphere for the dam-construction and the onset of rainy season. Markandaya offers technical descriptions of the construction work and the machines and the cranes. Prof. Iyengar corroborates the statement when he remarks thus :

> There is a quiet efficiency in the technical descriptions, and there is an eerie quality, in the early-morning adventure in bird-catching. Kamala Markandaya writes with increasing mastery of the medium, and although there is some obvious contriving and some ingenious formulations of contrast, the novel as a whole is a deeply disturbing protest against the onslaught of modern technological ruthlessness against the simplicity and humanity of an earlier order of life.[11]

At places Markandaya displays her remarkable descriptive and narrative powers.

In *The Nowhere Man,* Markandaya depicts two Indians — Srinivas and his wife Vasantha — as victims of British tyranny and terrorism. Afraid of undue harassment at home, the couple leaves for Britain and settles down there for good in an uncongenial surrounding. They are treated as 'aliens' there, especially by Fred and his companions. The end of the novel is tragic, and the novelist's vision of life is evidently pessimistic to the core, recalling Hardy to our minds. There is also a moral in the story — that too much of hostility is harmful to both the East and the West. Mrs. Fletcher, Mrs. Glass and the men in the pub provide "a chorus in the neighbours"[12] of Srinivas, and the chorus recalls the practice of Greek tragedians and that of T.S. Eliot (as in *Murder in the Cathedral*) in quite recent times.

As already mentioned, *Two Virgins* is undoubtedly a hopeless novel with a slight theme and a low-keyed technique. Even the details furnished herein are loose and incoherent. The narrative is meandering, and the plot ill-conceived and mismanaged. One, therefore, feels great relief when one leaves behind this frustrating novel and goes forward to the historical narrative of *The Golden Honeycomb* (1977). This stupendous work is divided into three parts — and each part being preceded by an epigraph, contains a prologue quoting from Lord Randolph Churchill and an epilogue referring to the formation of the Indian Union after our Independence, and minutely portrays at least three generations of Indian History as represented by Bawajiraj I to III. The attitude of Britishers and the King of Devapur is nothing different with regard to Indian masses, and the tables are turned only by Rabi, the rebellious son of the Maharaja, and Usha, the enlightened daughter of the Dewan (Chief Minister of the King), and their followers. True to the grain of history, the narrative is carried forward here with utmost detachment and impartiality. There is no effort on the part of the fictionist to twist the historical background of the novel, and her viewpoint remains perfectly patriotic and nationalistic throughout. At times the novelist resorts to an ironical mode of expression in dealing with the British or the Maharaja, and its presence is marked by Margaret P. Joseph in her critical study of Kamala Markandaya's fiction.[13] Thus, the British is almost always mentioned as 'Bania' (Merchant), and the grand Durbar of Delhi as a 'bun-fight' and a 'circus.' And all the spicy remarks come through some other characters, not directly through the author. Markandaya does not insert the use of 'I' anywhere in the work, and in this she is to be contrasted with such novelists as Mulk Raj Anand (*see* his *Private Life of an Indian Prince,* 1953) and Manohar Malgonkar (look up his *The Princess,* 1963). This speaks of the individual, independent approach of Markandaya to the matter of technique, without toeing any other novelist.

The latest novel of Markandaya, *Pleasure City* (1982), employs the third-person narration. Neatly divided into 51 chapters of varying length, the work highlights the British co-operation with India after her political freedom, participating in the latter's developmental plans and programmes and constructive expansions. The multi-national organisation called AIDCORP takes up the invitational assignment of building a holiday pleasure-resort known as Shalimar in a coastal village of South India. Shalimar is successfully completed with the willing co-operation of Britishers and Indians, and offers grand opportunities of familiarity and friendship between Tully, one of the Directors of AIDCORP, and Rikki, a hardworking Indian boy of barely sixteen. These two further cement their friendship by working together in the renovation of Avalon, that deserted castle which was once built by Tully's own grandfather who was then Proconsul to the Southern province. Until the completion of Shalimar, the novel seems to be moving in the right direction, but once the work is over, it becomes highly fragmentary and episodic in character. A kind of Smolletian spirit pervades it thereafter, and the content appears to be fragile and slippery. Without solid content, technique goes awry and structure become loose and lax.

A chronological survey of Markandaya's novels reveals the truth that she has used flashback and flashforth techniques in them. This is why most of her novels follow a 'circular' pattern and a reminiscential mood. But in *The Golden Honeycomb* this technique is discarded in favour of a direct, linear technique. The historical narrative actually requires it to be so.

In plot-construction, Markandaya adopts a neat, clean and straightforward approach. Generally, her plot is well-knit and properly balanced, but in such novels as *Nectar in a Sieve, Two Virgins* and *Pleasure City* it is superseded by story. Elsewhere, her plot is meticulously executed. There is room for wit and irony (though not for humour) in her plot; for example, in *The Golden Honeycomb,* Markandaya employs at least three things in her plot-structure — a personal story, a social background and a wider conflict. There is a kind of 'classical' quality about her art, as noted down by Uma Parmeswaran :

> Each novel is organised as a classical play. A microcosmic equillibrium is upset giving rise to conflicts; the focus is always on the main character, the plot is unfolded step by step, there is a rapid denouement after the climax. Some classical 'machinery' is also used. There are symbolic forewarnings in each story.[14]

And in a 'classical' play, the story of a Markandaya novel is usually complete in itself. There is hardly any scope for a secondary plot in her novels. Similarly, they also lack philosophical ruminations, lyrical outbursts of feelings, and extraneous characters. As a result, her thoughts occasionally tend to be shallow and unimpressive, but she makes no compromises on the score of her fictional narratives, which often gush forth without any barriers. Her language is markedly free from unnecessary embellishments and decorations. Since she offers no authorial commentary on events or characters, she commands a commendable objectivity and detachment in her novels.

Markandaya's art of characterization draws its sustenance from her wide-ranging experience and knowledge of the world around her. Her characters, like Chaucer's in English poetry, belong to different sections of society — the poor and the rich, highclass gentlemen and ladies and down-the-earth rustics and vagabonds. They are both British and Indian — both well within her range and experience — whom she studies minutely in their inter-cultural and inter-racial relationships. There is no consideration of caste, creed and clime in the portrayal of her characters, who happen to be both types and individuals. In her 'God's Plenty,' Rukmani and Nathan, Mirabai and Richard, Dandekar and Sarojini, Lady Caroline and Valmiki and to a lesser degree the Swamy, Ravi, Clinton and Helen and Bashiam, Srinivas and Vasantha and Mrs. Pickering and Fred, Saroja and Lalitha, Rabindranath and Usha, and Tully and Rikki : all are living characters of flesh and blood. But there are others like Nalini in *A Handful of Rice,* Rawlings and his wife Millie in *The Coffer Dams,* Chingleput in *Two Virgins,* the Swamy in *A Silence of Desire,* and Janaki, Das, Jaya and bearers in *The Golden Honeycomb* who never grow fully and act individualistically. Markandaya does not seem to be a novelist of 'the inner workings' of the mind, nor of the emotional and intellectual turmoils of an individual. At best, she is a novelist of sensitive individuals placed in certain piquant situations and of their ensuing actions and reactions in the given social and cultural context. She admirably succeeds in drawing her protagonists with a few masterly strokes.[15]

In the matter of technical adjustment of expression of character and situation, Markandaya can't be fully vindicated. Although she handles her medium of expression with the unmistakable touch of a consummate artist, she occasionally slips into the error of forgetting the real status or rank of her character. She has been praised for her "simple and effective language,"[16] and rightly so, but the truth also remains that she has misconceived the real nature of her rustic characters, such as that of Rukmani, throwing as she does a kind of aura around them by making them speak in what is often termed as 'anglicized idioms.' This is decidedly an inexcusable flaw on the part of a writer who very well knows the subtle nuances and delicacies of the English language. One of the redeeming features of Markandaya's language, however, is that it remains chaste and flawless almost to the last detail, and it displays no trace of the abuses or undue Indianisms of Mulk Raj Anand and Khushwant Singh. There is no need to search for them in a well-mannered and well-cultured lady of the stature of Markandaya. Some scholars have endeavoured to find fault with her because she does not always stick to Indian setting, character or expressions, but this is an unjust demand from her by all means, keeping in view her peculiar position. Aren't we satisfied with her continued use of her maiden-name 'Markandaya'? With regard to the question of the use of unnatural language by certain characters in her fiction, such as by Janaki in *The Golden Honeycomb*, we may construe it as an obvious result of her alien situation — "the price the expatriate writer has to pay."[17] Markandaya, on the contrary, sounds very natural and impressive in putting proper words, phrases and expressions in the mouths of her British characters. How forceful and effective her medium becomes when she comes to delineate the characters of Sir Arthur and Lady Mary Copeland in *The Golden Honeycomb* and to reproduce their living English speech and rhythm!

Then follows the question of style and its execution by Markandaya. What we need to underline here is the fact that style is not something static but dynamic, and that it has to modulate itself from time to time in keeping with the demands of the story. Besides, style is also an index to the inner workings of a man's mind to which the vehicle of expression is tailored in a suitable manner. The use of tenses, inversions, hyphens or hyphenated expressions, and truncated or intricate dialogues are all of secondary importance. Markandaya's style is quite dynamic in nature and peculiarly suited to capture effectively the varying moods and fancies, feelings and thoughts, of her character. Occasionally it tends to be impressionistic (as in the description of the colourful Holi festival in *The Golden Honeycomb*), but usually it is character or situation oriented. How skillfully she pen-portrays the divergent views and tempers of the Maharaja, the Dewan, Rabi and Usha in *The Golden Honeycomb*! It is likely that Markandaya sometimes slips and does not show "sufficient attention to small details,"[18] like the location of a particular village or the site of a dam-construction. A scholar like Shyamala Venkateswaran is highly sore over this,[19] but her concern goes in the extreme. Markandaya's style does not entertain aberrations of mind and distortions of facts. Speaking of her style, Uma Parmeswaran has rightly remarked :

> Kamala Markandaya's is not a translated language. She does not attempt to adopt vernacular idiom or tone; the language of her earlier work is always unobtrusively pure. Yet she succeeds in bringing out the texture of the social classes by varying the degree of simplicity and articulation. A distinct note of experimentation with prose style is present in *The Coffer Dams* and later novels....[20]

Being shorn of superfluities and unwanted details, Markandaya's style moves between the twin polarities of simplicity and complexity and thereby draws a dividing line between her earlier and later works. It is totally devoid of rhetorical raptures and lyrical effusions (which one finds in plenty in Anita Desai), and is almost free from philosophical speculations and metaphysical abstractions (which are abundantly witnessed in Raja Rao, B. Rajan and Arun Joshi). Although it admits of the ardent social considerations of Mulk Raj Anand, Bhabani Bhattacharya and Ruth Prawer Jhabvala, it is not committed to any particular ideology or doctrine. And though it makes use of wit and irony at appropriate places, it does not demonstrate any propensity for humour or comics of the type of R.K. Narayan and Ruth P. Jhabvala. Markandaya's style follows a rather middle path and strives to transmute the disparate experiences of her characters into an artistic whole of charm and beauty.

In the final reckoning, the narrative technique of Kamala Markandaya does not adopt a certain definite mode of expression and keeps its options open like the free mind of a dispassionate reader. Her technique springs from the valued position of a detached observer, which Markandaya is, and freely modulates itself according to the needs and demands of the situation and character. Hence, sometimes it takes to a third-person narration and at others to a first-person narration. Both narration and description form the fibre of her technique. Markandaya also makes use of flashback and flashforth techniques in her novels, giving a rounded, circular shape to them in a convincing manner — a thing which recalls the practice of Arun Joshi in his fictional works. Her art of characterization, her plot-construction, her medium of expression, and her style are all bound together in the firm knot of her dynamic technique to enhance the overall effectiveness of her novels on the minds of her readers and to reaffirm the validity of her claim to the title of 'the Big Four' in Indian-English fiction.

NOTES AND REFERENCES

1. E.M. Forster, *Aspects of the Novel* (Harmondswarth, Essex Penguin Books, 1964), p. 45.
2. Robert Payne, "The Homesick Shepherd," *The Saturday Review,* 46, No. 21 (May 25, 1963), 34.
3. Uma Parmeswaran, *A Study of Representative Indo-English Novelists* (New Delhi : Vikas Publishing House, 1976), p. 92.
4. K.S. Narayan Rao, "Kamala Markandaya : The Novelist as Craftsman," *Indian Writing Today,* III, No. 2 (April-June 1959), 33.
5. R.S. Singh, *Indian Novel in English* (New Delhi : Arnold-Heinemann, 1977), p. 138.
6. *Ibid.,* p. 140.
7. K.R. Srinivasa Iyengar, *Indian Writing in English* (Bombay : Asia Publishing House, 1973), pp. 442-3.

   —Its later editions are being brought out by Sterling Publishers of New Delhi.
8. *Ibid.,* p. 445.
9. Parmeswaran, *op. cit.,* p. 103.
10. *Idem.*
11. Iyengar, *op. cit.,* p. 449.
12. Margaret P. Joseph, *Kamala Markandaya* (New Delhi : Arnold-Heinemann, 1980), p. 78.
13. *Ibid.,* p. 99.
14. Parmeswaran, *op. cit.,* p. 91.

15. Joseph, *op. cit.,* p. 155.
16. Parmeswaran, *op. cit.,* p. 90.
17. Joseph, *op. cit.,* p. 209.
18. Shyamala Venkateswaran, "The Language of Kamala Markandaya's Novels," *The Literary Criterion,* 9, No. 3 (Winter 1970), 60.
19. *Ibid.,* p. 62.

    —Here this scholar remarks thus : "...in a novel employing first person narration, the beauty of the style in itself is not as important as its appropriateness."
20. Parmeswaran, *op. cit.,* p. 90.

3

"THE GOLDEN HONEYCOMB" : A CRITICAL APPRAISAL*

The Golden Honeycomb divided into three parts sums up the trials and tribulations of our country under a foreign governance through a succession of moving events, pitiable strikes, and round-the-clock agitations and lockouts. It is undoubtedly Kamala Markandaya's memorable *fait accompli* in which she turns her all-absorbing mind to the momentous historical events shaping and affecting India's fate during the British regime. This historical novel, precisely speaking, follows a certain chronology in recording the dates and years of these events, and reflects the spirit of the age faithfully. Before the story proper begins, we encounter a Prologue, and at the close we read an Epilogue, a Note, and Acknowledgements. All these appendages should not be construed as mere accessories, but as important organs in the body of the text intended to reveal the purpose of this work and the author's choice of a particular time, the tense drama enacted on the national stage and its eventual outcome in the form of Independence, — the explications to avoid certain probable confusions, and to reveal the sources of the novelist's material.

The Prologue pinpoints the importance of India as a dominion in British possession. It becomes all the more incumbent upon Britishers to hold on after the Declaration of Independence by the United States of America in 1776. The popular statesman,

---

* Reprinted with permission of the editor of *Perspectives on Kamala Markandaya*, ed. M. Prasad (Ghaziabad : Vimal Prakashan, 1984), pp. 208–220.

Lord Randolph Churchill, delivering his speech to Members of Parliament appealed to them :

> ....to watch with the most sedulous attention, to develop with most anxious care, to guard with the most united and undying resolution, the land and the people of Hindustan, that most truly bright and precious gem in the Crown of the Queen, the possession of which, more than that of all your Colonial dominions, has raised in power, in resource, in wealth and in authority this small island home of ours....has placed it on an equality with, perhaps even in a position of superiority over, every other Empire either of ancient or of modern times.[1]

Keeping this fact in mind, the rulers conquered the princely states scattered throughout India one after another.

The story treated in the novel concerns the Devapur State whose ruler, Bawajiraj I, is deposed for his so-called seditious activities. The Agent, an Englishman, and the Dewan, a shrewd Brahmin serving the State as Chief Minister, select a young man of eighteen belonging to the Kshatriya caste who is just married to a girl of thirteen. He succeeds to the throne of Devapur State as Bawajiraj II. He is actually a commoner — a landowner's son — elevated to the highest position in order to execute the British design. The Britishers wanted only puppets rather than talented and independent persons to work under their control. But Bawajiraj II meets an accident while hunting and ultimately dies, leaving behind his young, beautiful wife and a son. The son ascends the *gaddi* as Bawajiraj III under the supervision of the influential Dowager Maharani and the British Resident, Sir Arthur Copeland.

Bawajiraj III and his son, Rabindranath (who is affectionately called Rabi), are the central characters in the story. In due course, the Maharajah is married to Shanta Devi, the daughter of a neighbourly princely State, and has four daughters from her. But he is drawn more towards his mistress, Mohini, who gives birth to Rabi, rather than to his cool and sedate wife.

Like his father, Bawajiraj III has received European education through English tutors, and has attended the Chief's College, the Military Academy, and the special coaching in civil administration under an experienced I.C.S. officer. He is, therefore, well-suited to carry on British interests even at the cost of his own people and their resources. He may suitably be dubbed as an intermediary between the rulers and the ruled, being himself a 'figurehead' or 'a pinhead.' He sometimes feels the progressively growing levies and restrictions on his people, but is helpless to offer them any relief. Many a time he grows indifferent to such matters on the pretext of his *izzat*, his prestige, and his promise, and that of his predecessors. The Chief Minster of his State also reminds him of his kingly duties but he snubs him.

As Rabi grows up, a Pundit is engaged as a tutor. Rabi does not attend the Chief's School or College; he refuses to go to the Military Academy. But he learns a lot, through his tutor and mother and grandmother, about the golden past of his land and about the heroic deeds of his ancestors. He has occasions to mingle with the commoners and their children (such as Janaki) in the playgrounds as well as in the open countryside. Naturally, Rabi develops as a contrast to his father. He is devoted to the Dewan along with his father and other members of the family, but he is not worried about the official or princely duties there, as his father is.

After the grand Durbar, the Maharajah and his family and followers return to Devapur, and leave afterwards for Simla for a sojourn. There they decide to proceed to Bombay to receive the delivery of three Rolls-Royces which were ordered earlier. But Bombay is troubled these days due to strikes of mill-workers and dockers. The royal family has no experience of facing such a tense situation, and the Maharajah and Rabi get injured badly in two separate incidents. While the Maharajah recovers at the Imperial Hotal, Rabi is looked after by a mill-worker named Jaya in her hut, where he has his first experience with a woman.

The royal family then returns to Devapur, where, too, the national awakening has made its inroads. The Maharajah is so loyal to the Empire that he raises a force and leads it to the western Front during World War I. He shows his mettle there and wins awards for his gallantry. He takes the opportunity to get Sir Arthur Copeland reinstated as the Resident of his State in place of the stubborn and offensive Mr. Buckridge.

In the final scenes, the national awakening grows very sharp and tense. The Indian masses are in no mood to cooperate with the foreigners, who levy heavy, new taxes on them day by day and render their lives miserable. In Devapur, too, things seem to be going against the Maharajah, who does not resist these taxes and harassments, and the Resident, who is the representative-head of the Empire. Rabi is on the side of the masses. He derives strong support from Usha, the youngest daughter of the Dewan. Usha once stages a subversive play showing the rulers as monsters to the horror and distaste of the Resident (who is now Mr. Buckridge) and the Maharajah. But Rabi and the Dewan like it immensely. The people become totally restless. The Maharajah, the Resident, and the Dewan realize the change of time. Mohini, Rabi, and Usha — the symbols of independence — emerge triumphant at long last, as India attains Independence on August 15, 1947.

Kamala Markandaya shows her deep insight in the handling of situations and characters in *The Golden Honeycomb*. Her art has grown subtle and suggestive in this novel. She displays an exemplary courage and determination in grappling with an enormous situation created by the Indo-British struggle. She ably produces both round and flat characters in this novel. The Maharajah, the Dewan, Mohini, Rabi, and Sir Arthur Copeland are really memorable and well-developed characters in it, while the Dowager Maharani, Shanta Devi, Janaki, Jaya, Mr. Buckridge, Miss Sophie, the daughters of the Dewan, Ramdas, and many others are undeveloped ones appearing before us only in patches. Evidently the two most dominant characters in the entire story are Bawajiraj III and Rabi. Often Markandaya presents her characters with vivid outlines of their physical and mental make-up.

We have already partly considered Bawajiraj III. But it remains to be mentioned that he is not merely a ruler conscious of his official duties and high privileges, but also a fond lover of his family and his subjects. There are individuals for whom he can sacrifice all, such as Mohini and Rabi. He never says a word against his mother. He counts on the devotion of his people to him. He knows that the Dewan is a man with an unquestionable record of sincerity to the State and of honest dealings with one and all. His deep attachment for Mohini and Rabi becomes quite evident when the two leave the Palace and go out on a countryside tour in the name of earning fresh experiences outside. He becomes very restless and dull counting hours and days of their possible arrival. On the occasion of the Delhi Durbar, he insists on their participation in it and succeeds. He also prevails upon them to join him in his Simla trip, whence they proceed to Bombay to take the delivery of the Rolls-Royces. He actually never wants to be separated from them, though he is reasonably loyal to his wife too. The following extract from the novel will amply demonstrate the bond of love existing between him and Mohini :

> 'Ah Mohini!' he sighs again. He has taken to pleading with her, it is becoming quite an exhausting business. 'I beg you, will you not marry me?'
>
> 'No.'
>
> 'It would make me the happiest man alive.'
>
> 'I can make you happy without that. I have no wish to be your second wife either.'
>
> 'Can you not think of the child?'
>
> 'I often think of the child. It is precisely because I think of the child.'
>
> 'I cannot understand your objection.'
>
> 'I've explained it to you.'
>
> 'I must say I find it difficult. Even princesses do not baulk at becoming Junior Maharanis.'
>
> 'I am not a princess.'

> 'You could be a *queen.*'
>
> 'I don't want to be your queen. I want to be free' (p. 32).

And his fatherly anxiety and affection for Rabi is nicely manifested in the following :

> 'I'm sure he's safe and sound. He says he is.'
>
> 'Safe! What does he mean?'
>
> 'Naturally he means what he says.'
>
> 'He says don't worry!'
>
> Bawajiraj smacks the disreputable chit his heir has scribbled and sent.
>
> 'Is it possible for a father, considering everything?'
>
> 'My love, there's no need to be upset. Rabi's not a child any more. Why can't you trust him to look after himself?'
>
> 'Leaving the hotel — running off as if he were a rickshawallah — does that inspire trust' (pp. 284-285).

In truth, the Maharajah finds many occasions to complain of Rabi's growing wild habits and of his connections with the riff-raff, but deep down in his heart he bears unspeakable love for his son.

Mohini is one person before whom Bawajiraj III is helpless. She is full aware of her physical charms which have ensnared the Maharajah. In any argument with him, she often emerges triumphant. Though she also loves him deeply, she has the guts to face him and convince him of the validity of her point. She does not like his unflinching loyalty towards the foreign rulers. She usually calls Sir Arthur 'Bania Sahib.' She tells her paramour that the Britishers are here for their financial and territorial gains, and that they are least interested in the uplift of the Indian populace.

Mohini's strong views are also shared by her son, the Pundit, and the Dewan. The powerful, irrepressible Dowager Maharani, Manjula, is also on her side. All of them rally around the

Maharajah to advise him what is right and dissuade him from what is wrong. They tell him that he is the father of his subjects and has nothing to fear but only his extra-allegiance to the *firanghis*, with whom his mighty ancestors had fought. Manjula enlightens her grandson at times and fuses into him anti-British feelings. That shows her deep love of the future heir to the *gaddi*. Similarly, the Pundit and the Dewan are deeply attached to Rabi. The Pundit injects nationalistic feelings and thoughts into the boy and prepares him for fight ahead. For this reason, the Maharajah does not like the tutor and expressed his displeasure with him in a conversation with Mohini :

> 'Arrange what?'
>
> 'A tour. For him to see the world. Panditji has travelled widely throughout the country; we can safely leave the arrangement to him.'
>
> 'You know I don't mean that.'
>
> 'What do you mean?'
>
> 'I mean his education. He ought to be under a proper tutor.'
>
> 'Panditji is a proper tutor;
>
> — or go to a proper boarding establishment' (p. 73).

And ultimately the father-king back-tracks because he does not like to send away his only son.

The Dewan, now Tirumal Rao, is a shrewd person entirely devoted to his Maharajah and to the people of his State. He is one who can favourably compare with the Englishman in talent and manipulations. So was also his father, Narasimha Rao, and so were his sharp ancestors. This illustrious race of Brahmins is conscious of its intellectual superiority over others in the given surroundings. The following is a pen-portrait of Tirumal Rao's father :

> The Dewan, who has an interest, which he does not declare, has also dispatched emissaries whose commissions are equally strict. His concern is to secure a union which will strengthen the realm, which by means he hopes to trim the sails of the

> British, whose power, he fears, has grown overweening. At the same time he has no wish to strengthen the realm to the point where he, the Dewan, is rendered a cipher. The balance to be struck is a delicate one, requiring some agility and considerable skill. Narasimha Rao does not doubt himself but he is a preoccupied man (p. 20).

And this is a threadbare analysis of the character of his son :

> Having been groomed for office virtually from infancy, Tirumal Rao slips smoothly into his father's shoes. Bawajiraj, whose prerogative it is, has nominated him. The Resident has confirmed the appointment. He has no reason not to. Tirumal Rao is a man of outstanding ability who has held virtually every portfolio in the realm (p. 50).

Tirumal Rao is a practical and alert Chief Minister who dares advise the Maharajah and the Resident against the newly levied Salt Taxation, which has irritated the people considerably. When one of his farmers, Ramdas, comes to inform him of its unbearability, he cooly replies that he has full knowledge of it. Later, the same Ramdas turns one of the staunch agitators against the British. The Dewan knows his duties and performs them well, supervising the civil administration of his State, its resources and revenues and its liabilities towards the subjects on the one hand and towards the Resident and the Viceroy on the other. The novelist has made known her admiration of the Dewan and his skilful management of the State affairs. At one place, she writes :

> The Dewan appoints his ministers; but he is a shrewd man (another Brahmin; the Brahmins have collared the best brains — they have proved it can be done by a system of sufficient ingenuity and singular dedication) who is very well aware of the presences in the Cantonment and Residency; and he chooses his men accordingly (p. 37).

The Dewan sometimes shares his top secrets with his wife or with Rabi (whose access to his house is free and unfettered). In fact, two of his daughters — Vimala and Usha — are taken up with Rabi, and Usha is specially suited for him. Both of them provide support and inspiration to the fighters for freedom. Towards the close of the novel, after the initial objections from her mother, Vatsala, Usha is seen with Rabi planning for the future which will presumably result in their wedlock.

Rabi is a very fascinating character in the novel. He is born in the Palace, and grows before our eyes. He gets his early education and training by Punditji, and develops ideas and tendencies prejudicial to the British and at times to the Maharajah, although he loves his parents very much. Like his mother, Mohini, he feels he is one of the commoners, and seeks opportunities to mingle with them. He has scoured the country extensively. The Dowager Maharani also shapes his mind and attitude to some extent. While his father is identified with Salt because he does not protest against Salt Taxation, Rabi is identified with Water, as he undertakes to build a dam for his people. He does not like the rotten British Raj, which relentlessly pursues the 'divide and rule' policy. Though his father is annoyed at this, he does not bother even a fig and carries on his activities until success is attained. Even his father seeks his advice with regard to the agitators' programmes and policies, and the Resident consults him in connection with his family's participation in the Holi celebrations. When Rabi along with his parents visits Bombay, they face a violent mob of striking workers and dockers, but Rabi alone knows the filthy language of the rabble and by using it instantly he rescues his injured father. The Maharajah thanked him for saving his life, but Rabi simply rejoins : "No, I didn't show them anything. I spoke to them in their language, that's all" (p. 261). Afterwards, Rabi takes a leading role in the mass-struggle for India's freedom. In truth, his control over his people is complete and appreciable. The Bombay strike of mill-workers and dockers was of a different nature, and so it fizzled out. But the mass-struggle with obvious far-reaching consequences in the history of the nation is much more powerful and organized due to the willing cooperation and participation of the masses. That is precisely what we gather from a conversation between Usha and Rabi :

> But that was before — That crowd didn't know its own strength. This one does. There have been one or two discoveries since (p. 462).

And this is the authorial commentary :

> This crowd is not going to make the mistake of mill crowd, or any other crowd, or strike. It has discovered muscle. Further, it has found out that muscle is a mesh of physical and mental fibre. It intends to use this strength, which is founded, even more basically, on its human spirit.
>
> It intends to stay. It, or if not, its heirs and successors. Time is on its side (p. 463).

Like Mohini and the Dewan, Rabi has the courage of his conviction, which inspires people to win freedom ultimately. The information of India's freedom is given in the Epilogue.

One aspect of Rabi's character that remains unnoticed so long is his affairs with girls. He develops an adolescent love for Janaki, a working girl in the Palace garden, and sees her ribs and rips, her clothes. She accompanies him on his trip to Delhi, and he buys a yellow sari for her as a gift. In the meantime, she disappears mysteriously and nothing is known about her. But while his love for Janaki remains mainly pure and untainted, his second love with a mill-working girl, Jaya, in Bombay is not so, and with her he has the first experience of a woman. Perhaps the circumstances are unavoidable, both living in the same hut and rolling over each other in the dead silence of the night. Jaya also takes it easy, her husband having been imprisoned for five years on the charge of active participation in strikes. Rabi has a handsome and tall personality which attracts girls. Vimala, the Dewan's second daughter, unsuccessfully attempts to lure him, but her father comes to know of it and he immediately arranges her marriage with a Brahmin of the neighbourly State. But the same father allows concessions to his youngest daughter, Usha, for her *amour patrial*, and she freely moves and acts with Rabi. When the curtain drops, Rabi and Usha are seen together planning their future programmes. For a time, Rabi also carries on with Miss Sophie. Although she is the smart, pretty daughter of the Resident, Sir Arthur, she has no inhibitions and goes with him hunting and boating.

The British Raj holds its sway over the Indian princes and states through its Agents, Residents, Commanders, I.C.S. officers, Governor-Generals and later Viceroys. In the name of maintaining law and order, it keeps garrisoned forces in all the Indian States which can easily be used for purposes of coercion, subversion, or deposition. The Viceroy is the supreme authority governing the Indian sub-continent on behalf of the Queen or King. Lord Curzon as India's Viceroy is very popular because he is identified with Justice, and he does not spare even the Englishman from punishment. He functions with utter dignity and composure. Sir Arthur is also a similar kind of person, least interfering in the State affairs and yet looking after the English interests very well. Although his wife, Lady Copeland, is made of different stuff, Sir Arthur is always judicious, sincere, honest, and compassionate towards Indians. He has, in fact, profound respect for Bawajiraj III. Because of him, the Residency becomes accessible to all those who need. Sir Arthur sees nothing objectionable in the ever-growing contacts between his grown-up daughter and Rabi. But he has to go to England for a short period during World War I, and is replaced by Mr. Buckridge, a tough man of few words and haughtly temper, who is never liked by the natives. Mr. Buckridge is instrumental in imposing a new levy of Salt Tax on Devapuris, who resist it tooth and nail and who finally succeed in overthrowing the British government and installing their own in its place. Mr. Buckridge is a total contrast to Sir Arthur, and Bawajiraj III is fully justified in recalling the latter form England once again in the same position.

There are certain important occasions when the Britishers and the native Indians function in close proximity. Thus, the Agent and the Resident work in harmony with the Maharajah and the Dewan and his retinue of ministers. The Delhi Durbar is a grand exhibition of their unique co-operation. Both the English rulers and the native rajahs attend it punctually, and compete with each other in pomp and show. This is how Bawajiraj III is portrayed here :

> His performance is flawless. When he goes over it, afterwards, he cannot really fault himself. He walks with a firm easy tread along the aisle, ascends the steps without a hitch, and advances to within six paces of the throne before which His Excellency is standing. Here, holding himself with dignity, he pays homage to the King-Emperor's Representative, and, in a few well-chosen words, asks for his felicitations to be conveyed to his Majesty on the occasion of his Coronation. Then he bows deeply, three low bows, and retires in good order (p. 160).

And yet another glimpse of the closeness of the two distinct races is to be had in the hunting spree of Rabi and Miss Sophie. The two peoples also come very close to each other during the wild yet harmless Holi celebrations in Devapur State. Of all English men and women present on the occasion, Miss Sophie enjoys this festival best.

The most charming feature of Markandaya's prose is her command of the English language. She does not write like Mulk Raj Anand whose language seems to course down tempestuously, or like Raja Rao whose writing meanders tortuously highlighting the anguish of the soul. Markandaya rather picks up her words and phrases carefully and makes use of them without any conspicuous linguistic distortions. Her language is not laboured. It is usually simple, chaste, and crisp. The sheer necessity of description or narration sometimes forces her to ignore the insertion of articles and the completion of sentences. The following extract will possibly illustrate this point :

> He indulged her, he knew. Fond father to all his children, but this child had a special place. He

> found time for her. Put aside the State, look her on his knee. Little girl unimpressed by august personage, enchanted by her father. Demanding. Sunny about it though. Huge smiles and airs of ravishing expectancy. Huge appetite for stories (p. 332).

Her language runs on smoothly like a racy river. She has also a propensity for short and clipped expressions and sentences, offering us a delightful feast of precise and pointed words. This is clearly seen in dialogues between two or more characters in *The Golden Honeycomb*. Occasionally, she employs Latin, French, and Indian words and expression. Some fine examples are :

(1) 'He is quartermaster *par excellence'* (p. 3).

(2) 'Appreciation, possibly, *le mot juste*?' (p. 233).

(3) 'You're only a *nam ke vaste* king' (p. 36).

But these insertions are neither too many, nor do they mar the overall impression; instead they add to the richness, variety and intellectuality of the work.[2]

The technique of Kamala Markandaya in *The Golden Honeycomb* is one of forceful narration and occasional description. Her style reveals the person behind the work. It tells us a lot about the author's educational and cultural background and about her love of the mother-land. She changes her scenes frequently, and each change is indicated by three asterisks. It appears as though we are sitting in a cinema hall, witnessing frequent changes of scenes on the screen. Sometimes a scene is a little lengthy, but sometimes it is very brief, say of barely four or five lines. Obviously, the eyes of the novelist are set on the exigencies of plot,[3] and S.P. Appaswamy rightly remarks that "it is indeed a saga, told by a master story-teller — a modern saga."[4]

Markandaya succeeds well in *The Golden Honeycomb* simply because she could tailor her method to the strict demands of a truly historical novel — and one such demand is the adherence to chronology, and in this she ranks with Thackeray and Trollope in English fiction and Mulk Raj Anand and Manohar Malgonkar in Indo-English fiction. She is decidedly a consummate artist, and critics have invariably praised her. Prof. Iyengar pays tributes to "the sufficiency and suggestiveness of her prose..."[5] K.R. Chandrasekharan discovers an "implied message in Kamala Markandaya's novels,"[6] which is that India should confidently pursue her own path holding fast to her traditional values and using methods appropriate to her culture. To Uma Parmeswaran, Markandaya "is, undoubtedly, one of the major novelists of the Commonwealth scene."[7] The Russian critic, Kalinnikova, echoes Parmeswaran when she remarks that Markandaya "is undoubtedly an outstanding creative artist."[8] Prof. R.S. Singh thinks that "Markandaya is a sensitive fabulist, and her depiction of the clash of the two attitudes, the Eastern and the Western, is authentic...."[9] Meenakshi Mukherjee and S.C. Harrex also express an identical opinion in their respective books. H.M. Willams brackets her with Anita Desai in exploring "the anguish" in modern society.[10] And Margaret P. Joseph considers her to be "not only the earliest Indian woman novelist of significance — in fact William Walsh calls her 'the most gifted' of them — but also one of the most distinguished writers on the Indian literary scene today."[11]

To conclude, *The Golden Honeycomb* is yet another feather in Markandaya's literary cap, though it finds no mention in the critical studies of K.R.S. Iyengar, K.R. Chandrasekharan, Meenakshi Mukherjee, Uma Parmeswaran, A.V. Krishna Rao, S.C. Harrex, H.M. Williams, R.S. Singh and Elena J. Kalinnikova, because they were written before this novel came out. But S.P. Appaswamy in his article and Margaret P. Joseph in her book-length study on Markandaya have dealt ably with this novel. It is unquestionably Markandaya's *magnum opus* because it shows "the poise and balance"[12] of her maturity.

NOTES AND REFERENCES

1. Kamala Markandaya, *The Golden Honeycomb* (London : B.I. Publications in association with Chatto and Windus, 1977), p. IX. Thereafter, all textual quotations figure in the body of this essay.

2. In an article published in *The Literary Criterion*, IX, No. 3, (Winter, 1970), Shyamala Venkateswaran finds fault with Marakandaya's early novels (barring *Some Inner Fury*), but this does not apply to *The Golden Honeycomb*.
3. Trying to explicate the wide significance of plot, Elizabeth Dipple observes : "More significantly, it is a word which establishes a liaison between reader and literary text.... In other words, it is a term which when justly used, asks that every reader participate in the movement of the form and through this participation become himself a critic. Its stress and life are nevertheless in the work of literature — in its interior dynamics." — *Plot* (London : Methuen & Co., 1970), p. 67.
4. S.P. Appaswamy, "*The Golden Honeycomb* : A Saga of Princely Life in India by Kamala Markandaya," *The Journal of Indian Writing in English*, Vol. 6, No. 2, (July 1978), p. 63.
5. K.R. S. Iyenger, *Indian Writing in English* (Bombay : Asia Publishing House, 1973 ed.), p. 449.
6. K.R. Chandrasekharan, "East and West in the Novels of Kamala Markandaya," *Critical Essays on Indian Writing in English*, eds. Naik. Desai and Amur (Dharwar : Karnatak University, 1972), p. 328.
7. Uma Parmeswaran, *A Study of Representative Indo-English Novelists* (New Delhi : Vikas Publishing House, 1976), p. 89.
8. Elena J. Kalinnikova, *Indian English Literature* (Ghaziabad : Vimal Prakashan, 1982), p. 163.
9. R.S. Singh, *Indian Novel in English* (New Delhi : Arnold-Heinemann, 1977), p. 147.
10. H.M. Williams, *Indo-Anglian Literature* (New Delhi : Orient Longman Ltd., 1976), p. 83.
11. Margaret P. Joseph, *Kamala Markandaya*, Indian Writers Series (New Delhi : Arnold-Heinemann, 1980), p. 11.
12. *Ibid.*, p. 210.

4

THE HISTORIAN AS A NOVELIST : MANOHAR MALGONKAR*

I

In a critique of *Kanthapura* (1938), C.D. Narasimhaiah once remarked that "Indian fiction in English can make headway by continuing the Raja Rao line, which is to say one must have not merely his technique, but his amazingly high intellectual equipment and awareness of the Indian tradition."[1] Considered in the light of this remark, Manohar Malgonkar (born 1913) though does not follow the Raja Rao line, especially his technique, he has still made a mark in Indo-English fiction as a writer. He rather stands apart from other Indo-English novelists, in that he portrays distinct phases of Indian National Movement and its stirrings with the irresistible tenacity of a historian turned novelist. Whereas a strong humanitarian attitude enlivens the novels of Mulk Raj Anand, an acute social awareness bristles the works of R.K. Narayan, Ruth Prawer Jhabvala, and Bhabani Bhattacharya, and a cross-cultural conflict persists in the novels of Kamala Markandaya. Raja Rao, and B. Rajan, there is an ever-growing historical consciousness in the writings of Malgonkar. The fact to be borne in mind is that he was a historian of the Marathas even before he entered the domain of Indo-English fiction. Some people might take it as the paucity of his imaginative and inventive

* First published in *Perspectives on Indian Fiction in English,* ed. M.K. Naik (N.D. : Abhinav Publication, 1985), pp. 135-149. Reprinted with permission of the editor.

powers, but the truth remains that he is a writer who moves with a consciousness of the area of his operation and the period of his depiction.

Malgonkar is unquestionably a prolific writer with a number of novels to his credit. Although he has published quite a few books of history and several collections of short stories to date, it is as a novelist having a technique and language of his own and being grounded firmly in the rich Indian tradition that he will survive in literature in the days to come. The novels on which his abiding fame is to rest are : *Distant Drum* (1960), *Combat of Shadows* (1962), *The Princes* (1963), *A Bend in the Ganges* (1964), and *The Devil's Wind* (1972). These novels, on the whole, tend to consolidate the proposition that Malgonkar is a novelist endowed with "a wonderful knack of weaving plots of singular originality."[2] This he could be because of his inclination towards historicity, his ability to commingle fact with fiction, and his skill in yoking together recorded truths and elements of romance and adventure, in his works. After all, he is a historian with a difference, a historian blessed with creative mind and fertile imagination.

II

The first novel, *Distant Drum,* which is divided into three Parts and runs into 270 pages in print, is dedicated to a group of three persons — Duggie Sawhny, Pattie Somdutt, and Pat Totterdell — and is based on Malgonkar's own experiences in the Indian Army as a Colonel. This novel hailed by K.R. Srinivasa Iyengar as one of "unusual distinction"[3] recounts the story of a Regiment — the 4th Satpuras — that had maintained its equanimity and reputation in the face of crushing defeats as well as glorious victories. Throughout this novel, Kiran Garud, the CO of the 4th Satpuras, is the central figure, and the story revolves round him. He is a young, enthusiastic, and hard-working officer, who has a sense of human values above and beyond the military laws. His relationships with the 4th Satpuras, with Abdul Jamal, and with Miss Bin Sonal form the crux of the matter. He had fought against the bloody Japanese in Burma and crossed twice the Sittang Bridge spanning a very dangerous river in a shaky raft. The reward came after the war in the shape of the command of the 4th Satpuras. When shifted to the HQ in Delhi, he had to face certain teething problems created by the jealous army officers. He then opted for an operational area, namely J & K, for his posting. And when things got rotten to the core at Raniwada, where the 4th Satpuras were stationed, Garud was summoned by Gen. Spike Ballur to take over the reins once again and build the Regiment from the shambles. How persuasive Gen. Ballur is may be inferred from the following : "I am depending on you, Jacko. I want the 4th to become exactly what it was in Ropey Booker's time. Second to none. But we must all work for it, we old tigers."[4] Garud took up this assignment with all enthusiasm and responsibility, but this time he went to Raniwada along with his beloved, Miss Bina, who had earlier rejected Mr. Arvind Mathur, a multi-millionaire of Bombay against the wishes of her adored father. The conversation of Kiran and Bina is worth recording here :

> "Oh," Kiran said, "Darling, will you marry me?"
> "Yes. If you love me. Do you?"
> "I can never tell you how much I love you. How much I have missed you....I only wanted to make things easier for you..." (p. 269).

As regards Col. Kiran's relationship with Col. Abdul Jamal, it is cemented with perfect understanding and faithful friendship. The scale rather swings in favour of Col. Jamal, a true specimen of the reliable Muslims, who had not only once lied to save Kiran from the murder trial of Mr. Bob Modley, with whose wife Kiran once had an affair, but also guarded his life in the mosque when he was being surrounded by the fanatic Muslim mob. Even after the partition of India, their friendship continued unabatedly, though Jamal had joined the Pak troops. While posted on the borders of J & K, they once met under the Bushy topped tree in No-Man's land and chatted together for a while and emptied the glasses of champagne with the old, prestigious war-slogan of the Satpuras :

"Come on Jawans!"

"Tigers don't live for ever!" Abdul said (p. 238).

Abdul being senior to Kiran always took initiative in his dealings with the latter and remained honest and straightforward throughout. Their counterparts in the novel are : Kamala Kant, Namdar, and Rawal Singh, who are just parasites on the government exchequer and nothing more. One can't close an account of the novel without mentioning that it is heavily loaded with the writer's personal experiences in the Army, both in peace time and during the war.

Malgonkar's second novel, *Combat of Shadows,* takes an epigraph from the *Bhagavad-Gītā,* verse 27, and runs into 35 chapters in all. This sizzling story of adventure, romance and lust has Henry Winton as its principal character. Winton is one of the British managers of the Brindian Tea Company having his headquarters at Silent Hill. In this novel he is pulled by the mutually opposite drives — 'shadows' as the author calls them — of Desire and Aversion. The drive of Desire takes him to a number of women — to Guari, Ruby Miranda, and Jean — turn by turn, and in his search for a purpose and meaning in love he is eventually engulfed by the yawning jaws of Death. He obviously does not like Gauri, as he had once caught her red-handed while stealing a sackful of tea leaf and warned her : "If I ever catch you robbing my garden again, I'll give you a thrashing, understand? I'll flog you with a horsewhip, and then hand you over to the police."[5] There is a stage when Jugal Kishore brings her to him with the bad intention of corrupting him morally, but Winton rebukes and turns them out of his official residence. In the latter part of the novel, the married Gauri re-emerges on the scene suddenly when Winton is trying to track down the one-tusked elephant, a very dangerous creature by all means that has taken so many lives in its stampede, particularly those of Kistulal (father of Pasupati) and Eddie Trevor (son of the old John Trevor). She takes him to a place called Wallach's Folly where she shows him his wife, Jean, and Eddie making intense love to each other. The shock of what he sees is so overpowering that he fractures his own leg while attempting to give a hard blow to this naughty woman. Winton does like Ruby Miranda and Jean from the core of the his heart, and with both he has had sexual contacts as occasions demand, but his marriage materialises only with the latter, who not only betrays him in preference to his stockman — Eddie — but also grows completely indifferent towards him and ultimately deserts him and leaves for Poona to lead a separate life there. Miranda, who is given employment and promotions by Winton, wants to marry him, but the *pucca-sahib* that he is and the British officials in India — Sir Jeffrey Dart, Capt. Cockburn, Col. Waters, Henderson, etc. — come in the way and prevail upon him to accept Jean as his wife; otherwise, Winton knows it well that "that was the woman he now longed with all his being to get back to; the rare mixture of the submissiveness and surrender of oriental womanhood with the freedom and gaiety of the West...." (p. 116). But in the last chapter it is tacitly suggested that Ruby in connivance with Sir Dart and Pasupati wreaks revenge upon him and burns him alive in the same cottage in a helpless, hapless condition, and this shows that she never forgives him for the wrong done to her. More to blame is Jean who grows unexpectedly fond of him, and is drawn to another Englishman as the object of her love, and lastly chooses Winton as her husband and comes to live with him at Silent Hill, where she somehow manages to learn of Henry's pre-marital affairs with Ruby, grows cold and stiff towards him, and is attracted much and more towards the dashing hockey player-cum-sportsman Eddie. She often taunts him with unseemly remarks, and her behaviour towards him is hardly justified.

The instinct of Aversion operates in the novel on a still larger scale, and it includes not merely womenfolk but also menfolk in its range. We have already spoken of the swinging see-saw of love in Winton's relationships with the three important women characters in it, but we have said nothing so far about his relationships with certain significant male characters like Jugal Kishore, Mahipat, Eddie Trevor and Sir Jeffrey Dart. Of these,

Winton has some affection and deep reard for Sir Dart's rational approach to the burning issues like strikes on the tea estates and for his indomitable courage (remember that he kills the tusker that has already taken two precious lives and that has ever deluded Winton's hunt for it), but he has no affection or consideration for others. Once he starts hating Kishore for his active role in inciting labour trouble for him, there is no end to it, even though the latter submits his resignation from his Company and goes away to be a powerful political leader. He even insults his sister, Gauri, twice or thrice, and at least once in his very presence. Winton looks upon Mahipat as a stooge in the hands of Kishore, having no guts of his own to stand and stare when he comes across him during the labour-management confrontation. He has no softness for Eddie Trevor, too, who is thrust upon him by Sir Dart, his superior, and who steals a march over him in shooting the incessantly and horribly crying python during the mating season, in playing stellar roles in the national hockey matches and club-dances, and in snatching away Ruby from him for good and his wife, Jean, to boot. The person who correctly reads this writ large on the conscience of Winton is no one else than Eddie's own father after his death. The old John Trevor tells Winton blatantly : "You never liked my... You did not like Eddie, did you Mr. Winton!" (p. 270).

And one untouched thread of the narrative is Winton's passion for hunting, letting us wonder occasionally whether he does not resemble Jim Corbett in this respect. He has shot biscons and birds, and has even attempted to prey upon mating pythons, dangerous tigers and wild elephants, though without any notable success. He has taken a fancy to the killing of the mountainous one-tusked elephant, a great terror in the areas of its operation — the forest and along the river Koyna, but he fails to accomplish it as he has broken his leg badly at Wallach's Folly.

Another craze for Winton is to join the military commission in the ensuing course at Belgaum, but this also remains unfulfilled. His competitor in love, Eddie, gets the commission and is to join the Academy within two weeks before he gets killed by the bumptious elephant, but Winton's wait without hope for a call up never materialises. For this, too, he envies Eddie, and subtly plots his murder. The only natural justice for him is what he meets with at the hands of his own people at the close of the novel.

The third novel, *The Princes,* evokes a vivid picture of the partition days in India when the aristocratic rulers of the Estates were put to untold sufferings and hardships owing to their uncertain future. These rulers initially thought that they would be safeguarded and their interests promoted by the verbal assurances and announcements of the British Crown, but later they were disillusioned when the Britishers left them in the lurch, to the whims and freaks of the mushrooming national leaders of all castes and creeds. The title of the novel is actually a pointer to these rulers in general and not to one single prince of Begwad Estate. Abhayraj, who is reared in the lap of feudal luxury, joins military for a few years but comes back to his native place when the activities in the Estate seem to slip out of the hands of his father, whom he as well as the affectionate public loves to call 'Dadaji.' Abhay develops love for Minnie, whom he incidentally meets in Mussoorie in one of its royal hotels, and with whom he carries on his affairs till the very end even after he is wedded to Kamala and has fathered two children — one female and the other male. But when he accuses her of being an accomplice in the booming business of her husband, Mr. Punch, she cannot tolerate it and slaps him and breaks her relations with him, saying; "You swine!" and again : "You bloody, lowdown swine!"[6] At this juncture, his father is no more, having been killed by the kalaras giant tiger in the forest on a shooting spree; his mother has deserted him for ever to join Abdulla Jan in Pakistan as his wife — a shock too deep to absorb for him; his step-brother, Charudutt, who is now the Inspector-General of Police, has betrayed him cooly yet methodically; his despised classmate, Kanakchand, a cobbler's son, has now emerged victorious in the struggle between monarchy and nationalism. But he has his wife and children, his palace and Chief Minister — Harikishore — with him, and these are enough to give him strength and solace at the times of test. In fact, this prince has a peculiar softness for the nationalists, even for Kanakchand, who later becomes K.C. Gaur as the leader of Prejamandal against the king and his forces, but when the latter denounces his noble father in the public, he has courage in him to come forward and flog the babbler. In this context, the speeches of the two are worth recording here. This is Gaur :

> "What has happened to the man, who flogged me? His power is gone, his money is gone, he himself is gone. I, whom he whipped, have the honour to be one of your Ministers. It is they who are finished : it was we who finished them...we were determined to wipe them out. This we had sworn — this we have fulfilled" (p. 342).

To this the pert reply comes from Abhay, who has just whipped Gaur in the presence of all :

> "This I have sworn...This have I fulfilled" (p. 343).

This novel, like its predecessors, contains the adventurous story of hunting in its texture. It has a Prologue and an Epilogue, signalling thereby pre-Independence India and post-Independence India respectively.

The Princes captured the attention of the world-famed Caribbean novelist, V.S. Naipaul, who took it as a glaring example of "withdrawal, denial, confusion of values."[7] Speaking at some length about this work, Naipaul remarks : "*The Princes* is the medieval tragedy of a medieval Indian petty prince who loses power with Independence and feels the humiliation of his fall so deeply that he goes out unarmed after a wounded tiger and is killed. It is an honest book, and the writing is not without skill. Malgonkar has a feeling for outdoor life and his descriptions of hunting and shooting can convey the enchantment of these pastimes even to those who do not practise them."[8] And a little afterwards Naipaul comes out with a horrible lash : "The poverty of India is quivering...the narrator sees his father denying 'basic rights' to 'the people,' he talks of the 'collective wish of the people'.... This is the Indian withdrawal and denial; this is part of the confusion of Indian Anglo-India."[9]

The fourth novel, *A Bend in the Ganges*, is dedicated to Vibhakar and carries a citation from M.K. Gandhi. It became immediately popular and successful. E.M. Forster, the noted English novelist, found it as one of the three best novels of 1964, and Richard Church in his review of the book in *The Bookman* compared it with Leo Tolstoy's *War and Peace,* while the B.B.C. of London branded it as 'a very exciting story told with great skill'. This novel is written on a grand scale and depicts the Gandhian era in all its manifestations. Its title is derived from a sentence in the *Ramayana* : 'At the bend in the Ganges they paused to take a look at the land they were leaving,' and is symbolically applied here. In it the two principal characters, Debi-dayal and Gian, also pause and look longingly at their land while they are getting deported for the Cellular Jail of the Andaman Islands. Lord Rama had once left Ayodhya behind for fourteen years and Debi and Gian have also to serve a term of fourteen years in exile. This may also apply to the multimillionaire businessman, Tekchand Kerwad, the father of Debi and Sundari, who has, at the close of the novel, to leave his home in Pakistan with a very heavy heart, nostalgically recollecting the dying words of his wife, Radha : "Please don't leave me here, darling, please take me with you...,"[10] to which he had given the reassuring reply : "No, I shall never leave you... Now rest" (p. 380). In his brief Note, Malgonkar tells us : "Only the violence in this story happens to be true; it came in the wake of the bloodiest upheavals of history: twelve million people had to flee, leaving their homes; nearly half a million were killed; over a hundred thousand women, young and old, were abducted, raped, mutilated" (p. 6). This powerful story tries to highlight the truth that freedom is a hard-earned trophy, and that when it came to India in 1947 it was attended by violence, bloodshed, and betrayals. The history of the Indian Freedom Movement is typically represented by Gian Talwar, who is originally a follower of Mahatma Gandhi — "I am a follower of Gandhi" (p. 16) — but later gets involved in a revengeful murder of Vishnudutt (who had earlier killed his lovable younger brother, Hari) in a family feud. Gian is prosecuted and exiled to the Andamans, where he draws very close to Englishmen, particularly to Patrick Mulligan, and escapes with them in a boat bound for India at the time of the Japanese attack of the Islands, and concealing his identity earns a decent livelihood in Bombay through Tekchand and Sundari (who have come to know that he was with Debi in the Andamans Jail), but leaves it when the port of Bombay is bombarded and reduced to ashes, and once again back to Tekchand he helps his family in various ways, partly to expiate the sin of having betrayed Debi once in the jail and partly to serve the really needy and unattended old couple along with Sundari. In the end, the reward for him is the hand of Sundari which he so keenly desires. As a contrast to him is the hard-core, unyielding but faithful character of Debi-dayal, the terrorist, who is also an ardent lover of Mother India but who believes in the use of arms and ammunition against a mighty British Empire. He may be guessed to be the follower of Bhagat Singh, Azad and other martyrs in the cause of the country, and is once nabbed by the police for blowing up an aeroplane along with Shafi (before a misunderstanding arises between the Hindus and the Muslims), and is tried and deported to the Andamans in the same ship as carries away Gian too. Debi is a self-respecting person and once badly beats and kicks the abusive Gorkha sentry, Balbahadur, in the jail; he hates Gian for the latter's betrayal, and confides all this to his sister Sundari, who holds a very high opinion about her brother. Though he is of a steely heart, he recognises human values in Mumtaz, a Muslim woman picked up from the clutches of his erstwhile companion who is now turned a woman goer, — the woman who nurses him back to health from the severe wounds he has received from Shafi in a scuffle for her. Flouting the rigid family traditions, Debi falls in love with her and decides to make her his wife, and informs his sister all about this episode and seeks her assistance in placating the anger of the parents on this score which Sundari readily offers. Though Sundari arrives at her parents' quite safe and sound, her brother along with his wife does not, because on his way home near the Indo-Pak border he falls a victim to the fury of the Muslims and is permanently separated from his wife in the midst of her deafening scream : "Debi! Debi, my darling! I shall never live without you! I am coming with you too... I am coming..." (p. 369). The third important character in the novel is Sundari, who is though married to an army officer of Bombay, to one named Gopal Chandidar, is in half-love with her own brother, and encourages the advances of Gian towards her when he returns from the Andamans. Debi's arrival in Bombay brings a change in her attitude towards Gian, but the latter meets her again at her father's, and looks after the whole family during the riots, and fights with Shafi and his gang in its protection, and arranges for its despatch to India under his supervision, though on the way Tekchand deserts and disappears suddenly without letting anyone know about it. His disappearance keeps readers guessing where he might have gone. There are also some other occasions when the air of suspense hangs over the plot, *e.g.*, what happens to Mumtaz after Debi's death? But such unresolved strands are always to be found in Malgonkar's novels, and *A Bend in the Ganges* is not weakened by their presence in any way. This novel is rather Malgonkar's masterpiece which has immortalized him in the annals of Indo-English fiction.

The last novel to be considered in detail here is *The Devil's Wind*. This is the story of the first Indian struggle for freedom in 1857, in which Nana Saheb, the adopted son of Bajirao Peshwa II, took a leading part and fomented troubles for the British stationed in and around Kanpur. The struggle was called 'a mutiny' by the covetous and hard-hearted *firanghis* (Englishmen, as nicknamed by Indians), but it was countrywide in its scope and enveloped the whole of the northern plains, such places as Meerut, Delhi, Oudh, Jhansi, and Kanpur. The title given to this novel — *The Devil's Wind* — is very appropriately picked up as it suggests the rise of the Rebellion in the North exactly after a hundred years when the Battle of Plassey was fought — that was in 1757 — in which Lord Clive emerged victorious over the disjointed forces of Siraj-ud-Dolla. According to the novelist, the accounts of Nana Saheb are already there, but all of them invariably paint him as "infamous, dastardly, despicable, crafty demon, barbarous butcher, and arch assassin," and in England he replaced "Napoleon Bonaparte as the hate object of a nation."[11] Malgonkar, therefore, thought it proper to present his character and life-story from a truly Indian viewpoint, without twisting the truths about them. He observes : "This ambiguous man and his fate have always fascinated me. I discovered that the stories of Nana and the revolt have never been told from the Indian point of view.... It is fiction : but it takes no liberties with verifiable facts or even with probabilities."[12] The book being divided into three Parts and dedicated to Sunita keeps its hold on matter-of-fact descriptions and historical characters. There are distinct groups of characters in it — the Britishers and the natives, the rulers and the subjects, the masters and the servants, and the men and the women. Nana Saheb, like the other Peshwas, was addicted to beauty and sex, but was all the time illumined by the glittering rays of Freedom. A curse on the family had it that Bajirao's heir — Nana himself — would not be able to cohabit with his wife, and if he ever did so she would not survive. His two or three wives had died prematurely, and he never dared touch Kashi, the teenager queen from the South. He was satisfied with his two concubines — Champa (who had born a daughter, Gangamala) and Ajizan (who had died — a martyr's death at the hands of the British immediately after the mutiny) — and later with Eliza, the charming daughter of Gen. Wheeler. It is the last-named who was with Nana Saheb on his voyage to Mecca in the last ladder of the story. And though he succeeded in reaching Mecca, where he got all the facilities due to the generous arrangements of Jayaji Scindia, the Maharaja of Gwalior, and where his trusted lieutenant, Azim, rejoined him making his life easy and comfortable, he could never forget his motherland, and nostalgically recalled that "The vivid colours my land and the profound silence of the Ganges are somehow closer to me than my surroundings [in Mecca]" (pp. 305-306). This, however, should not create the impression that Nana was runaway having no guts or tactics of the great Peshwas. On the contrary, he was brave and courageous, took active part in the people's awakening against the mighty Britishers, and fought thrice before Kanpur fell to the enemies. In his noble mission he was ably assisted by his brothers — Baba Bhat and Balarao — and his secretary — Azim — and his estate manager — Tantya Tope, and he never showed the cruelty and brutality of the blood-thirsty Britishers like Renaud and Neill. Though his mission flopped, it is the salutary efforts of patriots like him that paved the way for India's freedom after a long heroic struggle.

III

These are the full-fledged and mature novels of Malgonkar. The others that come from his pen are the espionage thrillers — *Spy in Amber* (1971) and *Bandicoot Run* (1982) — and the film-scripts — *Shalimar* (1968) and *Open Season* (1978). The novelized version of *Spy in Amber* owes much to the "initiative and talent"[13] of Suniti Malgonkar, the daughter of the author, and is all about a Tibetan monastery and China's designs on its fabulous wealth and the concerns of monks to dispatch it to a safe place in India. *Bandicoot Run* is about a file missing from the Army Headquarters in New Delhi. The CIA wants it in America, but it is sold to Pakistan through an unexpected intrigue and rivalry in the corridors of power. It derives its title from 'ban' di-koot,' meaning 'the largest species of rat, found in India and Ceylon, called also '*Malabar rat* and *pig-rat.*' It signifies an intelligence operation through "a tunnel running all the way from the innermost sanctums of the Indian Army's Headquarters at New Delhi, to the office of the Director of Inter-Services Intelligence in Rawalpindi, Pakistan. It worked for just over a year...."[14] *Shalimar* was originally a screenplay by Krishna Shah but later novelized by Malgonkar as faithfully as he could. Speaking of it, Malgonkar writes : "I have taken absolutely no liberties with the plot, done my best to incorporate the changes made while the film was being shot, and have left much of the dialogue of the screenplay as it was."[15] *Open Season* is a film story that was commissioned to Malgonkar by one of his friend-producers for the New York World Fair of 1964-1965. It was completed within two months. Writing of this work, the author remarks : "*Open Season* was not written as a novel, and it is being offered in that garb only because the film was never made."[16] One more work should be mentioned here, and that is *The Sea Hawk* (n.d. — but published definitely between *Open Season* and *Bandicoot Run*), which is really more of a biography than a novel.

IV

Manohar Malgonkar usually writes about romance, sex, adventure, military life, hunting, partition of India and other historical events. These themes are neatly pressed into creative service, producing the effect of a harmonious whole. In organizing them, the novelist displays an enviable skill. It is not that there are no strands of story left out or unresolved, but that such strands are needed to produce an atmosphere of suspense and mystery, and Malgonkar often succeeds in introducing the elements of suspense and adventure into his works. One incessantly absorbing subject for this writer is the history of the Marathas — that of Kanhoji Angrey, the valiant Admiral, and of the Puars of Dewas Senior and of the Chhatrapatis of Kolhapur, but mostly such attempts lie beyond the range of novel proper. Malgonkar does not attempt so much psychological, sociological, or anthropological themes as he does historical ones.

Malgonkar is at his best in plot-weaving and story-telling. His stories are often eventful and entertaining. He is absolutely conscious of his objectives as a writer, and observes as follows :

> ....I do strive deliberately and hard, to tell a story well : and I revel in incident, in improbabilities, in unexpected twists. I feel a special allegiance to the particular sub-caste among those whose caste-mark I have affected, the entertainers, the tellers of stories. Novels that do not conform to this basic pattern, however well-written they may be,

> are to me like unending cheese-straws, they may tickle the taste buds, but they cannot constitute a square meal — at least not to one who is used to curries and chutneys.[17]

Malgonkar's novels, as a result, are well-planned and well-constructed. And since he is very close to Indian history, his novels tend to be quite informative and knowledgeable.

Malgonkar's narrative technique comes out vividly in his novels. In describing an event or in unfolding a plot, he is unquestionably superb. Most of his stories are told in the third person and in the past tense, but *The Princes* and *Bandicoot Run* are exceptions to this. In these two works, the narrator is the 'I,' the principal character in the story. Nowhere in the works of Malgonkar do we witness the formlessness of *The Serpent and the Rope* or the puranic style of *Kanthapura*. Though in *A Bend in the Ganges* he becomes multifaceted and epical, like the author of *War and Peace,* he does not reach that height elsewhere. And as a historian, he does not remain detached and dispassionate at times. The obvious results are the occasional distortions of facts and figures. In this context, Meenakshi Mukherjee rightly remarks : "*A Bend in the Ganges* is not so much a story of men and women as of places and episodes, not an integrated human drama but an erratic national calendar."[18] Malgonkar takes Englishmen as the ideal figures of honesty and integrity, and sometimes pulls down Indians for lack of sincerity and sense of justice (remember that Gian praises the English judge who acquits him of the charge of murdering Vishnu-dutt).

This naturally leads us to a consideration of the art of characterization in Malgonkar's novels. In them we come across both types and individuals. Of the first category are the army men and the courtiers, the loyal ministers and the opportunistic leaders, the courtesans and the harlots, the prisoners and the businessmen; and of the second are Col. Kiran Garud, Henry Winton, Debi-dayal, Gian Talwar, Abhayraj (the Prince), and Nana Saheb. Sometimes the same character occurs in more than one novel, *e.g.,* Kiran Garud appearing in both *Distant Drum* and

Bandicoot Run. We do find women and children in Malgonkar's novels, but usually they are not allowed to develop fully. As for women, they appear in them as the symbols of sex and comfort, be they queens (like the mother and wife of Abhayraj in *The Princes* and Kashi in *The Devil's Wind*) or the ordinary ones (like Sundari in *A Bend in the Ganges,* Ruby and Jean in *Combat of Shadows,* and Miss Bina in *Distant Drum*). Obviously, women play second fiddle to men in the works of Malgonkar, and they are not generally granted the freedom of will or movement.

The lingustic achievement of Malgonkar is definitely commendable. Long ago, Raja Rao visualised the difficulty of an Indian writer in English when he pointed out the characteristic contrast between thought and medium of expression, between "the tempo of Indian life" and "an alien language."[19] The objection of scholars to the use of English, such as McCutchion raises,[20] has been due to the fact that such a non-native English lacks the 'fineness of nuance.' The English of Malgonkar is mainly traditional and conservative, but it is full and exact, as the B.B.C. correspondent John Morris has reported. Though Malgonkar is fully aware of the linguistic dilemma of an Indian writer in English, he has used English in a natural and spontaneous way, drawing his nuances from his close contacts with the British officials in the Indian Army and with the other ranks of Britishers outside. He may not be as innovative as Raja Rao, or as impressive as R.K. Narayan, or as vernacular as Mulk Raj Anand, but he is almost always readable and enjoyable. The reason for this is that Malgonkar keeps an eye open for a ready market and prefers "acceptability" to "experimentation."[21] He claims to have acquired 'a fairly full vocabulary of raw words' which he uses effortlessly. Here is an instance of the natural conversation of a drinks party in one of the Delhi restaurants :

> "Not another, no."
> "Nonsense, I insist; gin's quite harmless."
> "Sam's absolutely wizard."
> "Absolutely."

> "If you really swear gin is harmless; then just a wee little one."
> "Moochoo's terrific, absolutely terrific!"
> "Who says so?"
> "Abdaaaar!" (*Distant Drum,* p. 180).

In this extract, the language has become completely truncated; not a single word is used more than needed. And the last word in this conversation catches up the air of reality and naturalness; it is a vernacular by all means. Similar expressions may also be traced in Malgonkar's other works too, particularly when he tries to recapture the real speech of British officers in the Indian Army or that of hardcore hunters. In *Combat of Shadows,* Winton, who is a curious mixture of the two kinds of people specified above, exclaims as follows on hearing the death-news of Eddie Trevor : " 'Boy!...Boy!' Where's that damned brandy-pani? Juldi" (p. 268). This is the living speech of a typical Anglo-Indian saheb. It is no wonder, then, that the novelist's linguistic excellence made a correspondent of the *Times Literary Supplement* once write that a "new Malgonkar in a Piccadilly book-stall puts the seal on British achievement."[22]

Malgonkar's Indianness can hardly be questioned. He had, no doubt, read English and served with the Britishers in the Army, but he was "no lover of the British Raj."[23] His admiration for the British officers does not go without qualifications, and he shows a deep awareness of his cultural heritage and national history. *The Princes, A Bend in the Ganges,* and *The Devil's Wind* present India's historical events with impeccable accuracy and perfect understanding. Most of his leading characters are Indians, and almost all the events take place on the Indian soil, barring a few stray scenes here and there — a Burma operation in *Distant Drum,* or a Cellular Jail in the Andamans Islands in *A Bend in the Ganges,* or a Mecca Voyage for Nana Saheb in *The Devil's Wind.*

Malgonkar has been compared to John Masters, the celebrated author of *Bhowani Junction* (1954). To some extent, the comparison is apt, as both the authors write about certain identical themes — love and romance, sex and revellery, brave adventures and successful situations, *thugee* and highway robbery, etc. In *A Bend in the Ganges,* we have plenty of these things. But the comparison should stop there, because Malgonkar is no imitator of anyone. He is rather endowed with a creative intelligence of the first order and a distinct individuality of his own. Prof. Iyengar is not altogether wrong when he remarks : "Malgonkar is not an indigenous John Masters; nor is *Distant Drum* an Indo-Anglian variation of the Anglo-Indian *Bhowani Junction.* There is, on the contrary, an authentic quality about Malgonkar and his novel that can stand scrutiny without reference to the Masters recipe."[24]

V

To sum up, Manohar Malgonkar is one of those Indo-English novelists who have shown a keen awareness of rich Indian tradition and her hoary history, — the novelists like Mulk Raj Anand, Bhabani Bhattacharya, and Kamala Markandaya. The noted Caribbean writer, V.S. Naipaul, aptly observes that Malgonkar is outstanding for his fondness for outdoor life. Other writers might sound bookish or imitative, but Malgonkar does not. Though most of his recent works tend to be thriliers and entertainers, his popularity as a novelist is already established on a sound footing. It may be that, for chronological, historical and other related reasons, he does not rank with 'the Big Three' in the field of Indo-English fiction, but he is still a force, and a living one at that, to reckon with and not to be forgotten by the posterity. Khushwant Singh rightly places him among the select band of seven Indo-English writers and characterizes his monumental work. *A Bend in the Ganges,* as one of the few books that are "samples of good writing by Indo-Anglian writers of today."[25] For his unmistakable historical sense, for his outdoor freshness, and for his flawless plot-construction and engrossing story-telling, Malgonkar remains almost matchless in contemporary Indo-English fiction.

NOTES AND REFERENCES

1. C.D. Narasimhaiah, "Introduction," *Kanthapura* (Madras : Oxford University Press, 1974), p. xviii.
2. P.P. Mehta, *Indo-Anglian Fiction : An Assessment* (Bareilly : Prakash Book Depot, 1968), p. 244.
3. K.R. Srinivasa Iyengar, *Indian Writing in English*, 2nd ed. (Bombay and London : Asia Publishing House, 1973), p. 425.
4. Manohar Malgonkar, *Distant Drum* (New Delhi : Orient Paperbacks, 1960), p. 267.
5. ——, *Combat of Shadows* (Delhi : Hind Pocket Books Pvt. Ltd., 1962), p. 8. Subsequent references to this novel are absorbed in the body of the article itself.
6. ——, *The Princes* (1963; New Delhi : Orient Paperbacks, 1970), p. 355. All textual references are taken from this edition only.
7. V.S. Naipaul, *An Area of Darkness* (Harmondsworth, Middlesex, England : Penguin Books, 1964), p. 62.
8. *Idem.*
9. *Ibid.,* pp. 66-67.
10. Manohar Malgonkar, "Author's Note," *A Bend in the Ganges* (New Delhi : Orient Paperbacks, 1964), p. 379. Subsequent textual quotations are taken from this edition.
11. ——, "Author's Note," *The Devil's Wind* (New Delhi : Orient Paperbacks, 1972), p. 5.
12. *Ibid.,* p. 6.
13. Iyengar, *op. cit.,* p. 434.
14. Manohar Malgonkar, *Bandicoot Run* (New Delhi : Orient Paperbacks, 1982), pp. 325-326.
15. ——, "Prologue," *Shalimar* (New Delhi : Vikas Publishing House Pvt. Ltd., 1968), n.p.
16. ——, "Author's Note," *Open Season* (New Delhi : Orient Paperbacks, 1978), p. 3.
17. *The Times Literary Supplement* (June 4, 1964), p. 491.
18. Meenakshi Mukherjee, *The Twice-Born Fiction,* 2nd ed. (New Delhi : Arnold-Heinemann, 1974), p. 60.
19. Raja Rao, "Foreword," *Kanthapura* (O.U.P. ed.), pp. v-vi.
20. David McCutchion, *Indian Writing in English* (Calcutta : Writers Workshop, 1969), p. 11.
21. G.S. Amur, *Manohar Malgonkar* (New Delhi : Arnold-Heinemann, 1973), p. 18.
22. *The Times Literary Supplement* (October 22, 1964), p. 966.

23. Amur, *op. cit.,* p. 122.
24. Iyengar, *op. cit.,* p. 423.
25. Khushwant Singh, "Art and Literature," *Khushwant Singh's View of India,* ed. Rahul Singh (Bombay : IBH Publishing Co., 1974), p. 284.

5

'THE PRESENCE OF TWO CULTURES' : EAST-WEST ENCOUNTER IN THE NOVELS OF B. RAJAN*

In one of his brilliant essays on "Identity and Nationality," which John Press included in his edited work *Commonwealth Literature* (1965), Balachandra Rajan (born 1920) suggests that it may be an advantage for an Indo-English writer to be aware of 'the presence of two cultures'of the East and the West in his mental make-up which will provide him with the necessary fillip for creativity. To quote Rajan himself :

> ...the presence of two cultures in one's mind forms a wider and therefore saner basis on which to originate the quest for identity, and...the discordance between these two cultures can be creative as well as merely confusing. Perhaps one can go further and suggest that the man with mixed allegiances is contemporary Everyman....[1]

The cross-cultural conflicts for which Rajan seems to plead here are helpful not only in creative activities but also in one's quest for identity. They are also indicative of a writer's contemporaneity. The suggestion made above apparently sprang from the necessity of self-defence by an expatriate (that Rajan is) living too long in the West and yet unable to forget his native roots and relations.

---

* Reprinted with permission of the editor of *New Literary Horizons,* 3, No. 1 (Jan. 1988), 58–67.

The dilemma resulting from the East-West encounter forms one of the intrinsic charms of Rajan's novels, which are otherwise so diverse and inconsistent in treatment, technique, and quality.

B. Rajan educated in the West (having obtained his Ph.D. from Cambridge, England), like the hero of his first novel, reversed the sequence of careers by joining the Civil Service first and then turning to Professorship. As a novelist, he has contributed only two novels in English — *The Dark Dancer* (1958) and *Too Long in the West* (1961), but as a critic on John Milton and T.S. Eliot, he has established himself in the academic world so securely that no attempts at dislodging him are ever likely to succeed. And though his novels do not guarantee him a place besides Mulk Raj Anand, R.K Narayan, Raja Rao, Kamala Markandaya, Anita Desai, Nayantara Sahgal, Bhabani Bhattacharya, and Manohar Malgonkar, they are significant studies in the revelation of culture-tossed and tension-ridden expatriates and native-aliens who find themselves ill-suited and ill-adjusted in their own motherland. It is this revelation that binds them together, otherwise they are quite different in attitude, style, plot-structure, story-telling, and characterization. And when we approach them this way, they do not come under fire from Rajan's critics, who are mainly concerned with his "mannered prose"[2] and "insensitivity to language."[3] In fact, one feels that the necessary suspense and tension created by Rajan's novels is the only redeeming feature to be discovered in them. Both the novels of Rajan open with the central characters returning to their ancestral homes in India after several years of stay at a Western University, and both concentrate on their growing sense of alienation from their own culture and country.

The Dark Dancer, a compelling story of V.S. Krishnan, moves through a world of swift violence and change, throwing problems and challenges for the protagonist. This Cambridge-educated man returns to India after spending ten years abroad to be put into an arranged marriage with Kamala, an M.A. in Sanskrit and a sober girl by all means. At first Krishnan wants to become a teacher, but being reminded of the insignificant social and financial position of a teacher, he joins the Government Secretariat in New Delhi. Here he meets in a club his old girl friend, Cynthia Brainbird, and dances with her. Thereafter, they meet regularly on one or the other pretext, until a time comes when Kamala has to go to the South to see her ailing mother, promising to return in a fortnight. When she comes back to Delhi, she is taken aback on Krishnan's disclosure of his sense of deep attachment to Cynthia. Though he assures her to be fair and just to her and to look after her requirements, she slips away one day to Shanthipur, without telling anyone of her whereabouts. Krishnan's friend, Vijayaraghavan, informs him where she is. In the meantime, Krishnan has severed his connections with Cynthia. He goes to Shanthipur to find Kamala in a tent with an adopted child, someone's orphaned son, and doing her duties carefully in the hospital there as a nurse under a considerate and compassionate medical officer. Krishnan discovers Kamala a changed person with a mission. On the eve of Indian independence, riots break out everywhere, even in the town of Shanthipur, resulting in horrors of mass-killing, looting, arson, and rape. The cholera also spreads in a part of this town, but the practical wisdom of M.O. and Kamala and Krishnan keep it well under control. In one of her evening walks, Kamala is savagely attacked by two drunkards with a knife and a lathi, and she dies then and there, leaving Krishnan badly injured. The drunkards are put to death by the irate mob, and thus the 'poetic justice' is dealt out. After ten days, Krishnan recovers and goes to Benares to immerse his wife's ashes into the holy Ganga. He also performs all the rites ordained by the *Shastras* under the supervision of Kruger and his parents and father-in-law (Shankaran). When his mother talks of his re-marriage, he coldly snubs her and announces that he will never remarry — "I'll stay single...God knows I've made enough mistakes."[4] Krishnan is now a transformed man, living with Kamala's memories (who had died a gallant's death in facing the two brats pursuing a Moslem girl), and deriving consolation from the *Gita.* This is the whole story recounted in *The Dark Dancer,* which definitely reveals the novelist's deep sensitivity, poetic impulse and seriousness of purpose.

The title of the novel so aptly chosen verily applies, by means of suggestion, to Krishnan, who always dances in the dark without having an idea of his right position in a tradition-bound society. He is the hero of the piece, and becomes a spokesman for the novelist himself. He is actually a victim of cultural ambivalence and psychological tension.

Krishnan who is a born South Indian Brahmin in a ritualistic family bound with convention and superstition, turns a rebel in his attitude and thought under the impact of his Western education. The conflict within him surfaces right from the beginning. He comes home, but to an uncongenial atmosphere — "It was where he was born, but where he was born didn't matter" (p. 1). And again : He was coming back, but not to an entity, a sense of being rooted, not even to an entity like that of sun and earth, a struggle against circumstances, a creative confronting, which would open his mind to its depths of repossession. He was coming back to an indifferent sky, an anonymous teeming of houses...(pp. 1-2).

The East-West encounter is so clear when Krishnan is seen torn between his loyalties for a Hindu wife — Kamala — and a Western Girl — Cynthia. With the former his contact is formal and yet spiritual, but with the latter it is informal and yet sensual. He wants to carry on with both, but that is not simply possible. In an upsurge of feeling when his wife is away, he enjoys his days with Cynthia, who is a matter-of-fact, intelligent, and possessive lady, but he is pricked deep down for Kamala who is a sober girl of deep understanding and compassion. Explicitly, Kamala represents the East, and Cynthia the West. Placed between these two women, Krishnan belongs to neither, as Cynthia seems to suggest when she says to him : "You're Karma.... The man who couldn't belong" (p. 130). Though in the rivalry between the soul and the matter, the former suffers for a time, but ultimately it emerges victorious. Credit goes to Kamala to have brought about a thorough transformation in the life of her husband and to have taught him a lesson of 'duty done in dispassion' (which originates from the GITA), come whatever may. Through her sacrifices both in life and death, Kamala showed to him the path "to do what was right" (p. 307). After this transformation, nothing evil or carnal could distract him, for we know that Cynthia re-appears on the scene when Kamala is no more, but she is advised : "Don't be a perfectionist. Go home and settle for ninety-eight per cent" (p. 305). And she, too, obeys Krishnan and goes away. The protagonist grown philosophical and resigned to his lot walks back slowly to "the strength of his beginning" (p. 308), to his loneliness and frustration, but only to explore the meaning and purpose of life and to continue his exploration of 'what is right.'

The presence of two cultures asserts itself in the form of Kamala and Cynthia. These two women in the novel are a study in contrast. While one is black, the other white in skin. While one is a living embodiment of 'acceptance' and tradition and normal decency, the other is a violation of these and a champion of 'stubborn individualism.' Kamala is undeniably submissive and dutiful, whereas Cynthia is defiant and independent. The soul beautiful is pitted against 'the body beautiful' (p. 151). Kamala is rooted deep in her soil and people and culture, but Cynthia is driven from pillar to post 'in her rootlessness' (p. 156). Cynthia does not have the tolerance or forbearance of Kamala, and when her people — Britishers — are attacked, she cannot ignore the rebuke' (p. 160). She considers her civilization as 'green, cool, soft-decorous.' She has a strong possessive instinct, but Kamala has none. Cynthia is ultimately rejected by Krishnan because she wants to possess him wholly, but his 'half' is Kamala, and also because she asks for 'a total commitment' (p. 171). And when Cynthia fails to have his 'whole,' she angrily retorts : "Go back to her" (p. 176) and "I hate you and I never want to see you again" (p. 176). But Kamala never says a harsh word to him, though he wrongs her at times. She even forgives his sins of 'desertion' and 'adultery' (p. 188). He is, after all, her husband, her DEVATA (God). In the final analysis, she succeeds, and not Cynthia, in making him choose 'the right path' of duty, which, in Vijayaraghavan's words, is "a world of responsibility, not of feeling" (p. 184). Thus, the East-West encounter represented by Kamala and Cynthia culminates in the 'world of responsibility' prevailing over the 'world of feeling.' And yet, this betrays the dichotomy of Krishnan's mind and heart, the psychological pressures on him.

If *The Dark Dancer* is "an intense story of the self-division and maturation of an individual and of a nation, of the cyclic phenomenon of fratricidal war and its message transmitted in the blood-consciousness of a people,"[5] *Too Long in the West* is, to Parmeswaran, "a hilarious comedy, a spoof of the absurdities in Indian and American social codes, of arranged marriage, and of the foibles and eccentricities of individuals."[6] In *Too Long in the West,* everyone is poked fun at, except Nalini, the heroine in this novel, who is the only charm in a sincere portrayal.

Nalini, the only daughter of Sambasivan and Lakshmi, has been to Columbia in America for her higher education. She returns to India after a long stay in the West, and braves the perils of Mudalur, a remote and featureless village selected by her father as his summer resort. Keeping in mind her age, Sambasivan has advertised in newspapers for her marriage. There are some responses to his advertisement from such suitors as the correct and miserable Satyamurti, the phenomenologist of arranged marriages, Kalyansundaram, the handsome and prosperous Kubera, and the stiff and stubborn Viswakarman. Later, Ernest Hamilton Jones, an American friend of Nalini, also joins the bandwagon of these suitors. They are all comforted at Hailview, the residence of Sambasivan, where the outer world's progress does not intrude upon. Mudalur is a cluster of mud houses, excepting those of Sambasivan and Guruswami with 298 inhabitants, which swells to 299 with the arrival of Raman, the village barber, a barbarous and blood-thirsty fellow. Raman does not like Sambasivan and his family due to their exploitation of the whole village for 32 years, and incites the villagers against them, blaming them for having invited the sinuous suitors who brought troubles to the entire community. Raman is particularly annoyed at the arrival and intimacy of Ernest with the Sambasivan family. He believes that Ernest is carrying on his sex-orgies with Nalini. The villagers approach Sambasivan and threaten him with dire consequences if he does not send away his daughter in marriage by tomorrow morning. Consequently, a kind of *Svayambara*[7] is held, and Nalini, to the surprise of all, puts her garland around Raman, pursuing the policy : "If you can't lick'em, join'em."[8] Politically, this may be a marriage of conveniences, but aesthetically this is a most unsatisfying and detestable union, quite unbecoming of an American graduate and her socially dignified status. By this marriage Raman's revolutionary fire is certainly quenched, but he turns into a nose-and-ear piercer of ladies. The ensuing peaceful atmosphere offers a facelift to the otherwise backward South Indian village.

It is in the person of Nalini that the East-West encounter takes place. She is, like Krishnan of the first novel, born in a South Indian Brahmin family of four members, but is sent to America for her higher learning and training by her pompous professor father. In the West, she becomes "a party to the American way of life" (p. 51). She likes New York and its people. In this city of plenty, she has "the will to be herself, the most self-evident and the most sky-scraping dignity" (p. 52). But she has to return to India, to Mudalur, after three years, and the problem of adjustment poses itself before her. Lakshmi, the mother of Nalini, is very careful and calculating about the prospects of her daughter, but she is worried that "She'll never fit in...She's been too long in the West. She's forgotten our language and will turn up her nose at our food. She'll want to bathe with soap instead of *sheyaka* powder and to clean her teeth with toothpaste instead of a *neem* twig. And worst of all she'll talk back to her husband" (p. 24). Though this is somewhat a miscalculation of an indulgent mother, it is true that she is not the same Nalini that she was before she had left for the States. This is hinted at so clearly by Kalyan in his conversation with Nalini in the train while returing to Mudalur : "You won't fit in. You've joined the lost generation, out of place everywhere and acceptable nowhere. You'll always be an exile and an alien, a self-created foreigner refugee from yourself. You can't belong. You'll live in two worlds and fall between two stools" (p. 55). And since she lives in two worlds, she is a divided self, a split personality, and almost an enigma to others. This makes her restless, lonely and frustrated, — "She sang to nobody, she sang alone, neither aware of herself nor of an audience..." (p. 111). She remains a riddle to all, — to her parents, to her younger brother, and to her suitors. The American suitor, Ernest H. Jones, proposes to her to leave India behind and get back to the States for her happiness and natural growth, pointing out to her : "You're so out of place here — a girl like you, vital and generous. You ought to be doing something constructive, something important, helping your country to move into its future or at least living your own life and really finding yourself, instead of which, you're stagnating in this backwater, waiting to be married" (p. 122). He also paints a rosy picture of the future before her by saying that their children will "mix the best of the two of us" (p. 117). But Nalini simply answers that this is not a question of happiness but of 'responsibility,' — an idea similar to that of Krishnan in the first novel. She seems to have grown stoic about her fate, and like Thomas Hardy suggests that 'Happiness is but an occasional episode in the general drama of pain'. And in the drama of her painful life, she goes in for Raman, the village barber, much against the wishes of her parents and other well-wishers. The over-powering sense of responsibility engineered probably by her pragmatic American training and education prompts her to select Raman as her life-partner, otherwise she 'detests' him from the core of her heart and makes it known to her spouse, "I'll need a lifetime to explain how much I detest you" (p. 186). It was the practical wisdom of Krishnan in the first novel which has led him to forsake his English girl, Cynthia, and here it is again this kind of commonsense which inspires Nalini to choose Raman as her husband. More, therefore, the novel is a chronicle of her inner struggle and crushed impulses against a rustic background than it is a triumph of hilarity and comic spirit. By bringing Ernest into the story, the novelist merely wished to highlight the intensity and poignancy of feelings within the central character. Considered in this light, the following statement of Uma Parmeswaran about its real nature is only partly ture — "The novel is a fantasia woven around an eccentric assemblage of parents, suitors and rustics. Realism and satire are thrown in for good measure but only to enhance the lively tempo."[9] As compared to this, the anonymous author of an article published in the *Times Literary Supplement* seems to be nearer the truth when he states that it is "a story about the clash of Indian and American cultures."[10] For it is against this backdrop that the novel assumes a meaning and a purpose and that the beginning and the end seem to be an organic whole, though it is suggested that the word 'clash' in the anonymous author's article be replaced by 'contact.' Nalini, thus, becomes the meeting-point of the twin cultures of the East and the West, and imparts cohesion and charm to the novel.

To sum up : B. Rajan is an Indo-English novelist who has largely dwelt on the theme of East-West encounter in his two novels by showing the 'presence of two cultures' in his central characters. By so doing he joins the select band of such eminent writers as Raja Rao, Santha Rama Rau, Kamala Markandaya, Nayantara Sahgal, and J.M. Ganguly. But in handling the theme, Rajan "comes closer to the crux of the problem"[11] than any of the novelists mentioned here. The alienation of Krishnan and Nalini form the social and cultural milieu of their land is quite apparent form the very beginning, and their East-West dilemma constitutes one of the perennial charms of Rajan's novels.

NOTES AND REFERENCES

1. B. Rajan, "Identity and Nationality," *Commonwealth Literature,* ed. John Press (London : Heinemann Educational Books, 1965), p. 108.
2. V.Y. Kantak, "The Language of Indian Fiction in English," *Critical Essays on Indian Writing in English,* ed. M.K. Naik, S.K. Desai and G.S. Amur (Dharwar : Karnatak University, 1968), p. 156.
3. David McCutchion, "Le Style C'est Homme," *Writers Workshop Miscellany* (May-June 1961), p. 21.

   Some other critics of Rajan's style and language are : Frederic Morton in "New Truths, Old Values" published in *New York Times Book Review* (29th June, 1958), p. 6; Prema Nandakumar in "The Achievement of the

Indo-Anglian Novelist" published in *The Literary Criterion* (Winter, 1961), p. 160; and C.D. Narasamhaiah in "Why This Animus?" published in *The Literary Criterion* (Summer 1966).

4. B. Rajan, *The Dark Dancer* (1958; New Delhi : Arnold-Heinemann, 1976), p. 301. All the textual quotations are taken from this edition.
5. Uma Parmeswaran, *A Study of Representative Indo-English Novelists* (New Delhi : Vikas Publishing House Pvt. Ltd., 1976), p. 125.
6. *Ibid.*
7. It is a word for 'self-selection', in which the bride in olden days was to choose her life-partner from amongst many claimants on the basis of merit. This practice was prevalent in ancient India, as in case of Damyanti picking up Nala.
8. B. Rajan, *Too Long in the West* (Bombay : Jaico Publishing House, 1961), p. 187. All the textual quotations are taken from this edition.
9. Parmeswaran, *op. cit.*, p. 127.
10. Anonymous, "Indian Ink," *The Times Literary Supplement* (19 May 1961), p. 313.
11. Meenakshi Mukherjee, *The Twice Born Fiction* (New Delhi : Arnold-Heinemann, 1974), p. 84.

6

THE DARK DANCER : A CRITIQUE*

The Dark Dancer (1958) created a ripple on the surface of the academic water because a well-known critic of English letters had turned to creative writing with a touch of warmth and gusto. But as there is too much intellectualism and sophistry in the work, it could not produce the intended impression on the minds of readers and reviewers. K.R. Srinivasa Iyengar, a very generous critic indeed, compares *The Dark Dancer* to Chinua Achebe's *No Longer at Ease* and finds fault with it for having introduced a very "sophisticated creature"[1] — Krishnan — as its hero, but he also hastens to add that "the novel certainly merits praise on account of Kamala who incarnates Shakti in her essential strength and unfailing gift of compassion and understanding."[2] Paul Verghese considers this novel as "not successful because the novelist's approach is too intellectual and detached to allow him (Rajan) to make imaginative use of the post-Independence riots for purposes of his novel", though he also admires "its excellent use of irony."[3] Those who have attacked B. Rajan on account of his so-called insensitivity to the language and style include Frederic Morton, David McCutchion. C.D. Narasimhaiah, V.Y. Kantak, and Prema Nandakumar. But this writer feels that most of these critics echo or re-echo one another, and that they ought to have found fault with his rambling method of story-telling rather than with his use of the language or sophisticated style. It

---

* Reprinted with permission of the editor of *Studies in Indian Fiction in English,* ed. G.S. Balarama Gupta (Gulbarga : JIWE Publications, 1987), pp. 68-76.

appears, they were out with a preconceived notion to attack the novelist right or wrong, and thereby dismantle his image in the academic world. They also forget the fact that Rajan was portraying a very sensitive and sophisticated young man of Western education, and Krishnan's sophistry is quite natural and life-like. A critic of the stature of B. Rajan is hardly ever likely to slip on the count of language, and his deviations, if any, from the Queen's English are simply deliberate and purposive. These possibly form a part of his technique to evoke a living picture of the South Indian social and cultural milieu.

Balachandra Rajan (born 1920), a brilliant scholar and distinguished professor of English, is now settled in Toronto, Canada, and has published two novels to date : *The Dark Dancer* and *Too Long In The West* (1961). As a critic on Milton, Yeats, and Eliot, he has already made his position secure in the literary world, and no attempts at dislodging him are ever likely to succeed. And though his novels do not guarantee him a place beside Mulk Raj Anand, R.K. Narayan, Raja Rao, Kamala Markandaya, Anita Desai, Nayantara Sahgal, Bhabani Bhattacharya, and Manohar Malgonkar, they are significant studies in the revelation of culture-tossed and tension-ridden expatriates and native-aliens who find themselves ill-suited and ill-adjusted in their own motherland. It is this revelation that binds them together, otherwise they are quite different in attitude, style, plot-structure, story-telling, and characterization. And when we approach them this way, they do not come under fire from Rajan's critics, who are mainly concerned with his "mannered prose"[4] and "insensitivity to language."[5] In fact, one feels that the necessary suspense and tension created by Rajan's novels is the only redeeming feature to be discovered in them. Both the novels of Rajan open with the central characters returning to their ancestral homes in India after several years of stay at a Western University, and both concentrate on their growing sense of alienation from their own culture and country.

The Dark Dancer, a compelling story of V.S. Krishnan, moves through a world of swift violence and change, throwing problems and challenges for the protagonist. This Cambridge educated man returns to India after spending ten years abroad to be put into an arranged marriage with Kamala, an M.A. in Sanskrit and a sober girl by all means. At first Krishnan wants to become a teacher, but being reminded of the insignificant social and financial position of a teacher, he joins the Government Secretariat in New Delhi. Here he meets in a club his old girl friend, Cynthia Brainbird, and dances with her. Thereafter they meet regularly on one or the other pretext, until a time comes when Kamala has to go to the South to see her ailing mother, promising to return in a fortnight. When she comes back to Delhi, she is taken aback on Krishnan's disclosure of his sense of deep attachment to Cynthia. Though he assures to be fair and just to her and to look after her requirements, she slips away one day to Shanthipur, without telling anyone of her whereabouts. Krishnan's friend, Vijayaraghavan, informs him where she is. In the meantime, Krishnan has severed his connections with Cynthia. He goes to Shanthipur to find Kamala in a tent with an adopted child, someone's orphaned son, and doing her duties carefully in the hospital there as a nurse under a considerate and compassionate medical officer. Krishnan discovers Kamala a changed person with a mission. On the eve of Indian independence, riots break out everywhere, even in the town of Shanthipur, resulting in horrors of mass-killing, looting arson, and rape. The cholera also spreads in a part of this town, but the practical wisdom of the M.O. and Kamala and Krishnan keep it well under control. In one of her evening walks, Kamala is savagely attacked by two drunkards with a knife and a *lathi*, and she dies then and there, leaving Krishnan badly injured. The drunkards are lynched to death by the irate mob, and thus the 'poetic justice' is dealt out. After ten days, Krishnan recovers and goes to Benaras to immerse his wife's ashes into the holy Ganga. He also performs all the rites ordained by the *Shastras* under the supervision of Kruger and his parents and father-in-law (Shankaran). When his mother talks of his re-marriage, he coldly snubs her and announces that he will never remarry —

"I'll stay single — God knows I've made enough mistakes."[6] Krishnan is now a transformed man, living with Kamala's memories (who had died a gallant's death in facing the two brats pursuing a Moslem girl), and deriving consolation from the *Gita*. This is the whole story recounted in *The Dark Dancer*, which definitely reveals the novelist's deep sensitivity, poetic impulse, and seriousness of purpose.

The title of the novel so aptly chosen verily applies, by means of suggestion, to Krishnan, who always dances in the dark without having an idea of his right position in a tradition-bound society. He is evidently pulled by the twin urges of love and duty. He is the hero of the piece and becomes a spokesman for the novelist himself. He is actually a victim of cultural ambivalence and psychological tension.

Krishnan, who is a born South Indian Brahmin in a ritualistic family bound with convention and superstition, turns a liberal in his attitude and thought under the impact of his Western education. The conflict within him surfaces right from the beginning. He comes home, but to an uncongenial atmosphere — "It was where he was born, but where he was born didn't matter" (p. 1). And again. "He was coming back, but not to an identity, a sense of being rooted, not even to an enmity like that of sun and earth, a struggle against circumstance, a creative confronting, which would open his mind to its depths of repossession. He was coming back to an indifferent sky, and anonymous teeming of houses..." (pp. 1-2).

The East-West encounter is so clear when Krishnan is seen torn between his loyalties for a Hindu wife — Kamala — and a Western girl — Cynthia. With the former his contact is formal and yet spiritual, but with the latter it is informal and yet sensual. He wants to carry on with both, but that is not simply possible. In an upsurge of feeling when his wife is away, he enjoys his days with Cynthia, who is a matter-of fact, intelligent, and possessive lady, but he is pricked deep down for Kamala, who is a sober girl of deep understanding and compassion. Explicitly,

Kamala represents the East, and Cynthia the West. Placed between these two women, Krishnan belongs to neither, as Cynthia seems to suggest when she says to him : "You're Karma… The man who couldn't belong" (p. 130). Though in the rivalry between the soul and the matter, the former suffers for a time, ultimately it emerges victorious. Credit goes to Kamala to have brought about a thorough transformation in the life of her husband and to have taught him a lesson of duty done in 'dispassion' (which originates from the *Gita*), come whatever may. Through her sacrifices both in life and death, Kamala showed to him the path "to do what was right" (p. 307).

After this transformation, nothing evil or carnal could distract him, for we know that Cynthia re-appears on the scene when Kamala is no more, but she is advised : "Don't be a perfectionist. Go home and settle for ninety-eight per cent" (p. 305). And she, too, obeys Krishnan and goes away. The protagonist grown philosophical and resigned to his lot walks back slowly to the strength of his beginning (p. 308), to his loneliness and frustration, but only to explore the meaning and purpose of life and to continue his exploration of what is right.

The presence of two cultures asserts itself in the form of Kamala and Cynthia. These two women in the novel are a study in contrast. While one is black, the other is white in skin. While one is a living embodiment of 'acceptance' and tradition and normal decency, the other is a violation of these and a champion of stubborn individualism. Kamala is undeniably submissive and dutiful, whereas Cynthia is defiant and independent. The soul beautiful is pitted against 'the body beautiful' (p. 151). Kamala is rooted deep in her soil and people and culture, but Cynthia is driven from pillar to post 'in her rootlessness' (p. 156). Cynthia does not have the tolerance and forbearance of Kamala, and when her people — Britishers — are attacked, she cannot 'ignore the rebuke' (p. 160). She considers her civilization as 'green, cool, softtoned, decorous.' She has a strong possessive instinct, but Kamala has none. Cynthia is ultimately rejected by Krishnan because she wants to possess his 'whole,' forgetting the fact that his 'half' is Kamala, and also because she asks for 'a total commitment' (p. 171). And when Cynthia fails to have him 'whole,' she angrily retorts : "Go back to her" (p. 176) and "I hate you and I never want to see you again" (p. 176). But Kamala never says a harsh word to him, though he wrongs her at times. She even forgives his sins of 'desertion' and 'adultery' (p. 183). He is, after all, her husband, her *devata* (God). In the end, she succeeds, not Cynthia, in making him choose 'the right path' of duty which, in the words of a prominent character, Vijayaraghavan, is "a world of responsibility, not of feeling" (p. 184). The East-West encounter represented by the two leading women characters — Kamala and Cynthia — in the novel culminates in the 'world of responsibility' prevailing over the 'world of feeling.' This also reflects the wavering condition of Krishnan's mind and heart.

But the East-West encounter forms only one thread of the story, the other thread being race-relationships during the pre-Independence days. The two threads are sometimes not happily blended together. In the first part of the novel, the first thread assumes importance, while in the second the other one becomes dominant. Rajan's depiction of the disquieting scenes of pre-independence riots may not be as forceful as that of Manohar Malgonkar in his *A Bend in The Ganges* (1964) or that of Chaman Nahal in his *Azadi* (1979), but it is no less truthful and natural. Unlike those two writers, he does not hang over them unduly and thus permits the novel to achieve its end — the emergence of the gradually brightening image of Kamala. When Cynthia rebukes Krishnan after their abortive visit to a temple in Mathura, saying. "There is something mean about non-violent people" (p. 176) and asking him to "Go back to her… Go back to your belonging and your bondage" (p. 176), he realises his mistake of getting involved neck-deep with the sensual, voluptuous Western woman, and turns back to Kamala, the living embodiment of self-sacrifice, who is now living separately far away at Shanthipur, a disturbed town camping a large number of refugees. He takes the train to Shanthipur, and on his way he is injured by a passenger in a scuffle. He, however, manages to reach Kamala, who accepts him without any grudge or grouse. For a few days they live together in peace and happiness, and this re-unification offers Krishnan "repossession of identity."[7] In this way, Kamala becomes a symbol of the "unifying force."[8] For the first time in their relationship as husband and wife the sensual and the spiritual get combined. But the communal frenzy breaks out again, and Kamala gets killed while trying to defend a Muslim girl from the clutches of murderous monsters. Her death, in the words of Harrex, symbolizes "the death of the illusion that man is an island and alienation the ultimate reality."[9] The martyred Kamala resolves the enigma of time, death, knowledge and evil. Her death is a pointer to the climax reached by the communal hysteria which, in its wake, brought about —

> The thousands that are dead and the millions that are homeless. The rich land abandoned and the lives we have left behind. That's been our sacrifice for making India (p. 199).

The brutality and the blood-bath generated by the confusion and anarchy of the prevailing situation in the Partition days are to be witnessed in the latter half of *The Dark Dancer*, particularly in chapters 6, 7 and 8. Kamala's death leaves Krishnan badly scourged, but he has, by this time, learnt a lot from her sense of duty, her detachment, her determination. In short, he has now discovered himself and is fully composed. The true meaning of the *Gita* has been grasped by him, as he has seen the 'selfless action,' which is also the right action, of his wife. He is now a changed person from what he was at the beginning of the novel. The wandering pilgrim has eventually come back home. *The Dark Dancer* has at long last emerged on the sunny atmosphere with the dawn of wisdom in him. In this context, we must take note of the recurring image of the Nataraja, representing the Cosmic Dance of Shiva. Though traditionally the Dance represents the Doom of the Universe, it also implicitly suggests the Re-creation after Destruction.

It has been mentioned that Rajan's language has evoked a sharp reaction among his critics, and that this reaction is misjudged and misdirected. The sophisticated language should not startle anyone, as language goes with character, and Rajan's language is quite forceful and expressive. It has the power to describe effectively persons and places, situations and characters, mental tensions and communal disturbances. He occasionally employs poetic and musical language too, as in the following :

> The circle of faces would cluck its assent, and he would shuffle off, ears burning, bored with playing marbles, back to the black morocco books where people spoke sense and spoke it in pentameters (p. 16).

Rajan's unique sense of punning is so evident in — "He had the strange sense of detachment once again, of being both the dancer and the dance, of being the ritual and the ritual's object" (p. 14). He is capable of using similes and metaphors, as in the following : "I have met you (Kamala) before, you of the *choli* of alarming brevity, with your midriff flat as the Rajputana desert" (p. 29). At times he becomes highly epigrammatic and aphoristic; for example, "Traditions die hard. The engines of repression are not easily abandoned. Power corrupts and absolute power corrupts absolutely" (p. 96). There are charming flashes of wit and irony in the exchanges of Krishnan and Cynthia. Take this as an illustration :

> "Why did you marry her?"
>
> "In order to get married,"
>
> "If I weren't so perceptive, I'd call that an unintelligent answer."
>
> "If you were perceptive, you'd realize that it wasn't meant to be intelligent."
>
> "It was supposed to be adequate" (p. 80).

This may also be found in the dialogue between Vijayaraghavan and Cynthia :

"I don't intend to survive an ordeal by fire."

"I was going to suggest you an ordeal by coffee" (p. 108).

In this novel, Rajan shows a refined sense of choosing words, phrases, and expressions. Even when he has to abuse, he simply says : "You pea-brained, babbling baboon" (p. 152), or merely "brat," "of a little hard-toned philosophy, my foot." Here is an instance of the alliterative and cadenced prose : "Put it away among the spiders and the scorpions, under the secret stone behind the storeroom vessels, in the black in box that no one has ever unpacked" (p. 136). Rajan's prose is an effective means of expression, and he does not falter in it unless it is deliberate and conscious.[10]

Rajan has been attacked by some critics for displaying his propensity to derive too much from T.S. Eliot, the literary giant of the 20th century. This attack is quite tenable, and there are several points of correspondence between them — theme, language, and landscape imagery are quite identical. According to the Australian critic, Harrex, "The main philosophical themes common to both the *Quartets* and *The Dark Dancer* — the reconciliation of past and present, creation and destruction, and the cyclic relationship of end and beginning — are crystallized in the dance symbolism of both works." To offer just one instance here : Eliot makes the following statements in "East Coker" — 'In my beginning is my end' and 'In my end is my beginning,' and Rajan gives us the following : 'Home was his beginning, no more than a point of departure' (p. 5) and 'He walked back slowly to the strength of his beginning' (p. 308). Unquestionably, Rajan has "digested Eliot with assurance and understanding," but Eliot himself had gone to Indian mysticism for "confirmation of his own vision,"[11] — to the *Vedas*, the *Upanishads*, the *Gita*, Patanjali's *Yogasutras*, and to Lord Buddha and his gospels to be specific.[12]

To conclude, of the two novels written by B. Rajan, *The Dark Dancer* is definitely the better one; it is better artistically, thematically, and linguistically. In truth, *Too Long in The West* is cast in a lighter vein and style. Uma Parmeswaran rightly remarks that it is "a hilarious comedy, a spoof of the absurdities in Indian and American social codes, of arranged marriages, and of the foibles and eccentricities of individuals."[13] Speaking of *The Dark Dancer*, the same critic observes that it is an intense story "of the self-division and maturation of an individual and of a nation, of the cyclic phenomenon of fratricidal war and its message transmitted in the blood-consciousness of the people."[14] *The Dark Dancer* unquestionably outshines *Too Long in the West*, and we only wish that Rajan should have continued his efforts on the lines of his first novel.

NOTES AND REFERENCES

1. K.R. Srinivasa Iyengar, *Indian Writing in English* (2nd ed. Bombay : Asia Publishing House, 1973), p. 506.
2. *Ibid.*, pp. 509-510.
3. C. Paul Verghese, *Problems of the Indian Creative Writer in English* (Bombay : Somaiya Publications (P) Ltd., 1971), p. 121.
4. V.Y. Kantak, "The Language of Indian Fiction in English," *Critical Essays on Indian Writing in English*, eds. M.K. Naik, S.K. Desai and G.S. Amur (Dharwar : Karnatak University, 1968), p. 156.
5. David McCutchion, "Le Style C'est L' Homme, "*Writers Workshop Miscellany* (May-June 1961), p. 61.
6. B. Rajan, *The Dark Dancer* (1958; New Delhi : Arnold-Heinemann, 1976), p. 301. All the textual quotations are taken form this edition.
7. S.C. Harrex, "Dancing in the Dark : Balchandra Rajan and T.S. Eliot," *The Fire and the Offering : The English Language Novel of India*, 1935-1970 (Calcutta : Writers Workshop, 1977), p. 195.
8. *Ibid.*, p. 191.
9. *Ibid.*, p. 192
10. *Ibid.*, p. 195.
11. *Idem.*
12. Those interested in this matter should look up the present writer's *Indian Thought & Tradition in T.S. Eliot's Poetry* (Bareilly : Prakash Book Depot, 1977), *and T.S. Eliot's Major Poems : An Indian Interpretation* (Salzburg, Austria : Publications Department of the University of Salzburg, 1982).
13. Uma Parmeswaran, *A Study of Representative Indo-English Novelists*, (New Delhi : Vikas Publishing House Pvt. Ltd., 1976), p. 125.
14. *Idem.*

7

FAILURE AND FRUSTRATION : A STUDY OF ANITA DESAI'S *IN CUSTODY**

Anita Desai, the most 'poetic novelist' of all in the contemporary era, seems to have written her latest novel, *In Custody* (1984), in a mood of gloom and disenchantment over human frailty and predicament. *The Times Literary Supplement* of London has remarked that her protagonist's "extreme sensitivity never alienates the reader" and that she handless her plot with "narrative suspense,"[1] but one wonders whether these remarks are applicable to this novel. Frankly speaking, we have neither the protagonist's 'extreme sensitivity' nor the 'narrative suspense' herein. The protagonist of the novel, Deven, is confronted with failure and frustration at every step, and is clearly sad, bitter and sardonic unto the last. Several obstructions come his way, and he does not know how to overcome them. He is the only character with whom the reader has some kind of sympathy, but he is befooled and cheated everywhere. The blurb page informs us that "*In Custody* is a sad, bitter, funny novel full of insight into human frailty and with some truly memorable scenes of comic catastrophe."[2] From this statement we may infer that it is a none-too-happy novel, that it is 'funny' and about 'human frailty,' and that only some of its scenes are 'truly memorable,' and not all.

---

* First published in *Indian Fiction in English*, ed. Prof. R.S. Pathak (New Delhi : Northen Book Centre, 1990), pp. 110-120. Reprinted with permission of the editor.

According to the noted British novelist, E.M. Forster, a novel usually has at least three components — plot (story-telling), people (characters) and pattern (design). Other things like setting and conversation are only secondary. Forster also makes a subtle distinction between 'plot' and 'story' and observes that "The king died and then the queen died," is a story, whereas "The king died, and then the Queen died of grief," is a plot.[3] Viewed in the light of Forster's essential components, *In Custody* fails to convince us as a novel.

Consisting of eleven chapters and 204 pages and dedicated to Alicia Yerburgh, *In Custody* has a fragile thread to hold it together. An impoverished, young college lecturer in Hindi called Deven comes from Delhi and settles down at Mirpore, a small town, along with his sullen and disappointed wife Sarla and small son Manu. He leads an unhappy domestic life. The place he lives in looks like a "cruel trap of prison"[4] for him. He discovers to his dismay that his surroundings are not in consonance with his high aspirations. His friend Murad arrives from Delhi and tracks him out at his College; both go out for lunch in a bazaar restaurant and discuss their financial problems. Deven complains to Murad about non-payment for his contributions — poems and reviews — to the latter's Urdu magazine, *Awaaz*, but Murad silences him by saying that his magazine has not been a success. He advises Deven to interview the noted Urdu poet, Nur Shahjehanbadi, for the forthcoming special issue of his magazine, and by agreeing to his proposal Deven falls into his well-laid trap, from which he can never escape. With a good deal of hesitation, Deven goes to meet Nur at Delhi. The latter rebukes him for being a lecturer in Hindi and yet interviewing an Urdu poet. Deven finds the atmosphere at Nur's home quite suffocating, cruel and vulgar. Nur's wife scolds the poet for drinking too much and the visitor for being selfish. Deven runs away from there in a huff. But the meddling Murad persuades him again to go and interview Nur with courage and determination. Reaching Nur's, Deven sees that a soiree-party has been arranged there to celebrate the birth day of his second wife, Imtiaz-Bibi, who bores the audience by her melodramatic and third-rate verses. Nur and Deven leave the soiree half-way and secretly retire to a room, where Nur reveals to the interviewer that Imtiaz has cheated him of all his belongings, including the audience. Meanwhile, the two wives of Nur appear there and start quarrelling most ferociously, and Deven has to flee from them. Once again Murad advises him to take the assistance of a tape-recorder in collecting the speeches and recitations of Nur and later edit them. Deven may even write a book like *My Days with Nur Shahjehanabadi* or a biography of Nur. The idea of tape-recorder clicks, and Deven seeks the help of Mr. Siddiqui, the Head of the Urdu Department at his college, in arranging funds for it. Murad persuades Deven to purchase a second-hand tape-recorder from the shop of Mr. Jain, with whom Murad has a secret deal. A raw technician, Chiku, is provided to assist him in recording. But a revealing interview of the poet is a remote possibility owing to the high temperature and diarrheea of Imtiaz-Begum. The first wife Safiya Begum, however, comes to the rescue of Deven and arranges his meeting with Nur at a hidden place. Chiku being a fool does not put the tape on and off, as required, during the entire conversation of Nur with Deven. He is more interested in his leave for home, in his sister's marriage, than in recording. The hard work of about three weeks goes wasted due to lack of technical expertise. Even the pruning of undesirable portions of the record tape does not succeed. The shop-owner, Mr. Jain, allots another technician, Pintu, to him. Any real help in the matter comes from his disciples like Dhanu who are trained in radio technology and electronics; they cut undesirable portions and sounds from the cassettes. Even then the recording remains a patchwork which is "completely useless from a scholarly point of view."[5] In the meantime, letters from Nur keep pouring in for financial assistance now for cataract operation, now for family maintenance, now for clearance of a bill of room-rent. Deven also receives a letter from Imtiaz-Begum, complaining of his utter ignorance of her poetic talent. When he approaches Murad for payment of some money for his contributions to his magazine, the latter gives him a blunt reply, informing him of the excessive bills on drinks and other materials from hotels and restaurants he himself has received and desiring the sole rights of the tape-recordings to sell them to HMV or Polydor in order to clear his bills and debts. Thus, Deven finds no truly sympathetic soul to console him or to draw him out of the woods. Instead, he meets failure and frustration from the beginning of the story to the end. The reader of the novel is left with the impression that the entire story is spun out just to trap the protagonist, just to put him in a cage — "still it was just a cage in a row of cages. Cage, cage, Trap, trap."[6] The plot is as indistinct and labyrinthine at the beginning as at the end. The beginning depicts the two friends, Murad and Deven, meeting each other in the College canteen beset with stares and noises (where they can't sit or talk properly), and the end shows the latter panting for breath, having an anxious morning walk, and pulling a branch of thorns from under his foot.

As for characterization, we do not have fully developed and three-dimensional characters in this novel, with the possible exception of Deven. As a protagonist, he is seen thrown from one problem to another, from one torture to another, without getting any solution or relief. He is drawn deeper and deeper into the project of interviewing India's greatest Urdu poet, Nur, but is fooled, cheated and bullied by all around him — by Nur's two wives, by the shifty Murad, by shopkeepers, amateur technicians, threatening students, and by the poet himself. Nur's verse having sustained Deven since his childhood ultimately lands him into troubles. The protagonist becomes an embodiment of failure and frustration in pursuing his ambitious project, and it is through him that the novelists' insight into human frailty may be sensed. If Mrs. Desai'a purpose was to present a really sad, bitter, and funny novel, this purpose is fulfilled to a large extent by the character of Deven, whose main fault seems to lie in his childhood fancy, which he can neither control nor overcome at this stage. The inevitable result is sneer and derision from all, even from his employers, friends like Siddiqui and officials like the Principal and the Head of the Department. His dismissal from the College service and the recovery of debts and bills from him are also imminent. Those whom he expects to assist him — like Murad and Siddiqui — come forward only with gibes and ironical remarks.

The selfishness of the Urdu poet, Nur, his wives Safiya and Imtiaz, and Murad is quite evident in the course of this novel. Nur is no more a celebrity; he is now a 'dissolute and rambling old man' residing in the bazaars of old Delhi and seized with weak eyesight and senility. He is now worried about his means of livelihood and tries to extort money from Deven for interviewing and recording him. His wives are garrulous and self-centred. Of the two, Safiya keeps a low profile. Imtiaz claims to be a nature-gifted poetess of talent and laments that Deven has not understood her properly. If Nur demands money from Deven for his cataract operation, the housewives send him bills for room-rent and medical treatment of the son. And Murad is a very cunning and crafty fellow. It is he who prompts Deven to have the interview of Nur and to record his speeches and recitations for the special number of his magazine. His motive is clearly selfish; he wants to promote the cause of his magazine and Urdu readers at the expense of Deven. He also exploits him in the purchase of the old and outworn tape-recorder, being in secret league with Jain Sahib, the shop-owner. And when Deven approaches him for some payment for his contributions to his magazine, he starts shouting belligerently at him, saying "Don't you try any more of that on me. I've already spent every *paisa* I could get from my mother on that blasted poet of yours—."[7] Even the attitude of the two technicians — Chiku and Pintu — towards Deven is perfectly selfish and money-oriented. While Chiku is quite inefficient and ignorant about his work, being more interested in leave and marriage of his sister, Pintu is slightly better and yet unable to set the records right. Deven's students assist him in anticipation of good marks, but once they know where they stand they hold out threats and abuses for him. Surrounded by such a pack of hounds from all sides, it is no wonder that Deven is totally crushed and depressed. Of course,

Deven as an intelligent man knows the cause of his ruin and destruction, and he tells Siddiqui Sahib that "it was not my fault! I worked hard...but I was fooled and cheated by everyone — the man who sold me the second-hand equipment, the technician who said he could do the recording but was completely inexperienced, by Murad who said he would pay and did not, by Nur who had never told me he wanted to be paid, and by his wives, all of them —."[8] But his knowledge does not help him, and he is hunted down by adverse circumstances like Hardy's Henchard in *The Mayor of Casterbridge*. We only wish someone should come his way and help him out, but that is not to be!

The pattern of the novel is geared up towards the gradual unfolding of the calamities and perplexities of Deven. He is its focal point and nerve-centre. The entire plot — what Aristotle calls 'action' in a play — rotates round him; he is to be seen at the beginning, middle and end of the novel. Other characters in it — Nur, his wives, Murad, Jain Sahib, etc. — play a subordinate role. We may say, they are just the cogs in the wheel. The remaining characters really do not matter much, — the technicians, the Principal, Mr. Siddiqui, Mr. Sharma, even the protagonist's wife Sarla and his son Manu, the students, etc. Of course, Mrs. Desai makes a notable departure here and creates a male protagonist instead of a female protagonist, as usual with her, but that alone does not change her general attitude towards mankind. There is the same agony, the same sadness, the same helplessness on the part of the protagonist here as elsewhere.[9] Even the prose remains poetic and musical here as in other novels; for example, "There was such a sound of splashing and spilling, then of clinking and clattering, of sloshing and giggling, one might have been quite misled as to the seriousness of this annual affair."[10] Such examples may easily be multiplied from the text. Mostly the novelist resorts to the method of description and narration in this piece of fiction, but sometimes she also takes the help of dialogues in furthering the story and portraying the character. Wherever she makes use of dialogues, they become sharp and revealing, occasionally even ironical and biting. At the very opening of the novel, we have the following incisive dialogue between Deven and Murad over the detaining of a devoted teacher from his class :

> 'But it's Monday – Not on Monday, Murad.'
> 'Oh, so friendship is only for Sunday, is it?'
> Murad boomed.[11]

How ironical in his remarks Mr. Siddiqui is when he hears the re-play of tape-recording in the staff-room. He terms it as 'charming' and smiles at Deven and rises from the sofa, indicating thereby that he has no more patience for it. He simply asks in a low voice, "Deven, is that all?"[12] This is certainly an instance of the novelist's understatement and terseness. As usual, Mrs. Desai divides her novel into chapters, but one feels that it would have been better had she given titles or sub-titles to them. That would have rendered the pattern more accessible and intelligible; that would have made a reading of the novel easier and happier.

By pointing out certain shortcomings in the novel, I do not intend denigrating Anita Desai as a novelist or her craftsmanship. Mrs. Desai can undoubtedly build 'a mountain-like novel on a mole hill like story.' I also do not wish to show that she totally fails in her artistic design and fictional mission in the writing of this novel. If *In Custody* she wanted to depict a protagonist in utter 'failure and frustration,' she has rather succeeded in it to some extent. Deven is definitely an unmistakable person who is waging a hard struggle with his insurmountable problems both at home and outside. The frequent breakdown of his plans and programmes at times raises him even to tragic heights, and his ceaseless struggle with the odds renders him adventurous and heroic, but the reader is surprised to see him helplessly slipping into the hands of mischief-mongers and conspirators and letting the situation go beyond his control. The amount of surprise is all the more increased by the knowledge that he is a well-read and well-ranked person — a lecturer in a college which is certainly a post of prestige and responsibility — and yet he allows others (like Murad, Nur and their entourage) to exploit him to the maximum. And the irony of the whole thing is that he pays no heed to the sound and worthwhile advice of his friends and admirers. By way of contrast, the novelist shows other intelligent persons busy in house-construction, contract work, or College build-up, and Mr. Siddiqui, the Head of the Urdu Department at the same Collage, is a living example of it, but this is not enough to open the eyes of Deven himself. He lives in a dream-world, behaves like an innocent angel, and in the end faces a hostile world of harsh realities around him. The whole dream-world crumbles and disappears by slow degrees before his vision, and he is left eventually a pathetic and helpless creature in the midst of millions. What is being suggested here is the truth that Deven is far-removed from the world of reality and commonsense and that he is not so practical as he ought to have been. Prof. R.S. Sharma's observation that "Her [Mrs. Desai's] protagonists are usually sensitive women who, haunted by a peculiar sense of doom, withdraw into a sequestered world of their own"[13] may also be applied to Deven with some reservations, for he is a sensitive man haunted by an overpowering sense of failure and frustration. The change of sex in protagonist does not bring a change in the artistic pattern of Anita Desai, who continues to write intensely with "the sensitivity and imagination of poet."[14] Her artistic drive goes with an amazing skill and intensity which demands a highly soaring imagination, and in the process she loosens her grip over her plot or story-line.[15] While her gifts as a prose stylist are now established on a sound footing, it is to be noted that her fictional canvas remains too small to be convincing.[16] Like Jane Austen, she carves out designs and patterns on 'two inches of ivory,' and seems to be lost in the exploration of the complex mental moods and psychic states of her dominant characters. By the time the harsh realities of life impinge upon her consciousness and shatter her dream-world abounding in music and poetry, it is too late to revert to the conditions of a happy living for them.

Even Anita Desai is not unaware of the thinness of her plot or story-line. In her interview given to Dr. Atma Ram, she makes the following illuminating statement :

> I start writing without having very much of a 'plot' in my mind or on paper — only a very hazy idea of what the pattern of the book is to be. But it seems to work itself out as I go along, quite naturally and inevitably. I prefer the word 'pattern' to 'plot' as it sounds — more natural — and even better, if I dare use it, as Hopkins' word 'inscape' — while 'plot' sounds arbitrary, heavy-handed and artificial, all that I wish to avoid. One should have a pattern and then fit the characters, the setting, and scenes into it — each piece in keeping with the others and so forming a balanced whole.[17]

The statement inevitably leads us to believe that Mrs. Desai gives her attention more to those little things that combine to produce an experience than to incident or experience itself, that she lays her emphasis more on 'pattern and rhythm' than on 'plot,' and that she is more concerned with the overall effects of a work of art, with the need of relating the parts to the whole, than with the artificial and arbitrary aspects of art. And in her practice, she is closer in spirit to a complex poet like G.M. Hopkins than to the straightforward story-teller Thomas Hardy (who invariably wrote with a clear-cut idea of his 'plot,' which scholars have termed as his 'architectonic'). Instead of stressing any other essential component of E.M. Forster, Mrs. Desai has chosen "pattern and rhythm," which "implies a balance, a synthesis and proportion."[18] So, *In Custody* also falls in line with her other novels in its slightness of plot and morbidity of recurrently agonizing feelings and experiences.

To sum up, it may be said that *In Custody* is a novel abounding in failure and frustration, bitterness of restlessness, and that the protagonist in it constantly leads a life of mental and physical tortures and financial hardships. The noted Indo-English poet, K.N. Daruwalla, has also found fault with this sad and sarcastic novel. While reviewing it for *The Hindustan Times*, he remarks that the novel is "built around a non-issue,"[19] and that its theme does not cope with its grand style. Commenting on the ending of the novel, he further remarks that "whether one takes it that Deven commits suicide or refrains from committing it, frankly left me surprised and untouched."[20] Though serious problems may arise from trivial incidents — such as in Pope's *The Rape of the Lock* (1712 and 1714 editions), it is least convincing that a Hindi lecturer, an intelligent and grown-up man indeed, falls into the inescapable trap of some Urdu lovers like Murad and Nur, paying no heed to the warnings of his friends and well-wishers and incurring the wrath of his employers resulting in his dismissal from service and untold financial miseries. Deven's fanaticism exceeds all bounds of decency and decorum, and he must continue to live in his self-created Inferno.

NOTES AND REFERENCES

1. Cited from the back cover of *Cry, the Peacock* (1963, New Delhi : Orient Paperbacks, 1980).
2. Quoted from the Jacket cover of *In Custody* (London : William Heinemann, 1984).
3. E.M. Forster, *Aspects of the Novel* (Harmondswarth, Middiesex : Penguin Books, Ltd., 1936), p. 45.
4. Anita Desai, *In Custody*, p. 19.
5. *Ibid.,* p. 180.
6. *Ibid.,* p. 131.
7. *Ibid.,* p. 188.
8. *Ibid.,* p. 199.
9. As, for instance, Maya in *Cry, the Peacock* (1963), or Sita in *Where Shall We Go This Summer*? (1975), or Nanda Kaul in *Fire on the Mountain* (1977).
10. *In Custody*, p. 95.
11. *Ibid.,* p. 95.
12. *Ibid.*, p. 181.
13. R.S. Sharma, *Anita Desai* (New Delhi : Arnold-Heinemann, 1981), p. 166.
14. *Idem.*
15. Prof. R.S. Sharma rightly remarks that —

    "Nothing escapes her eyes, not even the leg of a spider! This intensity and density of texture compensates for the absence of a strong plot or story line in her fiction. One reads her novels like long poems drawn mostly from those comers of life where no poetry seems to exist" (p. 166).

16. *Ibid.,* p. 167.
17. Atma Ram, "An Interview with Anita Deasi," *WLWE*, XVI, No. 1 (April, 1977), p. 101.
18. *Ibid.*, p. 100.
19. Keki N. Daruwalla, "Built on a Non-Issue," *The Hindustan Times* (Sunday Magazine, dated 13th January 1985).
20. *Idem*.

8

THE NOVELS OF ARUN JOSHI : A CRITICAL STUDY*

I

Arun Joshi is one of the younger Indo-Anglian novelists who excel in their themes and techniques and in their explorations of human psyche. He presents the aspects of Indian life so skillfully that it becomes universal in his creative smithy. We read the novels of Joshi and feel that the writer is opening out what is going within our own hearts. All of his novels are splendid, serious and powerfully disturbing. Through the simple knitting of the story, the novelist tries to explain, to make us understand Life, Love, God and Death. What is most exciting about him is the truth that he attempts a serious probe into the existential problems of mankind by fixing the lens of his focus on certain individualistic characters. In most cases, these characters are the protagonists of the novels — Sindi Oberai, Billy Biswas, and Ratan Rathor and Som Bhasker, but the minor ones are not ignored, *e.g.*, Bilasia, Mr. Khemka, Meena Chatterji. Joshi's inner explorations resemble those of Anita Desai and Chaman Nahal to some extent.

In all, Arun Joshi produced four novels to date. Of these four novels, *The Foreigner* (1968) is the very first one running into three parts and 18 chapters. It details the life and activities of Mr. Sindi Oberai, a Ph. D., but an orphan in Nairobi and educated

---

* First published in *Studies in Contemporary Indian Fiction in English* (Allahabad : Kitab Mahal, 1987), pp. 309–318.

in London. He finally settled down in New Delhi, the land of his forefathers. He seems to be an alienated person from his parents, from his friends and loves and finally from himself. Having come over to India, Sindi called on Babu's father, Mr. Khemka, who made him his assistant in his factory of electric appliances and other related manufactures, and when Babu's father, Mr. Khemka, ran into a rough weather after the dismissal of one of his employees, Mr. Ghosh, Mr. Sindi took over the control of the factory with the willing co-operation of his workers.

The second novel, *The Strange Case of Billy Biswas* (1971), is dedicated to the writer's father and runs into two hundred and forty-four pages. Billy is a psychic person given to consciences and sometimes to visions and hallucinations. He is a Ph.D. from New York in Anthropology with a peculiar bent of mind. When he returns to India, he gets married to a 'mod,' Meena Chatterjee, whose only concern is to make this man all the more restive. During one of his expeditions in Central India along with the students of the University of Delhi, Billy disappears from the camp and all attempts to trace him proved futile. The police reports that Billy is killed by a man-eater. But during one of his visits to villages, the narrator of the story who is the Collector's wife, Situ, falls seriously ill and Billy cures her for ever. But she repays him by reporting the whole matter to Meena and Billy's father, who come rushing from Delhi to take Billy back to the civilized world. Billy had already told his friend, the Collector, that any attempt to capture him would prove disastrous to him. And it so happens that a police party tries to capture him at the intervention of Chief Secretary at Bhopal at the request of Billy's old father. Billy defies it and ultimately dies of bullet injuries.

The third novel, *The Apprentice* (1974), dedicated to the novelist's mother runs into twelve chapters. In this novel, we have the story of Ratan Rathor who hails form one of the revolutionary families of Rajasthan, but is now settled in the foothills of the Himalayas. Ratan, a well-educated village boy, goes to Delhi to make his career, becomes a temporary clerk in the Army Store department where he gets confirmed in due course and rises to a special assistant and finally becomes an officer of the Government of India. How this honest, hard-working boy becomes a conceited man in the midst of the urban people — this is what the story is about. But he feels the pangs within, and his ever-alert conscience keeps on pricking him and he turns "to be of use" to others. He fulfils this desire by becoming a shoe-shine on the staircase of a Delhi temple.

The fourth and last novel, *The Last Labyrinth* (1981), is of good size and is dedicated to the three children of the writer. Here the central figure is Som Bhaskar, a multimillionaire married to a woman of his choice, Geeta, who has borne him two children. But Bhaskar is an ever dissatisfied, restless person, who is relentlessly driven by undefined hungers of possession — of an object, a business-enterprise and a woman. Later when he encounters Anuradha, a tall, beautiful but obsolete lady, he is irresistibly drawn towards her and frequently flies between Bombay and Banaras to satisfy his passions. In the meantime, Bhaskar is also drawn towards the problems of family life, of God and Death, and he takes a risky trip to the high mountains to pay a visit to a sacred shrine. There he gets possession of the business files and the jewellery of Anuradha. Though he gets possession of these materials, he is still restless and pulls out his revolver to finish himself off, but Geeta comes forward and rescues him momentarily from the dark mood of depression.

Thus, it is clear that the themes in the novels of Arun Joshi are largely full of struggle, tension and conflicts. In every novel, we find the articulation of these tensions and conflicts. There are fathers not satisfied with children and children, though they have great respect for their parents, are not content with their parents. In the first novel, *The Foreigner* (1968), the father, Mr. Khemka, sends Babu to America to study engineering. But Babu does not do well there and fails. The fear of an overpowering father disheartens him. He has no dreams of his own. He cannot marry a nice and noble girl because she is of American origin. Mr. Khemka becomes angry when he comes to know that Babu has married June — a fact which ultimately leads to the unnatural death of Babu. In *The Strange Case of Billy Biswas*, Billy studies anthropology, while his father, Mr. Biswas, thinks that his son is doing engineering in a western university. He becomes very much angry when he comes to know that Billy has done Ph.D. in Anthropology. Mr. Biswas is unhappy only because his son cannot be a Collector like Billy's friend, Romesh Sahay.

Secondly, there is a clash between husband and wife. In his *The Foreigner*, Sindi Oberoi is quite against the marriage. Though he loves June and cannot live without her, he tries to remain so much detached with the world that he denies the proposal of marriage by June. In *The Strange Case of Billy Biswas*, Billy is not satisfied with his wife Meena. He leaves his home and becomes a primitive where Bilasia makes him happy. While in *The Apprentice*, Ratan Rathor is tired of his wife, Som Bhaskar in *The Last Labyrinth* is totally neutral to his wife, Geeta.

Apart from this, there is a struggle in man's heart himself. He cannot decide what to do, whether one should confess one's guilt or not, whether one should reconcile with evil spirits or go hand in hand with one's soul.

The novels of Arun Joshi are the songs of the spiritual triumph of man despite the defeat of his physical powers. The very sight of death in each of his novels knocks at the door, but the strong spiritual pull affirms the existence of God. In *The Foreigner*, it is death of Babu and June; in *The Strange Case of Billy Biswas* the death of Billy; in *The Apprentice* the death of the Brigadier; and in *The Last Labyrinth* the death of the old man of the hills and his funeral, filling the heart of Som Bhaskar with realization of God.

But the novels of Joshi are not at all pessimistic in temper. On the country, they rejoice over man's capacity for enduring hardship. Man turns into shining gold coming out of the fire of hardships. He lives the life not for himself but for the social service. Sindi Oberoi becomes the bread-giver to the factory men, Billy is adored among the primitives as God, and Ratan

Rathor shines shoes at the gate of the temple to be of some good use to others.

Fate and Chance also play an important role in the novels of Arun Joshi. In *The Apprentice* at one place, the writer says : "Our character is our fate, my friend." Man cannot know its tricks. Billy leaves the civilized society of Delhi and becomes a primitive in a huff out of sheer restlessness possibly due to the irresistible drive of Fate.

Nature, a prominent factor in Joshi's novels, is presented in its various aspects. Its sensuous presentation is very charming. The novelist sees various colours in nature, enjoys the songs of birds, the steaming ponds, smells flowers like *Rat Ki Rani* and the smell of grass just after rain. The characters are children of Nature; for example, Billy Biswas, Bilasia, Dhunia in *The Strange Case of Billy Biswas* and the old man of the hill and his retinue and Gargi in *The Last Labyrinth*. Their friendship attracts so much that the America-returned, well-educated, civilized Billy rejects Delhi and enjoys the beauties of Nature. And Nature takes the form according to the sentiments of the characters.

The present social system of India is very well exposed by the novelist. Lying, hypocrisy, bribery, drunkenness, womanizing, and unfair distribution of money pinch the heart of the writer. The various problems have also come to light in the course of the novels, and the problem of unemployment, the growth of education, population explosion, housing problem etc., are some of them.

II

Most of Arun Joshi's characters are based on real life rather than on a utopian wishful thinking. The author lets them develop naturally and does not attempt to warp and distort them. They unquestionably suffer from a deep sense of depression and frustration, but eventually emerge heroic and triumphant. The death of Biswas should not be taken as the death of an isolationist but as the triumph of his ideals and principles. Mr. Sindi Oberai, a man totally alienated from his surroundings and society and even from his love, turns out to be the saviour of factory-workers. It is only at the close of the novel that he finds his chance to 'act' bravely, and it is here that he 'belongs.' The protagonist now gets over his inner pricks and mental pressures, and the hope of a successful, cheerful life brightens up. Earlier, he had resisted the seductive charms of June and her proposal of marriage with him due to her strong possessive instincts. His failure in love does not betoken his failure in life. Some other well-sketched characters in *The Foreigner* are : June, Mr. Khemka, and to some extent Babu. The remaining ones are mere types, not creatures of flesh and blood; for instance, Anna, Kathy, Karl, Mr. Ghose, Sindi's uncle, June's mother, Sheela, etc.

The Strange Case of Billy Biswas has Billy or Bimal Biswas as the central character, and the whole novels rotates round him. He is sick with the frenzied rush of the material world, and his deep-rooted 'existential' restlessness drives him far away from the madding crowd of money-minters and property-grabbers. This child of Nature joins the primitive community of tribals in Central India and lives happily there with Bilasia. He defies the attempts to recapture him and dies the death of a noble hero. He is definitely a 'strange case' for the psycho-analysts and psychiatrists to investigate, but such cases are not uncommon in India and other parts of the world. He renders the reading of this novel a pleasure, but other characters in it do not attract us much but for Bilasia. Meena Chatterjee, Romesh Sahai (or Romi), Situ, Billy's father, etc., are mere nonentities in the novel, having been drawn there simply for the expediency of the plot.

Like *The Strange Case….*, *The Apprentice* is a solo-character novel, dealing with the rise and fall of Ratan Rathor. He is called 'Mr. Crisis of Character.' This well-educated, honest and sincere village boy goes to Delhi and gets employed there, finally rising to the post of a Central Government officer, but in the process is lost. He becomes a cheat, a bribe-taker, a money-maker, a drunkard, and a womaniser. This reduces him to the status of "A Nobody" (p. 74). But his conscience pricks him constantly, and as an act of expiation be takes to shoe-shining at the door of a glittering temple in Delhi (the locale of the entire action). In this novel, there is hardly any other character worth the name, — the Brigadier, 'You,' the Officer Superintendent, Himmat Singh, and the Sheikh being only cogs in the wheel of the story.

The Last Labyrinth is definitely cast on a grander scale than *The Apprentice*, and the mystery shrouds the action here right from the beginning. This mystery relates not only to the taxing question about Life, Love, Death, and God, but also to those pertaining to the status of Gargi and Anuradha and the eventual disappearance of Anuradha from the story altogether. "Lal Haveli" of Mr. Aftab Rai is yet another point of deep mystery. In fact, the title of the novel is a pointer to all these mysteries, which seem to suggest that "In my end is my beginning" (T.S. Eliot). The action of the novel is surely 'circular' because the beginning and the close point to the same end. The dilemmas of Som Bhaskar, the protagonist, remain unresolved unto the very last. When the novel closes, Some is seen with a pistol in his hand pointing at his head, and in this moment of deep depression he is being rescued by his wife, Geeta. The role of Geeta is contrasted to the role of Anuradha in it. If Anuradha has been seductive and adulterous, Geeta has ever been enduring and tolerant. Geeta is the only remedy for a sick brain like that of Som Bhaskar, and by identifying with her he can realize true hope and peace (note the implied significance of her name — Geeta — as though suggesting directly the philosophical treatise of the Hindus!). The reader, however, feels that the novelist should have woven his plot on some solid substance rather than on the flimsy eternal triangle of love and treachery. Love-intrigue might have satisfied the emotional demands of an Elizabethan or of a Restoration man, but it does not look convincing and elevating to a modern man.

III

The novels of Arun Joshi hover between the opposing pulls of attachment and detachment, action and inaction, love and hate, possessiveness and dispossessiveness, down-to-earth materialism and eternity-bound urges of spiritualism. They constitute the perennial dilemmas of mankind, and Joshi explores them ceaselessly from the viewpoint of an artist. In maintaining a certain distance from his creations, he remains a detached, dispassionate observer of life around him, and herein lies his art. As someone has said, "Art lies in concealing art," Joshi is an excellent craftsman in fictional writing who knows well how to 'conceal' his art and how to create an atmosphere of suspense and mystery in it. In this respect, he is in utter contrast to another practising novelist of the day, namely Anita Desai, who identifies herself with her protagonists (who are all females — restless, tormented and alienated) and grows lyrical in describing their abnormal conditions and haunting passions.

Most of the novels of Joshi are tripartite (being divided in three parts), prosaic, and structured on the deeds and movements of a single outstanding character (inevitably the protagonist). Their action swings between gloom and light, sorrow and happiness, test and triumph (including release in death). The protagonists are not always the same, as in case of Anita Desai, who too is very careful in the structuring of her plot.

The fictional technique of Arun Joshi is kaleidoscopic, and moves forward and backward in a swift motion. That's why he does not give us so many sections or chapters in his novels; this is particularly true of the last novel, where the continuity of the action is maintained throughout by keeping above the impeding, artificial barriers of unnecessary divisions. In other novels, we do have chapters, but they are not too many. This characteristic is also shared by Anita Desai, especially in her *Where Shall We Go This Summer*? and *Fire on the Mountain*.

The Foreigner, which is decidedly modeled on Albert Camus' *The Outsider,*[1] is apparently theatrical both at the beginning and at the end. The novel begins with the death of Babu in a tragic accident, the cause of which is not known until the reader has finished two-thirds of it and closes with the overthrow of Mr. Khemka from his position and the installation of Mr. Oberai in his place. The story has sufficient potential in it to arouse the interest of the reader by means of a set of contrived episodes and a self-searching protagonist. What is most surprising in it is the fact that when a natural solution to the June-Sindi-Babu triangle in love is in sight, the voluptuous and lovable girl is removed from the scene for good.

As in *The Foreigner*, the probe into the depths of human psyche continues *in The Strange Case of Billy Biswas* too. But the narration here takes place through the mouth of the Collector, the bosom friend of Billy. Speaking of this novel, a scholar writes; "It is a compelling novel about a strange quest, drawing upon myth and folk-lore to reiterate its elemental concerns."[2] There is more truth in this statement than in what follows: "Arun Joshi's *The Strange Case of Billy Biswas* (1971) fails to tune the writer's sensibility to cultural subtleties."[3] What the latter fails to comprehend is the truth that the novel operates on more than one level, that it operates on elemental as well as metaphysical level. The question of 'culture' arises only after a thorough exploration of the peculiar psyche and mentality of Billy, who is otherwise highly educated and perfectly cultured. And 'culture' and its subtleties should not be equated with 'money-making' or 'worldliness', for it is in the latter that Billy is truly deficient. Billy's firm belief is : "the scratch for truth...was a lonely business" (p. 177).[4]

In *The Apprentice*, the narration is largely delivered by Ratan Rathor, who describes all events and persons in it; it is the first-person method of narration. The technique here is not different from James Joyce's stream-of-consciousness. The beginning is illustrated by the end, and hence the overall impression is one of compactness and cumulativeness. Its theatrical flashbacks and flashforths are remarkably reflected in the sentence : "You will notice that for all intent and purposes I was behaving as they do in the movies" (p. 134).

The first-person narrative is further continued in the next novel, *The Last Labyrinth*, where the narrator is Som Bhaskar, the protagonist. Through many a cinematic shot the plot is unfolded before us, not unlike the practice of an early Russian writer. The dialogues tend to be short and crisp, but their hurried motion is arrested by long, speculative or descriptive passages. A beautiful specimen of the speculative and philosophical prose is to be had in the conversation between Som Bhaskar and Dr. Leela Sahnis (see pp.75–79 in particular), and that of descriptive prose may be seen in passages depicting the journey of the old man over the mountains to the lake of his heart's desire (see pp. 191-194). Here it must be mentioned that Joshi contrives to diversify his language to suit different moods of speakers and different shades of meaning. Similarly, he fully understands that the formal language of an invitation or of a social gathering can hardly befit the language of domestic conversation by the fireside exchanged in a mood of perfect ease and relaxation.

IV

Arun Joshi seems to be in no hurry to produce a number of raw novels. Consequently, whatever he produces bears the unmistakable stamp of his talent and craftsmanship. His work is usually chiseled and artistic, and compels the attention of the reader. No wonder that he has been offered the coveted Sahitya Akademi Award for Literature on *The Last Labyrinth*. The only drawback in him as a novelist is that he hardly ever accommodated humour or comedy in his works. He does employ irony now and then but he can't be another R.K. Narayan or Ruth Prawer Jhabvala. Otherwise, his fictional art is flawless and poised, and we only hope that he will advance from strength to strength in the days to come. Even if he does not, he has still secured a permanent place in the annals of Indo-English fiction of today.

NOTES AND REFERENCES

1. K.R.S. Iyengar, *Indian Writing in English* (Bombay : Asia Publishing House, 1973), p. 512.
2. Meenakshi Mukherjee, *The Twice Born Fiction* (New Delhi : Arnold-Heinemann, 1974), p. 203.
3. R.S. Singh, *Indian Novel in English* (New Delhi; Arnold-Heinemann, 1977), p. 178, f. n. 6.

4. The details about Arun Joshi's novels are :
   (i) *The Foreigner* (Delhi : Hind Pocket Books, 1968).
   (ii) *The Strange Case of Billy Biswas* (Delhi : Hind Pocket Books, 1971).
   (iii) *The Apprentice* (New Delhi : Orient Paperbacks, 1974).
   (iv) *The Last Labyrinth* (New Delhi : Orient Paperbacks, 1981).

9

THE NOVELS OF MICHAEL CHACKO DANIELS*

Uma Parmeswaran goes wide of the mark when she remarks that Indo-English Literature "seems destined to die young"[1] and when she sets A.D. 2000 as "the dirge date"[2] for this brand of literature. Her pessimism generated by the peculiar concatenation of political circumstances prevailing in India in the Sixties has no solid base today and may be taken simply as ill-timed and untenable. David McCutchion is rather nearer the truth when he observes : "By a strange irony, Indian literature in English has been flourishing since Independence more successfully than it ever flourished before."[3] Obviously, some of the best works in Indian writing in English have been produced after 1947. Even Harrex seems to be correct in his assessment of the current political and cultural situation in this country. He says, "Indian writing in English has emerged out of a confusion of cultural contexts."[4] Of late there has come about a spurt in the production of both fiction and poetry written in English, and fortunately it has not gone unnoticed in the literary circles. There are Indian novelists and poets in English who have attained considerable stature and recognition — Mulk Raj Anand, R.K. Narayan, Raja Rao, Bhabani Bhattacharaya, Manohar Malgonkar, Khushwant Singh, Ruth Prawer Jhabvala, Kamala Markandaya, Anita Desai, Balachandra Rajan, etc., as novelists, and Nissim Ezekiel, Dom

---

* Reprinted with permission of the editor and publisher of *Indian English Novelists,* ed. M. Prasad (New Delhi : Sterling Publishers, 1982), pp. 117–129.

Moraes, A.K. Ramanujan, R. Parthasarathy, K. Das, Pritish Nandy, Pranab Bandyopadhyay, etc., as poets. A number of qualitative translations (or 'transcreations' as P. Lal would have it) of Indian classics, both old and new, have opened up new vistas for Indian writers in English today. And whatever they are busy doing today vouches a smooth passage for Indo-English literature through the days to come, despite the doubts and distrusts raised about it by certain sceptical persons from certain quarters.

Though Michael Chacko Daniels does not fall in line with the established and well-known Indo-English novelists of today in that he is mainly preoccupied with the minority problems of language and service, he has yet contributed whatever he could to the growth and diversification of Indo-English fiction. As compared to the big personalities in the field, he is a major author with only two novels[5], so far, to his credit — *Anything Out of Place is Dirt* (1971) and *That Damn Romantic Fool* (1972). Daniels is a little known figure of talent who has received very little critical attention to this day. The present paper is intended to fill up this gap.

Daniels, born in 1943 and an M.A. in Economics from the University of Bombay, 1966, went to the United States in June 1967, earned his M.S. in Journalism from the Northwestern University, Illinois, in 1968, and worked as an assistant editor in San Francisco until he returned to India in 1972. He is an Indian citizen and lives in Bombay.

His first novel — *Anything Out of Place is Dirt* — is set in Bombay and Bangalore. The first part of the novel is placed in Bombay and the second part in Bangalore. The first part has four sub-divisions : (1) Barthalowmew and Narayanan, (2) Liz and Po, (3) Samuel and (4) I am what I am. The novel is more a study of persons rather than of situations. Barthalomew is the focal point here. The title of the novel is aptly chosen and applies to him. He is one of the minor community in India trying hard to find a safe anchorage in a conservative society. He wants to belong to such a thing which does not own him. His problem, therefore, is the problem of 'belongingness,' — a problem similar to that of the Hairy Ape (or Yank) in the famous play of that name by the celebrated American dramatist Eugene O' Neill. His quest is the quest for identity, for self-recognition. He always feels like a fish out of pond, to use a Chaucerian expression. His predicament is clearly conveyed in "...it is very difficult for a person from a minority community to survive in India."[6] He constantly asks himself : "What would I have done if I were in his place?" (pp. 17 & 25).

The plot of the novel is very slim and slight. It rotates round Barthalomew and his physical and mental wanderings in Bombay and Bangalore. It begins with his meeting with Narayanan, and moves through a description of the two charming girls, Liz and Po, to that of a youngman named Samuel. There are reflections about the protagonist and his dreary, disturbing situation. This is all that we find in the first part of the novel. In the second part, Barthalomew is out to carve out his career as a journalist; he attends the *Daily* as a trainee in Bangalore. Here too, he meets nothing but fear and frustration. At long last, he reaches the land of his forefathers and parents — Kerala, and pointedly recalls his mother's usual saying : "Anything out of place is dirt" (p. 105).

Most of the narration in the novel takes place through the mouth of Barthalomew. He speaks not only about himself and his friend Narayanan, but also about the two girls and Samuel and his unexpected madness. But Barthalomew seems to be a man of flitting moods. He does not dwell long in the same place and does not converse long with a person. He goes to see Narayanan and Samuel on different occasions, but leaves them in a few minutes. This might have suited the design of the novelist to bring about a change in scene or character,[7] but this also leaves much to be desired.

Daniels's art of characterization is minute and lively. He portrays a character slowly but steadily. His Barthalomew is a round character, the axis of the plot. The novelist has drawn both round and flat, developed and undeveloped, characters in his works. They are both individuals and types, both males and females, drawn from different strata of society. However, I have no hesitation in saying that he has not succeeded well in portraying female characters. While Barthalomew, Narayanan, and Joseph are depicted painstakingly, Liz and Po, Estella and Leela, receive no more than a cursory treatment from the novelist. No insight is revealed in depicting them, and they largely remain the objects of passion and beauty to be appreciated and dismissed at will.

Barthalomew is a Christian from Kerala, of thin placid body, bearded, having smoke-burnt lips and white teeth. He uses a skull cap to settle his long, loose hair. He detests crowds and rush for bus or shelter. He looks a little diffident before Narayanan, who is a calm, quiet man and a lecturer in Mathematics and Ethics in one of the Bombay colleges, and who belongs to a large family of twelve persons, having five brothers and four sisters, all younger to him. He reads meanings in pictures, such as those when he sees pictures of Indian freedom fighters along with that of the king of Iran pasted on the glass front of the counter in an Iranian restaurant. He likes dust, loves colours, and believes in symbols. He is a little moody, with poetic temper and journalistic leanings. Of the two girls in his contact, Liz and Po, he likes the latter, who has 'golden breasts,' and who has touched his imagination. He actually waxes lyrical in remembering her beauty :

> He remembered Po had golden breasts. Sometimes they join together and become more golden and bigger in his imagination. When he had talked to Po he had looked at her in the eye. He had burned with hot fires. He wrote verses about her great beauty (p. 8).

He thinks too much of himself, of India, of minorities, of Indian Muslims and Christians and feeds himself with illusions — "after Nehru the Christians in India would be massacred" (p. 31). He feels lonely, while his brother who lives and moves in a group does not. Is it not that his loneliness is born of his unsocial habits? And when he goes to Bangalore to learn journalism, he still feels acute frustration. He is disillusioned with the rowdy and ludicrous behaviour of the Councillors of the

Municipality who are, in fact, a pack of dishonest people trained in shouting and raising slogans and concerned with only their own survival and honour, with the opening and closing ceremonies of wards, with the subscription to the Swami Vivekanand Black Rock Committee, etc. He feels completely laid aside there. He is certainly the central figure in this novel who makes his presence felt everywhere.[8]

Putting apart Narayanan, there are some minor characters too in this novel. They appear here mostly to show their relationship to Barthalomew. We have, thus, Liz and Po, the two beautiful girls, one Christian and the other Gujarati. Liz, who belongs to a minority community, has 'full breasts and blue skies', with long buttocks controlled by a thick skirt and her rounded legs balancing on her high heels. She has got brown hair, face, and rounded lips. Po (who is partly described above) has brown shoes, bag and skirt, and a light brown blouse. She has the colour of wheat and tired eyes. Barthalomew can't look Liz in the eye, but he can do so in case of Po.

There is also Samuel, a Christian — a Syrian Catholic — of lean and thin constitution, who hails from Kerala and who lives in a hostel in Colaba. Being religious, he tips the beads of Catholic rosary. He has the ability to write a play, but suffers from tropical esonophilia. He is rich, but wants to be richer; he has bought 'a new binoculars,' made in Germany. The ideals of Indian myths and legends have tied him down to inhibitions in sex matters and marriage. Evidently, his megalomania arises from his inhibitions. He does a bit of yoga and a little bit of dumbbells. He is for 'mental yoga' between the sexes. He is preparing for the Master's degree. He is an instance of a romantic youth living in the world of illusions. He pleads for secularism in the country, and vigorously argues on this topic with Narayanan.

Then, there is the self-praising Mr. K., who is over sixty. He is dark-complexioned and physically very strong, and ever talks of his own achievements. He enjoys dance, especially with his 'gori' wife, of whom he is proud. His two sons are well settled in England, and he seems to be fully content with his physical and material possessions.

The second novel — *That Damn Romantic Fool* — is a little bigger in size than the first one and is a story of Narayanan and Joseph. It is dedicated to the novelist's parents, and carries his brief note which runs thus : "Any resemblance in this novel to living persons is purely coincidental." This resemblance is so clear in his reference to 'the learned men and women of the Department of Economics' in the University of Bombay. Some characters of the previous novel are taken over in this one too for the furtherance of the story on a familiar ground. Of such characters, Narayanan and Barthalomew stand out. While Narayanan is the nucleus of this novel, Barthalomew appears nowhere physically in it though he is remembered nostalgically by his friend time and again. To Narayanan, Joseph has come as a substitute for Barthalomew, but Narayanan cannot forget Barthalomew because of his mental and ideological closeness to him. This is how Narayanan comments on his friend :

> Barthalomew should have read my volumes by Bertrand Russell. It would have made him a positivist. Besides, he would have learnt how to conquer happiness.[9]

That Barthalomew so much obsesses the mind of Narayanan is quite obvious in the following :

> Barthalomew sat on the same sofa about a year ago.... What has become of him? He was then about the same age Joseph is, he wanted to do the same things Joseph wants to do. Both of them are of Syrian Christian origin. How is it that I draw to me persons who are so similar? (pp. 31-2).

This is a highly revealing soliloquy of Narayanan, and it demonstrates that Joseph is actually a continuation of Barthalomew from the first novel.

The plot of the second novel, too, rotates round the two principal characters of Narayanan and Joseph. It is, so to speak, free from the complexity and ponderousness of a novel like

James Joyce's *Ulysses* (1922) or a novel like Somerset Maugham's *Of Human Bondage* (1915) or *The Razor's Edge* (1944). It is a simple, straightforward story of the two dominant characters noted above. It has five sections : (1) One of Those Days, (2) The Day After, (3) Another Day, (4) Other Days and (5) He Rushes to the Terminal. The first section begins with a description of Narayanan as a lecturer in Mathematics and as an avid reader of one of the cheapest English dailies. It shows his father's affection and respect for him and his views, his dislike of the Communists (but later he decides to become one), his visualization of himself as a revolutionary, his abhorrence for the religious atmosphere in his Christian college, and his love and admiration of Joseph. It also depicts the terrible quarrels between Joseph's parents. The second section describes Joseph's meeting with Narayanan at the latter's residence, their 'quiet penises,' their walk and talk on the film *The Yellow Rolls-Royce,* the role of the revolutionary Omar Sharif in it, the two's stances with regard to revolutions and social reforms, and Ronny's headache causing a concern for Narayanan. The third section highlights Narayanan's departure for the library, his fondness for the 'golden' crow flying in the sky at the sunset, his disbelief in violent revolutions, his meeting with Leela, a calm, quiet part-time worker in the library, his close male friendships, particularly with Barthalomew and Joseph, his adverse attitude towards the form and content of the English literary tradition, his inclination towards the proper use of language, his dislike for gold and jewellery, his unquestioning submission to 'society ways' (p. 56), his dream of Estella in a nap, his opposition to the United States and its information service, his growing interest in the common people and their harrowing tales and burning issues. The fourth section brings out Narayanan's anxiety for a knocked-down beggar about to die within three days, his preference for co-operatives to private shops — "a way of outwitting the capitalists" (p. 95), his deep love for Estella, his appreciation of the Soviet system in which "Democracy and socialism can walk hand in hand" (p. 110), his sudden encounter with Joseph at the

U.S.S.R. information board and out in the street, his passionate memory of Estella. The fifth and last section details Narayanan's meeting with Joseph and their exchange on the social order and the national parties, Narayanan's jeers and sneers at journalism and fiction-writing, Joseph's full-blooded and defensive reply to him, and his disclosure of the plan to visit America next year, Narayanan's declaration of his resolve to join the Communist Party of India, his vision of "masses of men and banners in his mind" (p. 133), his oneness with all people, especially the poor and the downtrodden, his rejection of "individualism," Joseph's uncontrollable irritation at Narayanan's resolve to join the Communists, his decision to go to the woods and shoot himself as conveyed to Narayanan in his letter, and, finally, Narayanan's rush to the terminal to stop Joseph from doing any harm to himself. Though the beginning of the novel is somewhat casual and unimpressive, the ending is really suggestive and striking.

The title of the novel applies to Joseph. It is used thrice for him by Narayanan towards the close. It is quite appropriately chosen, Joseph banks too much on his illusions and his idealistic concepts of friendship and human relationship, and when they are dashed to pieces by a hard-hitting announcement of his friend, he is left with no more power within him to face the harsh realities of life. So he hurriedly decides to commit suicide. Hence the title to him.

Daniels reveals the characters of Narayanan and Joseph slowly but steadily. Of the two, Narayanan receives greater attention. This lean and thin lecturer of Mathematics is aged 30, having thick lips and handsome features. His liking of the 'golden' crow and Russell and Nehru is well pronounced in the novel. He does not go by reports. He realises that most of the trouble in the world is due to "a misuse of language" (p. 2). He imagines himself as a revolutionary, and burns at the injustices of the world. More than a man of action, he is a man of thought and feeling. He regards his college as a place of work, though he is not ready to accept its religion. He also speaks against Gandhiji and his self-purification for one full period. He loves Estella

Corienda Diaz, a young Catholic girl who is not willing to give up her religion. For a while, Narayanan wishes to be a Catholic for her sake, but that will shatter his entire family whose well-being he always keeps in mind. He reads the *Marxist Outlook,* and believes in revolutions, violent or peaceful, social reforms and the uplift of the poor and the country. Thoroughly gentle, he cherishes the ideal of considering himself to be common. To set corruption and begging right, he wants a radical change in people's outlook that can easily effect a social change. He is a bit of poet too; three full poems are to be had in the book. He feels warmth for Leela, and at a stage thinks of marrying her. He has a deep rooted anger against the United States and its information service, though he is a member of the American library for Mathematics books only. He at times thinks of the importance of manual labour, of exercise, of relaxation and concentration. He likes the common people — "We should think of the whole world as one family....one person should not accumulate to the disadvantage of another person." (p. 89). But he seems not to have been a widely experienced person; for instance, he has not seen a swan or a seagull at close quarters, nor has he slept with a woman. But he shows an increasing curiosity in two things at least — in the Communist Party of India and in his sweetheart Estella. Ultimately, he decides to join the former and to take the latter as his wife. He is all praise for the Soviet system where democracy and socialism go hand in hand. He detests literary persons and journalists because they have no useful purpose to serve in society (p. 130). In joining the C.P.I., he thinks, his relations with his family and with Estella will remain intact. The emotional letter of Joseph touches him deeply, and he rushes to the terminal to save the precious life of his friend. At the close of the novel, Narayanan stands as a very human and generous person trying to serve and save others in all possible ways.

Joseph is another important character in this novel. He becomes a bosom friend of Narayanan after the dapartures of Bathalomew to Bangalore. Joseph has the respect and affection of Narayanan. He is a lonely but lovable man. He is short-sized, curly-haired, fairly rounded in a sort of muscular way, with chubby cheeks and large eyes. He tries to keep his distance from others. But he is not like a stunted nail, as he keeps growing inward. He grows in intensity of feeling and thought. He is fed on English lyrical poetry, novels and films. To those who are affectionate to him, he is also affectionate, loyal and steadfast; but if he is once betrayed, he breaks off all his relationship for ever. His most intense feelings are reserved for such abstractions as people, nation, democratic socialism, non-alignment, and world peace. He has love and admiration for Narayanan, and talks with him on economic and political matters without much originality. He is attached, besides Narayanan, to his family and the *Times of India.* In sex matters, he is a little perverted; to quieten his extended penis, for instance, he resorts to masturbation. He has the desire to become a novelist and a journalist. He is ashamed of his parents for their terrible quarrels. He is a voracious reader of the *Encounter.* He is a product of "a strong tradition of seeking individual perfection" (p. 42), and lives in "a state of perpetual tiredness and loneliness" (p. III). To Narayanan, he has "none of the attempted sophistication, the pretensions, the snobbishness or the condescension of people of his background" (p. 37). In his eyes and lips, he resembles Barthalomew. He values Narayanan's opinion more than anyone else's in the world, but Narayanan considers him as a little self-conceited and much too westernized. Narayanan thinks that Joseph is "a mindless blotter taking in second-hand experiences" (p. 117), that "he has not adjusted to reality" (p. 116), and that he "loses the ability to interact with people" (p. 117). He, in a way, likes his privacy, and holds the view that perfection is nothing but a "mere union with an ideal member of the opposite sex" (p. 120). He wishes to visit America next year. At a stage, Narayanan feels that Joseph is lost (p. 136), but when he receives the latter's letter near the door, opens it, and reads it, he immediately rushes to the terminal to save his friend from destruction. Joseph seems to have taken this extreme decision because Narayanan had totally shaken his faith in him by his unexpected announcement the last day to join the C.P.I. and because Joseph used to look to

Narayanan for the spiritual support, and now the two stand divided in camps.

There are some minor characters in the novels too. Estella is one of them. She is a Christian who has been to the States where she comes to realise her darkness. She loves Narayanan, but her religion stands in the way. Narayanan, however, decides to accept her, help her, and transform her, and thereby complete himself. She is a lovable girl with advanced manners but firm to her word. Narayanan warmly hugs her and kisses her, and she is "fully ready to receive his penis" (p. 121). Another girl who appeals to Narayanan is Leela, a part-time worker in the library. She is aged 21-22, and her interests are books. Later, Narayanan drifts towards Estella. There are also the members of Narayanan's family — Ronny, his youngest brother whom he loves deeply, Sheilla, his sister who is fond of interfering with other people's business and who likes good manners and rich people, Krishnan, his third younger brother, and two other brothers and three sisters and parents.

The technique of the novelist is to describe persons, places and things at some length with intermissions rather than to reveal them through dialogues or conversations. There are occasional dialogues no doubt, but they hardly tell much about someone's feelings, thoughts, and psychological pressures. The two novels look like a sequence, for there is a continuation of characters and their stories. When Barthalomew is left, Narayanan and Joseph are taken up. Daniels's technique reminds one of the noted novelist P.G. Wodehouse against whom the charge was levelled that he was no writer at all because he repeated the themes and characters in his works. Further, Wodehouse was long neglected by literary critics, and only George Sampson noted his existence in the literary world. Though I have no intention to become a George Sampson for Daniels, I feel that this works deserve a careful scrutiny and assessment. Daniels makes topical allusions at times in both the books, giving a sense of being up-to-date and modern. Thus, he refers to Bombay and its immense new opportunities to people, to the Sino-Indian conflict in 1962 and the Indo-Pak war in 1965, to the depression in India that comes with 'sickness, poverty and insecurity,' etc. There is yet one more way in which the author tries to sound somewhat modern or ultra-modern — the way he repeatedly mentions the quietening or extension of penises and the masturbations by male characters in the novels. There is a dearth of wit and humour in them, but no dearth of exposing situations and mental worries of characters, — the characters who are treated with all earnestness and seriousness. Though the plot-structure is not up to the mark, the novelist has admirably portrayed his characters and their likes, dislikes and tensions. The mode of writing adopted by the novelist is to start on a slow and limping note and to end with a remarkable pace and fluency. This becomes so clear when one studies the second novel cautiously. As Narayanan's consciousness of the human world deepens and quickens, the slow, cumbersome style yields place to the swift, racy one. This is what we find in the beginning of the novel :

> Crow is in view. Crow is in view, he registers.
> He squints.
> The sun strikes it.
> "Could it have been gold?" Narayanan asks himself.
> He squints at the rays of the sun. He registers (p. 1).

and this is what we find towards the end :

> A crow caws
> A light wavers
> A pair of legs move toward him
> A hand helps him up.
> He hears himself saying, "I must have slipped on that plantain skin. Thank you."
> He feels warm and moist.
> Two crows caw.
> Lights become brighter.
> People move, weave in and out.
> He moves toward home (p. 134).

A comparison between these two excerpts will bear out my argument.

For the novelist under discussion, language is no problem and he shows a comfortable command of it. Of course, there are attempts at punning here and there, but they are not frequent. There are apt similes and metaphors in both the books. Occasionally, the language tends to be symbolic, as in the following :

> There were snakes in his veins. A python was coiled round his middle. A succubus was at his throat. A brain-eater on his head (pp. 24-5).

At places, it becomes repetitive in words, phrases and expressions. But, on the whole, it is powerful and profuse. It abounds in sweet and charming expressions, such as "A mob in India is like fire on dry grass in summer" (p. 29) and "she is like a flower or a leaf in the wind. With the ripe wheat of her smile she is calm" [(p. 32) — both from the first novel], "without love life is not worth living" (p. 32), "The loneliness of one alien to his land" (p. 33), "its most sincere desire is to seduce my sensibilities" (p. 81), "...there is no better medicine than laughter for life's queer twists and turns" (p. 118), and "Black whores whirl" [(p. 118) — all from the second novel]. No doubt, such expressions may be easily multiplied, but they are sufficient to show the way the author worked at his language and craft. There are American spellings too, as in 'distill' and '*pan-colored* spittle,' but they are few and far between. On the count of language, I have an unfeigned admiration for the novelist.

Finally, Daniels is a novelist with potentialities in him, but those potentialities have not been exploited to the maximum. And as he has a long future before him, let us hope so, he may rise above his petty pitfalls, such as those of narration and plot-structure, and create for himself a niche in the temple of Indo-English fiction.

NOTES AND REFERENCES

1. Uma Parmeswaran, "Introduction," *A Study of Representative Indo-English Novelists* (New Delhi : Vikas Publishing House, 1976), p. 2.
2. *Ibid.,* p. 5.
3. David McCutchion, *Indian Writing in English* (Calcutta : Writers Workshop, 1964), p. 3.
4. S.C. Harrex, *The Fire and the Offering* : *The English Language of India 1935–1970,* I (Calcutta : Writers Workshop, 1977), p. 3.
5. Besides these, Daniels has also written a book of verse entitled *Split in Two* (1971) for the Writers Workshop.
6. Michael Chacko Daniels, *Anything Out of Place is Dirt* (Calcutta : Writers Workshop, 1971), p. 27. The textual quotations that follow are from this source.
7. I am deliberately leaving out a mention of the novelist's technique and language because I shall revert to them after analysing the second novel fully.
8. Narayanan is relegated to a subordinate position here to be treated fully only in the second novel.
9. Michael Chacko Daniels, *That Damn Romantic Fool* (Calcutta : Writers Workshop, 1972), p. 3. The textual quotations that follow are taken from this source.

10

KAMALA DAS'S *ALPHABET OF LUST* (1976) : AN APPRAISAL*

This is a novel all about lust and sex, — a theme valid enough for Kamala Das to handle adroitly. Dedicated to Jaisurya, the third son of the writer, and running into 148 pages, this Orient paperback publication has unity of purpose and thought, a good deal of irony and concentration. How far sex can go to secure the pride of place is to be witnessed here. Obviously, it is a sizzling story of a beautiful woman, who is also a famous poetess and her sexual surrender out of greed and ambition to some of the best-placed Cabinet Ministers in Delhi and her rise to power and pelf in an unimaginable manner.

Manasi, the protagonist of the novel, is married to Amol Mitra in a huff after the sudden and unexpected air-crash death of her fiance, the elder brother of Vijay Raje, by whom she has a child in her womb. Vijay Raje, a six years' junior to his elder brother, is in deep love with Manasi, and when he grows up into an adult he makes up his mind to seize political power and thereby win his love. Until Raje appears on the scene, the life for the Mitras is quite happy and carefree though not financially well-off. When he visits Manasi at her husband's after a lapse of two decades, he makes advances to her which she rebuffs scornfully. He goes away disappointed. Through the pull of Sadasivrao, an elderly but a conscientious politician, Raje becomes

* First published in my book, *Kamala Das and Her Poetry* (Delhi : Doaba House, 1983), pp. 133–140. Reprinted here with permission of the publisher.

a leader of youths and draws closer to the Prime Minister of the country. But afterwards, he elbows Sadasivrao out of the Central cabinet taking un undue advantage of the PM's displeasure with the latter, and steps in his shoes. On becoming a minister, he grabs power and influence in the capital, and sends off an emissary in Krishnan to Mansai with a concrete proposal of allurement for her — that she should spend a week with him in the best hotel in Simla and get in return diamond ear-rings. Ambitious as she is, she accepts the offer. Prior to this, she has been awarded, through the advocacy of Raje to the PM, the coveted Padmashri and a long citation for her enviable services to Literature, and she now thinks that she will be killing two birds with one stone. She will tell her husband that she is going to Delhi to receive her awards, and she will also take the trip to Simla in the company of Raje. She does so. In the meantime, the P.M. is drawn to Manasi, as she has been repeatedly praised by Raje, whose design apparently is to promote his beloved into the P.M.'s favour and be ever secure in his saddle. After spending a week in Simla with Raje, Manasi returns to Delhi and meets the P.M. at a dinner hosted by one of Raje's friends. The P.M. is left alone with her on the pretext of a severe headache, and she feels for him in his utter loneliness. And when he makes love to her, she does not resist it, since she has already decided to offer her body to him : " I rented out my body for a pair of diamond ear-rings. And hereafter for power I shall rent it out to the most influential tenant I can hope to get" (p. 41). Since then the P.M. meets her regularly and regales his life. Very tactfully Manasi is first made a member of the Rajya Sabha, then the Minister of Information and Broadcasting, and thereafter the Home Minister. Raje totally withdraws from her lest his boss be annoyed. She pays occasional visits to Bombay, but has no time to stay with her husband or to write letters to her only daughter, Suparna, who is now 19 years old studying in a boarding school at Lucknow. On her birthday, she asks Raje, who is going to Lucknow on some official commission, to call on her daughter and present a parcel of gifts to her. Raje's rapacious eyes fall on the beaming beauty that Suparna is and he invites her to a very good hotel in the city where he feeds her deliciously and tries to rape her then and there. Suparna is dazed and stunned at this, and sobs continually in the night, and in the early morning catches a train for Bombay to reveal all this to her sincere boy-friend, Cyrus Contractor. Sensing a sort of trouble for himself, Raje rushes to Bombay to calm her down. At her home she is all alone when he comes in, and she is greatly surprised to see him there. She tells him that she has not disclosed the matter to her parents nor has she any desire to do so. Raje again catches hold of her and begins caresssing her temples, locks and breasts, at which she waxes extremely emotional and accepts his offer of Simla visit for a few days. He tells her :

> My darling girl, I cannot live without you... caressing her breasts and her arms. Come away with me this minute. Come to Simla. We shall be happy together for a while. We shall get married. We shall be the happiest of married couples (p. 126).

Together they go to the same hotel where earlier her mother had made love to him, to the same room and to the same bed. What an irony of situation! They make intense love to each other and decide to get married soon. Suparna becomes pregnant too. When Manasi hears of this, she sadly repents her associations with Raje and complains of it to the Prime Minister after revealing her daughter's identity — that she was Raje's own niece. The Prime Minister who had earlier wanted her daughter to marry Raje asks her to divulge the secrets to the latter. Suparna is whisked away to Bomaby in a plane and is taken to a clinic for termination of her pregnancy, but she manges to run away from there to Poona along with her boy-friend, Cyrus Contractor, a truly well-meaning person. By the time they are located by the police at Poona, they get married and obtain a certificate to the effect and settle in a hotel. Manasi, who is now the Home Minister and the right hand of the Prime Minister, rushes to Poona in the company of Raje and blesses the new-weds and persuades them to return to Bombay and live there in peace and happiness. Meanwhile, her private secretary informs her of the illness of the Prime Minister, and she with Raje leaves for Delhi in a helicopter to attend on him. The party elders and bosses had already agreed to her name as the next Prime Minister, and she has "nothing on her mind now except her longfelt desire to be the head of the country" (p. 147). This is where the novel ends.

Parallel to this story of incest runs the sub-plot of political corruption rife in the government. On the death of the previous Prime Minister, the present one is installed in his place. A weak-kneed Prime Minister would be most acceptable to party bosses. The Prime Minister, Mr. Desai, who has a clean conscience, is somewhat irritable and short-tempered. He gets annoyed with Sadasivrao for no fault of his, rather for his frankness and honesty. But since Sadasivrao was a stumbling-block in the way of power hungry Vijay Raje, the latter coaxed the Prime Minister to shunt the former out of the cabinet. Raje took over his post as a representative leader of the youths of the country. He starts spreading canards about the older politician, and engaged men to hurl bombs at his public meeting in Bombay, and when after a month's hospitalization he is to return home he visits him with a bouquet and conspires with one of the medical men to inject poison to him. As a result, Sadasivrao dies. Cyrus complains of it personally to the Prime Minister, but Raje grows dramatically ignorant about it, saying that the old man was like his father and had been his political mentor once upon a time. Raje was instrumental in getting his beloved, Manasi, elevated to the highest government post, though in the end he becomes jealous of her when she is selected as the Prime Minister of the country.

Another instance of the political rot is that all the cabinet colleagues of the former P.M. are corrupt and blacklisted, and occasionally they cause pains and headaches to him. The Prime Minister is also not so pure, — he is exposed to love and lust and Manasi is his weakness. He has picked up a wrong man — Vijay Raje — as his adviser. It may verily be said that Raje is the villain of the piece who is despicably black and wicked to the core (more details about him will follow).

To please the politicians, the industrialists and businessmen play a seductive role. Krishnan is one of them, collecting beautiful girls from all parts of the land who are offered to Raje to keep him in good cheers, or his permits and licences will stop. Krishnan was the person who had come to Manasi as a messenger of Raje. Later, he sends Stella, a deaf and mute inmate of an orphanage, to him. Similarly, Srinivasachari, the ageing Chairman of a leading Public Sector undertaking, constantly encouraged by his mistress, Anasuya Devi, who is Principal of the best woman's college in Bombay, to trap Raje in by supplying the charming dancer, Sita, to him, otherwise he will lose his lucrative job.

Furthermore, the administrative class also comes under fire in this novel. Mihir Bandhopadhyay of the Indian Civil Service, who is hostile to the honest and hardworking Mitra, the husband of Manasi, tries to exploit the latter for his self-fulfilment. One has a very poor idea about the upper class and its sense of morality by reading this novel. This class is seen hatching plans to placate the corrupt politicians and the loose administrators, without ever attending the call of conscience.

One single man rotten to the core is Vijay Raje. Initially, Manasi considered him a "a corrupt man, an astute manipulator" (p. 19), but later she fell a prey to his freakish love-offer. As she herself is greedy and ambitious, she accepts his invitation of going to Simla for a week and enjoy life there. What is the most shocking in this novel is the seduction of Suparna by him. Raje is an irresistible womaniser who resorts to all sorts of tricks and policies in trapping the fairer sex in his net. His repressed desire for women erupts with a volcanic fire, and he goes to any extent to procure them, so much so that he misuses his ministerial coat. He kills Stella, an orphan, for no fault of hers, and Krishnan is to blame for having sent her to him for a suitable job. Krishnan is another rogue in the novel who is a befitting companion for Raje. Srinivasachari and Anusuya Devi are fully aware of Raje's weakness for beautiful women, and hence they plan to send the charming Sita to him. Raje has apparently made sexual encounter with many women, and his so-called love is nothing but his lust which he tries to satiate by fair or foul means. Also, he is responsible for the exit of so many politicians and ministers, having set his eye on his own security. He is very clever and cunning in offering tactful and timely suggestions to the Prime Minister. He wants to put an end to all dissenting voices in his party, and does not hesitate to advise the Prime Minister to wage 'a fake war' with a neighbouring country in order to win the public opinion to their side and thereby succeed admirably in the next elections, otherwise people know well that those who have the reins of the land in their hands are merely a pack of hounds, — a bunch of blacklisted, immoral politicians. To fulfil his aspiration of rising to the positions of power and pelf, he removes Sadasivrao from the scene for good. In short, he is a man who has no moral scruples whatsoever, though his accomplice, Krishnan, may prefer to call him "a saint" (p. 100) and a "man of great generosity" (p. 101).

The protagonist of the novel, Manasi, is a famous poetess of Bengal. She is young and beautiful, desired by some of the most influencial politicians of the land. She was betrothed to Vijay's elder brother, who dies in an air-crash, but before his death she had a brief love-affair with him. Consequently, she got pregnant, and when nobody accepted her for a wife, Amol Mitra, a struggling Government official who looked old enough to be her father, took her hand. This had made her a poetess, as the novelist suggests — "But then she would not have been a poetess, for her poetry had burst out of the mire of her utter hopelessness like a red lotus" (p. 9). Mitra was always honest and sincere in his dealings with her, and he never revealed her secret to anyone, not even during the moments of their strained relationship. She, too, was all happy and content until the appearance of Vijay Raje on the scene. Initially, she rebuffs Raje's advances towards her, but later when he becomes powerful politically as a youth leader and sends Krishnan to her with a tempting proposal of spending a week with him in the best hotel in Simla and get in return diamond ear-rings, she surrenders to him. She is also to blame for being very ambitious and power-hungry, and more than Raje it is her own inordinate desire that seduces her. She rises as a popular poetess, but her attitude of indifference towards her husband is hardly justifiable. This is what the novelist offers us about her character. "She felt pity for herself. She was still attractive. Her mind was active and very much alive. She was admired by the young as a revolutionary poetess. But her husband, the mild Mr. Mitra, had faded with the years, signing on millions of files, until he had become to her only a shabby appendage which she had to tot with her while she went to public function to preside." (p. 17). She actually repents to have married him : "She gave a rueful laugh. I am a sentimental ass, she told herself. I shall never be able to leave him for any other man. If at all I marry again he will accompany me to my new home as part of my trousseau..." (pp. 17-18). No doubt, she finds 'any other man' in her hunt for lust and authority. The 'other man' she finds is Vijay Raje, who is highly rotten and evil-minded. Having accepted his offer once, there is no going back for her. She is introduced to the Prime Minister, who loves her to do away his loneliness. She likes it at the cost of her husband, her family, neglecting her school-going girl at Lucknow. The result is perilous. The family-life is totally disintegrated; Mitra gets resigned to his lot; Miss Suparna, the daughter, follows in the footsteps of her mother, being trapped and ravished by the same Raje in the same hotel, nay in the same room and on the same bed, at Simla where he had once slept with Manasi. She herself knows that she has done a nasty thing, and she says to Vijay : "It is not as if I am a chaste woman now. A *pativrata.* You saw to it that I became a mere tart. I rented out my body for a pair of diamond ear-rings. And hereafter for power I shall rent it out to the most influential tenant I can hope to get" (p. 41). Thereafter, her torrid love-affairs with Raje and then with the Prime Minister become the talk of the townsfolk. She is awarded Padmashri; she is made a minister, she becomes 'a real bitch.' This is what the novelist gives us about her :

> Of course, her mother [Suparna's mother], after joining politics, had turned into a real BITCH.

> She had cut her hair short and waved it carelessly in the Adudrey Hepburn style. She took to smoking. Perhaps she had begun to drink too. She had certainly changed in her appearance. There were swellings under her eyes and an unhealthy flush on her cheeks. She had lost weight. She had picked up certain mannerisms which would have looked well in a lady like Miss Hepburn but was strange in a Bengali woman who had been for two decades the reigning queen of the literary scene (p. 86).

But in her case 'character is destiny,' which recoils when Suparna is raped by Raje. She now feels, Raje is an immoral man, who will never have the fruits of his misdeed. So, abortion is arranged for Suparna. Manasi is elevated to the highest post of the Prime Minister. Though 'defeated' by Raje in love-affairs and physical matters, she wreaks a revenge upon him by snatching away the Prime Ministership from him.

There are only two good and moral characters in the entire novel — Amol Mitra and Cyrus Contractor. They stand head and shoulder above others. Of these two, Mitra helps Manasi to get over her crisis at the beginning of her adult life, and Cyrus comes to the rescue of Suparna when she is badly let down by Raje. Mitra is aged 56, but is pure and honest and hard-working. 'Kindness' is his virtue (p. 18). As a student, he had won a scholarship, but is presently satisfied with his official job as a clerk. Again and again, he is mentioned as docile and mild, 'modest and unassuming' (p. 110). He is tolerant and does not open his mouth to his superior officers even when he is humiliated. He is quick to perceive the blunders of Manasi, and points them out to her when once she comes home from Delhi for a while.

Cyrus Contractor is a young man of 24. He is bold and fearless by nature. When Sadasivrao is wounded terribly in a bomb-blast on the public platform, Cyrus arranges for his medical treatment in a nearby hospital. It was during his absence that Raje could have the old man killed by a poisonous injection. So courageous and resolute is he that he decides to expose Raje in the eyes of the Prime Minister. He goes to Delhi for this. The Prime Minister, who is sometimes pricked by his inner urges, asks Raje about the death of Sadasivrao. He angrily says : "Stop it, Raje, shouted the Prime Minister. You know well that he was murdered. Did you set someone to do it?" To this Raje replies thus : "Nonsense,.... You are out of your mind today. Why should I get poor Sadasiv Chacha killed? He loved me like a son. It was on his knee that I picked up my political sense" (p. 128). Later Cyrus, who loves Suparna from school days, comes to her help in hours of need. Not only he releases her from the snares of Raje, but also accepts her as his wife through a court marriage. Manasi is left with no option but to bless the two young loving hearts. In accepting Suparna after her miserable condition, Cyrus once again shows exemplary courage. He does not bother about social customs and taboos.

There is also a whole set of minor characters in the novel. These characters are not fully developed, and they make their appearances in the text now and then to play subsidiary roles. They are like the contours of a picture. Of such characters, mention may be made of the Prime Minister Desai, Suparna, Sadasivrao, Krishnan, Stella, Anasuya Devi, Srinivasachari, Mihir Bandhopadhyay, Sita, etc. The Prime Minister, Sadasivrao, and Suparna are definitely creatures of flesh and blood, but others simply do not matter as they are merely 'pimps.' The P.M. is a man of conscience, while Sadasivrao an idealistic politician of the older generation. Suparna is just a teenager bubbling with life and laughter until Raje comes into the picture and spoils her happiness and modesty.

To conclude, *Alphabet of Lust* is a titillating story of 'an ambitious woman's rise to power through sexual surrender' (to use the blurb matter). It is a powerful novel of 'lust' and illicit love, with Raje and Manasi at the helm of affairs. If Manasi is an embodiment of sexual debasement, Raje is that of political corruption. Both combine to give a brilliant flash to the social and political malaise in the Indian context. There are certain truly tragic situations in this novel, such as the seduction of

Suparna by Raje, the killing of Stella by the same man, Manasi's negligence of her motherly duties towards Suparna and her wifely duties towards Mitra, and Sadasivrao's untimely expiry, and these again conglomerate into the texture of the piece to render it highly readable and enjoyable. And since the novel spans within the experiences of its creator, it is definitely authentic and convincing.

11

CONTEMPORARY INDIAN-ENGLISH SHORT STORY : AN OVERVIEW

I

Indian-English short story has not been able to make much headway in the literary world.[1] Often it has been treated casually by writers, resulting in the overall neglect of the *genre*. Mostly it has come out as a by-product of Indian-English fiction. This should not give us a surprise or jolt because both fiction and short story are the kindred branches of literature and both are related to each other in the same way as the big and small sisters to their parents. If Indian-English fiction originated in the 20th century, Indian-English short story can't be thought of earlier than this time. Of course, the short story is a simpler and more popular form of communication than the wide-ranging and complex fiction.[2] It is rather deeply rooted in our Indian tradition, which used to give us folk-tales and fables from the earliest times. And this tradition has always been enriched by oral as well as written tales. It is unquestionably as old as Indian society and culture.

II

The early short story writers of India had mostly found their source of inspiration and sustenance in the ancient tales of the *Panchatantra* and in the Buddhistic *Jataka Tales*, which are usually didactic in tone, gripping in narration, and epigrammatical in structure. Both the works may be said to be 'beast fables,' in which some animals symbolize human beings and their virtues or vices. There was yet another variety of tales, generally known as 'folk-tales,' in ancient India, and this variety is well-preserved in the *Kathasaritsagar* (which is based on the *Brihatkatha* of Gunadhya) and the *Dashakumaracharitam* of the noted Sanskrit author, Dandin. Apart from these, the ancient Indian tales are also found in several *Upanishads* and *Puranas* (like the *Bhagavata* and the *Brahmanda*), and in the well-known epics called the *Ramayana* and the *Mahabharata*. The Jains have not been lagging behind in this *genre*, and they have added such works to its stock as the *Padmapurana* by Ravisena and the *Mahapurana* by Jinasena and Gunabhadra. All these works provided stimuli and motivations to Indian short-story writers.

One has to bear in mind that the short story may be written in both prose and poetry. In truth, the medium is not so important as the subject-matter and style. A.J. Merson has rightly pointed out that "much of the popularity of the short story today is due to the diversity and unexpectedness of the subjects,"[3] and that "manner as well as matter further reveals the individuality of the writers."[4] Commenting on the wide range of the short-story, H.E. Bates has remarked that it can be anything from a prose-poem without plot or character to an analysis of the most complex human emotions, and that it can deal with any subject, from the death of horse, the loss of a cloak, to a girl's first love-affair. The theme may undoubtedly be 'anything,' but it must be presented in such a manner that it carries the impression of being 'unified' and 'whole' in a limited sense. The well-known American tale-teller, Edgar Allen Poe, has also laid great stress on "a certain unique or single effect to be wrought out." In England, R.L. Stevenson also insisted on the importance of an 'initial impulse' in the short story which recalls the practice of Poe. At best, a short story writer must visualize the end in the beginning, and then alone he will be successful in communicating an "impression" or "idea" (which is his primary concern). Even the language is reduced to the bare minimum to contribute utmost to the 'effect' intended. The general constituents of fiction proper — plot, character and setting — all are certainly present in the short story, but in the highly curtailed and condensed form for the sake of a memorable 'effect' or 'impression.' H.G. Wells correctly declares that a short story has to be read within twenty minutes (how contrasted it is to fiction in this matter!).

A relevant question arising at this juncture is : how to define a short story? This is surely a difficult question. One may hasten to state that the best course is to recognize it by its brevity, economy, short length. On a second thought, however, one pays a more serious attention to the *genre* and acknowledges, like a recent definer of literary terms, that :

> A relatively short narrative (under 10,000 words) which is designed to produce a single dominant effect and which contains the elements of drama. A short story concentrates on a single character in a single situation at a single moment. Even if these conditions are not met, a short story still exhibits unity as its guiding principle.... Dramatic conflict — the collision of opposing forces — is at the heart of the story.[5]

This is unmistakably a comprehensive definition for the short story, and is fairly acceptable but for a slight modification which is that it concentrates on "a single character" or on "a group of characters." The traditional notions associated with the short story are : continuity and design, though it has to expand its scope and texture in our own day to accommodate the truncation of ideas and the presentation of psychoanalysis, the obvious results of a tension-ridden age enveloped in 'discontinuities and disillusionments.' According to A. Walton Litz, the hallmarks of a well-made story are : consistency of style, rationality of structure, and steadiness in viewpoint.[6]

III

As with other *genres*, so with the Indian short story in English, the beginnings were made under the influence of Britishers, who had given us not only a steady nation but also an international language. It is, therefore, in the fitness of things to speculate that the Indian short story writer in English is an inheritor of British legacy bequeathed to him by such eminent practitioners as O. Henry, John Galsworthy, Somerset Maugham, Rudyard Kipling, who themselves were greatly inspired by the French author, Maupassant. It may be safely said that the Indian writer is in the direct or indirect line of Maupassant, with whom he shares certain intrinsic qualities — "uninterrupted narration, preservation of curiosity, and the resulting clear picture of life."[7] What is being suggested here is the fact that the Indian short-story writer in English began his work under the impact of the West, and that slowly yet steadily he spread his wings to incorporate the charms of a finished form and a natural prose style.

Thus began the history of Indian-English short story towards the close of the nineteenth century with the publication of Kamala Satthianandan's *Stories from Indian Christian Life* in 1898. Thereafter, some sporadic writings were done in this *genre* to arouse national consciousness, to effect social reforms or to have moral and philosophical broodings. Amongst those who cultivated this consciously in the early stages, we may mention K.S. Venkataramani and K. Nagarajan. While Venkataramani contributed two collections of short stories under the titles *Paper Boats* (1921) and *Jatadharan and Other Stories* (1937), Nagarajan gave us a single volume called *Cold Rice* (1945). Besides these two, a third important author of the early twentieth century was Rabindranath Tagore, an internationally known literary personality who wrote his short stories mostly in Bengali and then translated them himself or through others into English. Some of his popular stories are : "The Cabuliwallah," "Subha," "The Post Master," "The Babus of Nayanjore," and "The Castaway." There were also some lesser known figures writing tales in English who were largely reformists or sermonizers, such as A. Madhaviah who gave us *Kushika's Short Stories* (1924). Writers like S.K. Chettur and G.K. Chettur excelled in producing shorter fiction evoking the sense of awe and strangeness (including the supernatural) in us. If the public could digest such crude and weird stories, the tales of conspicuously moral bearings were supplied by A.S.P. Ayer, whose *Sense in Sex and Other Stories* out of a total of five collections captured its notice for boldly tackling some of the problems (such as evils of sex and marriage) faced by Indian women of the day. But for Shankar Ram coming out with two of his remarkable volumes, namely, *Children of the Kaveri* (1926) and *Creatures All* (1932), other early writers working in the area of shorter fiction are, for the most part, deficient in originally of conception and depth of characterization. Their propensity for moral instructions and social ameliorations tends to blind them to the inherent charms of the short story, and they helplessly end up in a fiasco aping the Westerns for want of vision and artistic sense.

IV

The mid-thirties of the twentieth century saw the publication of a genuine artistic work in this *genre*, and it is Mulk Raj Anand's *The Lost Child and Other Stories*, which proved to be 'an immediate success.' With Anand begins the era of big names, such as Manjeri Isvaran, R.K. Narayan, Raja Rao, Khushwant Singh, and Ruth Prawer Jhabvala. Anand is with the poor and the downtrodden, voicing the concerns and predicaments of the lower classes in our society and siding with the lost ones and the sufferers. The humanism of Anand is so evident in his short stories, and he lashes at 'the lies, shams and hypocrisies of our people' with relentless vigour and robust satire. The social injustices and the highbrow prejudices move him most, and he forcefully ventilates his strong feelings against them, as may be gathered from his stories like "The Cobbler and the Machine," "Boots," "The Old Watch," and "The Story of an Anna." In his long short story, "Lament on the Death of a Master of Arts." Anand takes to satire to hit at the rotten in human social customs and conditions — the proud parents, the child marriage, the stubbornness of the elders, hypocrisy, insanitation, and cruelty in education and many other things. Anand can be funny and humorous at time, such as in his stories "The Barber's Trade Union," "The Death of a Lady," and "Lottery." It is, however, regretted that Anand in some of his stories as well as in some of his novels resorts to mere propaganda, as in "The Power of Darkness" and "The Tractor and the Corn Goddess," and that he occasionally indulges in self-pity and melodramatic situations, as in his "Lament on the Death of a Master of Arts." But he touches new highs when he discards the mantle of propaganda or self-indulgence, and his story "Lajwanti" is a moving tale of the hopeless situation of a young village belle, who finds no anchorage either at her in-laws' or at her parental home. In the depiction of the variegated pictures of modern India, Anand is simply superb. His themes of the stories are wide-ranging and his treatment of them is varied in accordance with the expediency of the plot. He does not scruple to retain the flavour of the ancient Indian fable in his tales if the occasion so demands.

Of 'the Big Three,' R.K. Narayan occupies a prominent place as a writer of short stories in a lighter vein and style. Without allowing his stories to be loose in structure, he ends most of them on a happy note. Narayan usually fixes his gaze on those aspects of an incident or a character which are appealing to him. He is a fine painter of the ludicrous and the humorous in his stories like "Attila," "Engine Trouble," and "An Evening Gift." The stories contained in such collections as *An Astrologer's Day* (1947), *Lawley Road* (1956) and *A Horse and Two Goats* (1970) represent Narayan at his best, bringing out as they do his strengths as well as weaknesses. At times, Narayan is highly engaging and entertaining while dealing with the various facets of human life, but at other times he stoops to journalistic details and sensationalism. Occasionally he even slips into incidents of suspense and horror, as in "Old Bones," "An Accident," and "The Snake Song." He can also delve deep into child psychology and portray children with perfect sympathy and understanding, as in "Swami and His Friends," but he is decidedly weak in depicting women characters of flesh and blood, as one may gather from "Mother and Son" and from "A Willing Slave." Like his novels, his stories do not have political overtones or even undertones. They also avoid making reference to religion and belief. Like Anand, he reveals his situations or characters by means of narration, and not by means of dialogue. His cool-headed detachment is discernible almost in every story. His beginnings are often good and casual, but his ends are sometimes unconvincing. One of the typical features of his technique is that he does not bother to evolve an indigenous brand of English in order to cope with the local atmosphere or the social milieu. The sustaining power of a Narayan story is its unmixed comic sense and its pure delight in the art of living.

Raja Rao is definitely of a different mental make-up both in his novels and short stories. He is soberer and more serious in evoking a proper atmosphere for the flowering of Indian thought and tradition. He writes mostly on social and political scenes around him with a natural ease and philosophical resignation. Though he is not so prolific a writer of shorter fiction as Mulk Raj Anand or R.K. Narayan, he has certainly made a mark in the *genre* under review with his two collections known *as The Cow of The Barricades & Other Stories* (1947) and *The Policeman and the Rose* (1978), both published by the Oxford University Press. The long gap between the publication dates of the two collections of short stories is quite in keeping with the temper of the author. Raja Rao goes to the folk-tales and the epic legends to evolve a form of his own with 'all the simplicity and credulity' of a mythmaker. He often writes on such subjects as the popular myths, national upsurge, and rural characters. His story, "Narsiga," for example, brings to the fore an orphaned village boy saturated with Gandhism. He may not have a wide range of themes like Anand, Narayan and Isvaran, but he commands greater depth and philosophical probings in his works. His later short stories like. "The Policemen and the Rose" and "A Fable" confirm the statement. If "Javni" in the first collection is the charming tale of an untouchable woman widowed and despised by all and earning only a rupee per month for her livelihood, the short stories of a later day probe deeper into the metaphysical longings of man. True, the first collection remains unrivalled in the presentation of social problems and national stirrings. The story "Akkayya" in it is highly touching, portraying as it does the tortuous life of a high-class widow. Like "Narsiga," the story "The Cow of the Barricades" powerfully evokes the picture of the suffering motherland (symbolized by the cow Gauri) under the tyrannical rule of the red Englishmen. The stories "Kanakapala" and "Companions" highlight the popular snake myths, while "The Little Gram Shop" and "A Client" focus our attention on the cunning baniyas exploiting the innocent people and themselves wallowing in wealth and prosperity. As a short story writer, the real charm of Raja Rao lies in his profundity of vision and in his deep-rooted Indianness. He appeals to us for his onrushing narrative technique — as though the tale has gushed forth from a dark, deep cavern — and his masterly handling of the English language.

Manjeri S. Isvaran is slowly yet steadily gaining ground as a major Indian-English short story writer. Having published about ten volumes of short stories such as *Naked Shingles* (1941), *Sivaratri* (1943) and *A Madras Adminral* (1959), Isvaran "occupies a conspicuous place among our pioneers."[8] He is a typical Indian writer who confines himself to the life of the low and middle classes in the erstwhile Madras State. In his tales he observes fidelity to facts and his own experiences. He manages to write skillfully, from different angles, on a wide variety of subjects — the ravaging results of the Great Wars and the Indian National Movement (as to be seen in "Between Two Flags"), the naiveté of children (as in "Kolu"), the love-affairs of a confirmed thief or a motor driver (as to be had in "The Motorman"), the uninhibited exhibition of love leading to sensual gestures and sexy word-duel (as to be found in "Mango Lane"), the rape of the volatile Jagada by the crafty cart man (as in "Immersion"). But of all the subjects, Isvaran seems to excel in the sympathetic revelation of female psyche, ranging from a housewife to a school going girl, a mother-in-law to a daughter-in-law, from a young widow to a granny. In depicting the womankind, Isvaran is close to earth and keenly alive. But he does not succeed so well when he comes to deal with children and their delicate psychology. An Isvaran story usually begins leisurely but ends up with some authorial comments or philosophical reflections. What is tormenting, however, is the truth that he starts casting his views and reviews in the midst of a story. But for this weakness, he is a truly powerful story-teller, who is equally at home in narrations and dialogues. His total commitment to Indian life, especially to the life around Madras, is unquestionable. Isvaran is not an experimenter with the English idiom, as Anand or Raja Rao is.

With the dawn of Indian Independence, a new consciousness of one's nationality and people arose in writers. Khushwant Singh is a short story writer of free India, and he made his debut in this form with the publication of his work, *The Mark of Vishnu & Other Stories*, in 1950, to be followed by *The Voice of God & Other Stories* (1957), *A Bride for the Sahib & Other Stories* (1967), and *Black Jasmine* (1971). These four volumes greatly consolidated the position of Khushwant Singh as a short story writer of outstanding merits, — a writer who moves from this *genre* to fiction in due course, and not *vice versa* (as in case of many other authors). He and Attia Hussain are perhaps the two writers who began their creative career with the short story, — Hussain having produced *Phoenix Fled and Other Stories* (1953). Khushwant Singh comes down heavily on what is repugnant, repulsive, and hyprocitical. Thus, "The Mark of Vishnu" launches a scathing attack on blind belief which impels Ganga Ram, a pious and devoted Brahmin, to worship and feed with milk the black cobra (*Kala Nag*) which eventually bites him to death. "The Voice of God" highlights the inherent evils of a democratic system of government in which elections play a dominant role, but these elections are often won by hardcore criminals like Ganda Singh at the cost of deserving candidates like Baba Ram Singh. How hard-hitting is the irony of Mr. Singh when he remarks — 'The people had spoken. The voice of the people is the voice of God.' Another title-story, "A Bride for the Sahib", is a tragic tale of the schism between an Oxonian and his docile Indian wife, Kalyani Das. Some of the humorous and fantastic stories of Mr. Singh are : "Posthumous", "My Own My

Native Land," "The Red Tie," "Mr. Kanjoos and the Great Miracle," and "Rats and Cats in the House of Culture." Obviously, Mr. Singh's *forte* is irony and comic sense. V.A. Shahane has rightly pointed out that "The per-dominant quality of Khushwant Singh as a short-story writer is his comic spirit, informed by the sense of incongruity and the bewildering phenomena of contradictions in life."[9]

Another notable name in the field of contemporary Indian English short story is that of Ruth Prawer Jhabvala, who is a Polish by parentage, a German by birth, an Englishwoman by education, and an Indian by marriage. In a way, English is her mother tongue, and she writes her novels and stories in it with utter sincerity and command. Her portrayal of Indian life is sensibly executed, with the added advantage of a somewhat detached observer. So long she has written four volumes of short stories, namely *Like Birds, Like Fishes & Other Stories* (1956), *How I Became Holy Mother & Other Stories* (1964), *A Stronger Climate* (1968), and *An Experience of India* (1972), in addition to nine novels. From these volumes, it is evident that Jhabvala gets totally depressed and disillusioned in India, which she calls a country of 'heat and dust,' of slow movement and activity, of indolence and laziness. Her *A Stronger Climate* is a pointer to this fact. Even *An Experience of India* is cast in the same gloomy mood and in the same attitude of helplessness.

In addition to the above-mentioned established short story writers, we have some other memorable literary personalities of yesteryears. Of them, mention may be made of K.A. Abbas, G.D. Khosla, Bhabani Bhattacharya, Bunny Reuben, Chaman Nahal, Purasu Balakrishnan, Ruskin Bond, and Usha John. They have contributed in their own way to the growth and expansion of this *genre* in varying degree, — some with a happy-go-and-lucky stroke of mind resulting in a single volume and no more and others with a greater sense of dedication and commitment offering us more than one volume. K.A. Abbas is a well-known name in the film industry, but he has also created a place for himself in the niche of Indian-English short story by dint of his five collections. Abbas seems to be impatient with the present-day social set-up, which is dominated by poverty, ignorance, inefficiency, hypocrisy, selfishness, and unemployment. He is no less disturbed by the prevailing political problems like those of partition, bloodshed and refugee influx. His two volumes, *Blood and Stones & Other Stories* (1947) and *Cages of Freedom & Other Stories* (1952), treat these political issues, whereas his works like *Rice & Other Stories* (1947), and *One Thousand Nights on a Bed of Stones & Other Stories* (1957) highlight some of the glaring social evils in whose portrayal he sometime becomes enraged and furious and at others sentimental and melodramatic. His technique of narration is definitely coloured with strong urge for the visual cinematic effects, and as such he offers us a series of striking and memorable flashes of events and scenes. The overall impression that Abbas creates through his stories is one of harsh realism vehemently attacking the odd and the incongruous with the fond expectations of a zealous socialist who believes in setting things right in the last run, though sometimes he loses his grip over the medium of his art and slips into slipshod generalizations.

Another famous writer of short stories in English is G.D. Khosla, who gives us a peep into the multifaceted personality of Mother India through his wide-ranging themes. His characters are both types and individuals, and he portrays them with sensitivity and objectivity. All walks of people — from rickshawallahs to businessmen, from film heroines to defiant loving ladies : find a berth in his creative world. With his four volumes — *The Price of a Wife* (1958), *The Horoscope Cannot Lie & Other Stories* (1961), *Grim Fairy Tales and Other Facts and Fancies* (1966), and *A Way of Loving & Other Stories* (1973) — steeped in humour and realism, Khosla has undoubtedly earned an abiding place for himself in literature. Through them he hits hard at the social evils like untouchability and ill-matched marriage. His stories though have logical conclusion, they sometimes become too long and hence a bit dull. But his wit and humour come to his rescue and prove to be his saving grace.

While many Indian novelists like B. Rajan and Kamala Markandaya have never tried their hands at the story form, some others like Bhabani Bhattacharya, Chaman Nahal, Anita Desai, Arun Joshi have produced a single volume each and possibly deserted the *genre* for good in favour of the bigger sister. Bhabani Bhattacharya's *Steel Hawk and Other Stories* (1968) is as satirical in tone and social in theme as some of his novels. Neither he nor others in his company appeal to be 'big draws.' Sasthi Brata in his *Encounter* (1978) is somewhat interesting, but again bawdy and incestuous as usual. Ruskin Bond and Manoj Das are, no doubt, the redeeming figures for contemporary Indian-English short story, but the former is hardly accessible due to non-availability of most of his works and the latter is largely confined to a particular locale and the events taking place there. Arun Joshi and Anita Desai excel in laying bare some deep-hidden human motives and emotions and in making subtle psychological analyses of characters. Chaman Nahal's single volume does not add much to his reputation as a novelist.

Strangely, some Indian-English poets have also experimented with the short-story form, and Margaret Chatterjee, K.N. Daruwalla and Shiv K. Kumar are the significant names in this direction. Apparently, they have written their stories in a leisurely mood to relieve themselves of the burden of nerve-tingling and delicate and tense *genre*.

Nergis Dalal with her single volume, *The Nude* (1977), is out of print and a 'lost' case. One's worth is hardly known to the people unless the works easily reach them. Many short story writers are faced with this problem, but Ramesh Srivastava should have no such fears of natural extinction, having published all his volumes from the Writers Workshop (or, a publisher's workshop?), Calcutta.

V

A cursory glance at the state of affairs obtaining in Indian-English short story convinces the reader that it has traversed a long course of journey (nearly of one hundred years) and has now reached a stage, through the salutary efforts of a few talented writers, where it can make a breakthrough by exploring certain new areas and techniques. Despite the natural hardships of language and expression — remember, English is our acquired tongue, not mother tongue as such —, the short story has made some headway and has become truly Indian after shaking off the initial foreign influences. The short story writers have come to realize, and rightly so, that their own tradition of both tales and fables has been rich enough to feed and support them in moments of necessity, and that they have just to look around for their keen and lively subjects, to which they have tailored their modern techniques. So, while their sensibility and subject-matter are essentially 'autochthonous', their treatment of stories is moulded by such modern modes of expression as the stream-of-consciousness, the flashback and flashforth, the first-person narration, the point-of-view method, and the epistolary method. The traditional Indian tale used to be mostly didactic and descriptive in nature, but the modern story tends to be analytical and narrative. As against the omniscient author technique of a traditional tale, we find a number of other techniques (as mentioned above) in our day. This shows that the modern Indian short story in English has grown in variety and vitality, and credit for this mainly goes to 'the Big Three' and Isvaran and a few other gifted writers. But it would be a misconception if we think that their form has reached the pinnacle of artistic perfection and that nothing more is required to be done in it. Most of the writers have confined themselves to social scenes and events; they have ignored certain other burning issues of the day, such as the political awakening and upheavals during the Pre-Independence and Post-Independence periods. Also, they have largely overlooked 'the purely domestic situation,' but for Anand's "Lajwanti" and Raja Rao's "Akkayya" and Jhabvala's "The Interview." In their desire to be indigenous, these writers have occasionally grown over-enthusiastic and sentimental; in their inherent urge to be impressive, they have resorted to word-jugglery and verbosity. Many writers have felt the constraints of 'journalism' because they have to be readable to general public through the medium of magazines and periodicals. While such a tendency contributes lucidity and clarity to their writings, they come to suffer on counts of complexity, subtlety and suggestiveness, — a point which becomes crystal-clear to an alert reader making a comparative study of an Indian author with his counterpart in the West. Our writers have unquestionably added variety of theme and diversity of technique to this art-form, but they have yet to rise above some of the shortcomings listed above. They have yet to cultivate the qualities of brevity, economy and signification in their works in order to be able to compete with the international masters of the *genre* — Maupassant, Conan Doyal, Faulkner, Henry James, Hemingway, Galsworthy and Katherine Mansfield.

Finally, contemporary Indian short story in English is already standing at the crossroads, and it has to make cautious moves to pull itself through. Keeping in view the international standards, it has to strive consistently to arrive at a safe destination. For this, it will have to overcome its deficiencies and evolve fresh measures of invigoration and energization. We have only to 'wait and watch' for a better future of the short story, and not get bogged down in the morasses of unhealthy speculations and pessimistic tendencies, realizing the truth that 'The best is yet to come.'

NOTES AND REFERENCES

1. Murli Das Melwani, himself a short story writer, paints a similarly gloomy picture when he remarks that :

   "Indo-Anglian writers have neglected the short story. This is surprising considering that, next to poetry, the short story is the most flexible form of writing, and thus eminently suited to portray the variety of Indian life."

   —*Themes in Indo-Anglian Literature*, 2nd ed. (Bareilly : Prakash Book Depot, 1977), p. 23.

2. A.J. Merson, in his Introduction to his edited work, dwells at some length on the comparative merits of the novel and the short story. He observes :

   "The scope of the novel is usually wide; it may cover themes of several generations, and range in its setting from pole to pole. Its main theme is often complicated by numerous side-issues, only less important than the central plot, no one of which can be detached from the structure without a certain loss of continuity or of essential detail. The short story, on the other hand, is conceded with episodes and not with histories... it confines itself to what happened to one person or a small group of persons within a limited period of time and within a limited radius of activity. It may thus approximate more nearly than nay other literary form to the ancient idea of the Unties of Time, Place, and Action...."

—*Modern Short Stories : First Series* (Bombay : Macmillan India Ltd., 1981), p. ix.

3. *Ibid.,* p. xi.
4. *Idem.*
5. Quoted from *Major American Short Stories*, ed. A. Walton Litz (Bombay : Allied Publishers Pvt. Ltd., 1975), p. 4.
6. *Ibid.*, pp. 695-696.
7. C.V. Venugopal, *The Indian Short Story in English* (Bareilly : Prakash Book Depot, 1976), p. 13.
8. *Ibid.,* p. 31.
9. V.A. Shahane, *Khushwant Singh* (New York : Twayne Publishers Inc., 1972), p. 67.

12

THE SERPENT IN THE ROPE : SYMBOLISM IN RAJA ROA'S *KANTHAPURA*

Raja Rao happens to be one of the most talented and innovative Indian-English novelists of our day. He is a novelist who specializes in the handling of abstract themes and tense situations, such as we have in his very first novel entitled *Kanthapura* (1938). The mythical-cum-symbolistic design of this novel coupled with its political and social overtones prompts us to believe that the novelist was serious about his business in commingling fact and fiction, reality and illusion, the concrete and the abstract, and that by doing so he added an additional punch and meaning to his utterances. These utterances are made in *Kanthapura*[1] by an old brahmin woman, who is apparently illiterate but conscious of the latest developments in the surroundings. The old grandmother nostalgically recalls, while sitting by the fireside in a remote village-corner and narrating the "sad tale" of her village to one of the new arrivals, the happy and carefree days of the Kanthapurians before the Freedom Movement under the dynamic leadership of Mahatma Gandhi and the local Moorthy engulfed it totally. Naturally, it was a do-or-die fight against the mighty empire of Britishers, and symbolically this fight denoted a clash between the Good and the Evil. No doubt, *Kanthapura* is not that rich in symbolism as *The Serpent and the Rope* (1960) or *The Cat and Shakespeare* (1965), but it has its own storage of myths and symbols, which contribute to its suggestive quality and which enlarge its area of signification. The present paper endeavours to make an in-depth critical and textual study of *Kanthapura vis-a-vis* Raja Rao's use of symbolism in it, but before we come to the novel proper we should understand clearly the true meaning and significance of 'symbol' and 'symbolism.'

I

A 'symbol' usually employs one object to represent another in literature; for instance, 'cross' for 'Christianity,' 'rock' for 'Church,' 'moon' for 'a charming face,' 'water' for 'purity,' 'sunlight' for 'knowledge,' and 'darkness' for 'ignorance.' *The Princeton Encyclopaedia of Poetry and Poetics* defines a 'symbol' thus : "A symbol...resembles what are known traditionally as 'figures of speech' (*Cf.* Imagery), which themselves comprise 'tropes,' or departures (turns) from the commonplace modes of signification, and 'schemes,' or artful elaborations of the forms of words and sentences. A symbol is like a trope, in that a simile, metaphor, personification, allegory...., and so on, each represents a manner of speaking in which what is said means something more or something else."[2] And in their *Theory of Literature*, René Wellek and Austin Warren remark that a 'symbol' is used in "widely different contexts and very different purposes," and that it is to be found in logic and mathematics, in semantics and semiotics and epistemology, in theology and liturgy, and in fine arts and poetry.[3] According to these critics, in literary theory a symbol should be used in the sense of "an object" referring to "another object" and it demands attention also, in its own right, "as a presentation."[4] These well-informed critics have pointed out that there are three main categories of 'symbolism,' and they are : 'private symbolism,' 'traditional symbolism,' and 'natural symbolism.'[5]

Symbolism, which began as literary movement in France during 1870–1880, reached England in the Nineties of the last century, and from there it spread throughout the English-speaking world in creative writings. Its original theorist was Mallarmé, who was deeply influenced by Baudelaire, Verlaine and Rimbaud. Speaking about it, Edmund Wilson remarks that 'subjectivism,' is its quintessence and that it is a "second swing of the pendulum" of Ramanticism.[6] Another scholar, Charles Feidelson, Jr., things that symbolism involves much more than mere language or stylistic device, and that its physics depends on its metaphysics.[7] That's why this literary movement has a kind of prestige in contemporary philosophy. Evidently, it shows great interest in the medium of expression, and renders the abstract concrete, the inexpressible expressible, the obscure intelligible.

II

Kanthapura, as stated earlier, employs certain myths and symbols at times. When the novel is considered in the light of its symbolism, the observations of some scholars about it seem to be only partly true or tenable. Prof. C.D. Narasimhaiah, for one, remarks that "*Kanthapura* is a novel of village life — a village in the far interior of Mysore in South India, in the valleys of Himavathy…,"[8] but it is no less true that Kanthapura is India in microcosm and that what happens in this village on the social, religious and political planes also happens in other villages (and cities) of India. The statement of the novelist in his Foreword to *Kanthapura* is a pointer to this fact : "There is no village in India, however mean, that has not a rich *sthala-purana*, or legendary history of its own."[9] In his Introduction to *Kanthapura*, Prof. Narasimhaiah also agrees with this viewpoint. Therein he points out that there "are at least three strands of experience in the novel : the political, the religious and the social, and all the three are woven inextricably into one complex story of Kanthapura."[10] But Prof. Narasimhaiah does not inform us whether the novel has any symbolic significance or not. A similar line of approach has also been adopted by Prof. V.A. Shahane who observes that "the theme of *Kanthapura* is twofold: moral-cum-religious, and political."[11] Prof. P.P. Mehta, who praises Raja Rao for his "brilliance" in story-telling in *Kanthapura*,[12] neatly skirts the question of using symbolism in it.

In one of his essays titled "Books Which Have Influenced Me," Raja Rao acknowledge his indebtedness to various books written in various languages, French being one of them. We know, France is the country where Symbolism originated as a potent literary force. In that essay, Raja Rao states that the two great French poets who have influenced him are : Paul Valery and André Gide :

> In my maturer years two authors, both French (and incidentally friends of one another) have influenced me : Paul Valery and André Gide. Valery is not only one of the major poets of our century if not its only great poet, but is also a prose-writer of classical integrity. His critical essays and, especially, his short novel, *Monsieur Teste*, sharpened my intellectual processes.... André Gide brought, alongside Valery, a greater humanity and a more precise sense of the play of ethics and poetical sensibility. His *Porte Etroite*, with its anguished fervour and its accomplished simplicity of style is a minor masterpiece.[13]

Besides, Raja Rao also mentions Romain Rolland (especially his *Jean Christophe*) and André Malreaux (mainly his metaphysical novels and aesthetic essays)[14] in that essay. In writing *Kanthapura*, however, it seems that the novelist is more influenced by Ignozio Silone's *Fontamara* (1933) than by any other single source, and Silone's work is to be marked for combining folklore and politics and raising them to a new level of poetical experience.

Kanthapura, being a *sthala-purana* (a legendary history of a specific place), attempts to combine folklore and politics in its texture and tends to be symbolic at places. The novelist's device of mixing myth and fact proves to be advantageous in this imaginative work. According to Meenakshi Mukherjee, "This mythicising of facts serves a two-fold purpose in *Kanthapura*. Its narrator is an old illiterate woman, and mingling of myth and fact would be her natural manner of observation and reflection. Thus, it is a device of characterization. Secondly, Raja Rao adheres to the Indian classical tradition by idealising or mythicising the central character."[15] Obviously, *Kanthapura* displays Moorthy as an idealized character who, like self-effacing Jesus Christ, undergoes all the trials and tribulations of life and takes upon himself the offences of the people. He also fasts for three days with this objective in view. He organizes the Kanthapurians under the banner of the Congress and in the name of the Mahatma and infuses a new lease of life in them. Although a visionary by nature, he turns out to be a man of passionate action in the wake of the Freedom Movement launched by Mahatma Gandhi. As a Gandhi-man, he succeeds to rope in Range Gowda to his cause and makes Rangamma and Ratna (both being widows — the latter one of fifteen years only) his followers, and arouses the whole of the village consisting of brahmins, weavers, potters, and pariahs, into hectic political consciousness. He sets up the Panchayat in his village in order to coordinate the activities of the people with the Congress Committee at Karwar City. He inspires them to arrange for *bhajans, keertans,* and *Harikathas* (divine songs and religious discourses), and distributes spinning wheels (*charkhas*) to spin yarns of *khadi*, and spreads the message of Truth and Non-Violence (*Ahimsa*) among them. That's why the village women think of him as "the Small Mountain" and of the Mahatma as "the Big Mountain."[16] And the Mountain becomes a symbol of the saviour of the people as well as of the progenitor of the life-giving river called Himavathy. In this context, one should recall the truth that the Ganges "is born on the snows of high Kailas" (p. 176). Because of the Mahatma's visible absence at Kanthapura, Moorthy becomes "our Gandhi," as the strong man of the village Range Gowda states :

> "He is our Gandhi. The State of Mysore has a Maharaja, but that Maharaja has another Maharaja who is in London, and that one has another one in Heaven, and so everybody has his own Mahatma, and this Moorthy, who has been caught in our knees playing as a child, is now grown-up and great, and he has wisdom in him and he will be our Mahatma... (p. 106).

Clearly, Gandhi is always treated as a greater deity than Moorthy in the same way as Siva is greater than any local God or

Goddess (including Kenchamma). As for Moorthy, he represents the forces of Good struggling against the forces of Evil. The forces of Evil are so powerful that they repeatedly crush the forces of Good, reducing the entire village of Kanthapura into ashes. At the close of the novel, the village looks totally deserted and devastated, for its inhabitants are forced by the Government to run away for their lives and take shelter in the neighbouring village of Kashipura. If Moorthy, the *Satyagrahis*, and the Congressmen are the symbols of Good, Bhatta, the parish priest, Bade Khan, the policemen posted at Kanthapura and residing at the Skeffington Coffee Estate, the Police Inspector, Venkamma, who "roared day and night against Rangamma" (p. 5), and the Red-man managing the said Coffee Estate are all the unmistakable symbols of Evil (to this point we shall revert after dealing with the relevant myths of Siva, Krishna, and Rama-Ravana).

The myth of Lord Siva reinforces the idea of *Swaraj* (Freedom) in the novel. This myth is narrated by the famous *Harikatha*-man, Jayaramachar (who is somewhat different from other religious preachers like Belur Narhari Sastri and Vidwan Chandrasekharayya). Jayaramachar informs us that "Parvati in penance becomes the country and Siva becomes heaven knows what" (p. 14). Further, this talented priest mingles the myth with the freedom-fight, and observes thus :

> "Siva is the three-eyed," he says, "and *Swaraj* too is three-eyed : Self purification, Hindu-Moslem unity, *Khaddar*". And then he talks of Damayanti and Sakunthala and Yasodha and everywhere there is something about our country and something about *Swaraj*. Never had we heard *Harikathas* like this (p. 14).

The awakened priest also speaks about the descent of Mahatma Gandhi on earth from heaven as a result of the humble supplication of Sage Valmiki to Lord Brahma, the Creator of the Universe. Being pleased with Valmiki's noble plea, the Lord pronounced as follows :

> Siva himself will forthwith go and incarnate on the Earth and free my beloved daughter [Mother India] from her enforced slavery. Pray seat yourself, and the messengers of Heaven shall fly to Kailas and Siva be informed of it (p. 16).

And lo, Mohandas Karamchand Gandhi was born in a family in Gujarat, and years after he grew up to be "a saint," the Mahatma, a wise man and a soft man, and a saint, at whose feet "even his enemies fall" (p. 17).

The myth of Lord Krishna is also woven into the texture of *Kanthapura*. The narrator tells us that as soon as Gandhi was born, "the four wide walls began to shine like the kingdom of the Sun, and hardly was he in the cradle than he began to lisp the language of wisdom" (p. 16). And then, the image of Lord Krishna — of the valiant-cum-adventurous boy of Nand and Yasodha — swims before the narrator of the tale :

> You remember how Krishna, when he was a babe of four, had begun to fight against demons and had killed the serpent Kali. So too our Mohandas began to fight against the enemies of the country (p. 16).

The 'enemies of the country' referred to above are the British rulers who had "come to bind us and to whip us, to make our women die milkless and our men die ignorant" (p. 16). The Britishers are "the serpent Kali" (or, still better 'Kaliya Nag') who lets out deadly poison to kill the very spirit of Mother India. When Moorthy was a child, he had once quietly slipped into a deep meditation under the serpent Pipal-tree on the bank of the river Himavathy in the presence of his mother, who was then washing clothes there. In his meditation, he remembered the child Prahald who had said that Hari was everywhere. Later on when he took to fasting in the sanctum of the village-temple, he saw the vision of his mother, and spoke to her thus :

> "Mother, now you can throw me down the mountain," and she asked, "why, my son?" and…"I have seen Hari…" (pp. 90-91).

He had also seen a vision of the Mahatma and was filled with an unusual radiance. The visions of Lord Krishna or of the Mahatma are quite pertinent to the ongoing political hullabaloo because they come out as the destroyers of Evil and as the protectors of Good.

The myth of Rama-Ravana very aptly signifies a fierce battle between the forces of Good and those of Evil. The ten-mouthed ogre called Ravana had let loose the reign of terror and suppression in his kingdom as well as in the adjoining country. He had become a thorn in the eyes of saints and sages. During his reign, arson, loot and rape had become the order of the day. It was beyond the power of ordinary people to overcome such a dreadful demon. So, Lord Vishnu himself appeared as Rama on earth to free people from the terrors of Ravana. Similarly, under the powerful British governance, Mother India was held in shackles and her dear sons and daughters were denied freedom. Economically, Indian populace was poor and backward, though culturally they were far superior to their rulers. When Gandhi appeared on the political horizon of our country, he was looked upon as Ramachandraji. His humiliation in South Africa at the hands of the whites was compared with the humiliation of Rama at the hands of Ravana in the form of Sita's abduction from the jungle. Freedom was "like Sita sullied and dishonoured,"[17] for the sake of which the Mahatma had to wage a relentless fight against the British masters. Both Rama and Gandhi employed the same sort of weapons to fight the enemies, and these weapons were : Truth, *Ahimsa*, Self-control and Non-cooperation. The whole nation rose as a man on the clarion call of the Mahatma, and the mighty British staggered like a goat before a lion. The slogans like '*Mahatma Gandhi ki jai,*" '*Vande Mataram,*' and '*Inquilab Zindabad*' rent the air, and there was no stopping of the nationalistic forces when once they erupted. The Rama-Gandhi analogy became complete when Gandhi was vehemently backed by Pt. Jawaharlal Nehru, just as in the fight against Ravana, Rama was whole-heartedly supported by Hanuman. Pt. Nehru, an "equal distributionist" (p. 285), gave a practical shape to Gandhian ideologies. Instead of waiting for the wisdom to dawn upon the foreign rulers, Jawaharlal declared in 1929 that nothing short of '*Poorna Swaraj*' (complete freedom) was acceptable to the Congress. And we ultimately *did* achieve complete freedom on the 15th August, 1947 under the dynamic stewardship of our leaders.

In the text of the novel, we have direct references to the Rama-Ravana myth, which is so relevant in our given political situation. The old man, who is actually the Swami's paid man having come to Kanthapura to mislead the innocent villagers, airs out 'anti-national' thoughts and sentiments when he speaks in favour of the uninterrupted continuation of the British rule in India :

> All this is very good, but if the white men shall leave us tomorrow it will not be *Ramarajya* we shall have, but the rule of the ten-headed Ravana (p. 126).

This argument of the old man undoubtedly advances what we characterize 'wrong reason for a right cause' (to borrow an expression from T.S. Eliot's *Murder in the Cathedral*, 1935). The old grandmother who narrates the tale bristles with confidence and enthusiasm when she announces as follows :

> They say the Mahatma will go to the Red-man's country and he will get us *Swaraj*. He will bring us *Swaraj*, the Mahatma. And we shall all be happy. And Rama will come back from exile, and Sita will be with him, for Ravana will be slain and Sita freed, and he will come back with Sita on his right in a chariot of the air, and brother Bharata will go to meet them with the worshipped sandal of the Master on his head. And as they enter Ayodhya there will be a rain of flowers (p. 258).

This passage amply clarifies that Gandhi is like Rama in his heroic struggle against the Ravana-like British, and that Jawaharlal is like Rama's younger brother Bharata, a devoted and sincere follower, and that *Swaraj* is like Mother Sita. *Swaraj* (Freedom) can be achieved after Ravana is slain, and Ravana is an unambiguous symbol of evil and tyranny and oppression. The rejoicing Ayodhya denotes the whole of India gone into raptures over the attainment of hard-won freedom.

The mythical and symbolic design of *Kanthapura* calls for a passing reference to the local goddess Kenchamma who is sure to come to the rescue of the Kanthapurians whenever they are in dire straits. Immediately after mentioning the locale of Kanthapura — "High on the Ghats is it, high up the steep mountains that face the cool Arabian seas, up the Malabar coast is it, up Manalore and Puttur..." etc. (p. 1), the novelist hastens to introduce the river Himavathy and the goddess Kenchamma. Evidently, the river Himavathy originates from the Tippur Hill, the sacred resort of Kenchamma. Some people say that "the Goddess of the River plays through the night with the Goddess of the Hill. Kenchamma is the mother of Himavathy" (p. 2). The goddess Kenchamma is always invoked as a protector of the Kanthapurians "through famine and disease, death and despair" (p. 3). She is, naturally, kind and bounteous, and has never failed the villagers in woe or weal. The villagers sing a hymn in her honour which runs as under :

> Kenchamma, Kenchamma,
> Goddess benign and bounteous,
> Mother of earth, blood of life,
> Harvest-queen, rain-crowned,
> Kenchamma, Kenchamma,
> Goddess benign and bounteous (p. 4).

Kenchamma is their bread-giver, rain-giver, and their life-giver. Ages ago, she had killed a horrible demon in a long-drawn battle, and that's why the Tippur Hill is all red. If Kenchamma is the life-giver and saviour of the whole village, the river Himavathy is "a symbol of the continuous flow of life."[18] The river skirts the village and provides drinking water to people and their cattle. *Kanthapura* begins with a description of this river, and ends with a portrayal of Range Gowda visiting his dilapidated village and drinking "three handfuls of Himavathy water" (p. 259). Gowda also salutes Kenchamma while leaving behind his village in desperation. In place of the old inhabitants, Kanthapura will now have rich people from Bombay, but the benign Himavathy will continue to flow there and the bounteous Kenchamma will continue to be its presiding deity.

Like Himavathy and Kenchamma, the 'hill' and the 'temple' have their own symbolic significance. The 'hill' should not be taken as a mere static place, stable and strong, but also as a representative of the original face of Nature. In the novel, the Mahatma and Moorathappa (or Moorthy) are compared with mountains because of "their moral strength and firmness of mind."[19] They are the two vibrating souls having the original purity of heart and the rock-like unassailability of mind against the continual onslaught of devilish forces. The 'temple' has always been a seat of ancient culture, and it is still a source of solace and comfort for the troubled humanity. The Kanthapurians installed a 'lingam' in the sanctum of the temple after it was first sighted by Moorthy, and they come there everyday for *bhajans* and *Harikathas* and religious-cum-political meetings. Moorthy fasts on the verandah of the temple, which later becomes a centre of intense political activity.

Of the symbols of Evil, we have already mentioned two outstanding names — those of Bhatta (or Bhattare) and Bade Khan, while others like Venkamma do not matter much. Bhatta associates himself with Waterfall Venkamma, a fire-vomiting woman of foul tongue, with the Swami (who excommunicates Moorthy and his mother, hastening thereby the death of that old woman — Narasamma), and with the Government. We are told that he works as a Government agent for Rs. Thousand only, — he who began his life with a copper pot in his hand and with a loin-cloth at his waist. But as a ritualistic priest of the village, he grows rich and goes on adding money and lands to his name. "Money meant Bhatta" (p. 30), and he lent money at an exorbitant rate. He takes great delight in civil suits, and visits the city of Karwar with this motive. He is a very inconsiderate husband,

and cares little for his gaunt wife, who is devoted to him and who ultimately dies. After her death, Bhatta takes a girl of twelve and a half years. He goes to Kashi to wash away his sins and earn salvation. He is particularly against Moorthy because the latter mingles with the pariahs. Otherwise, he had sent Ramu for higher studies on his own money a few years ago. But by nature, he is usually greedy and selfish. During the political turmoil, he also suffers along with other villagers, and his house is gutted in the leaping flames of fire. One of the Satyagrahis called Satamma then blurts out : "Well done, well done; it is not for nothing Bhatta lent us money at 18 per cent and 20 per cent interest, and made us bleed…" (p. 219). The narrator of the story clearly expresses her disavowal of Bhatta and his conduct, and comments on his departure for Kashi thus : "But, don't they say, sister, the sinner may go to the ocean but the water will only touch his knees" (p. 135). The symbol of 'water' is "a time-honoured symbol of purification."[20] In *The Serpent and the Rope*, too, the Ganges is a recurrent symbol of purity. What the novelist suggests in *Kanthapura* is that the 'water' of the ocean (say, of the Ganga Sagar) is not enough to "wash this man's sins away."[21] Bhatta is, by all means, a great sinner and an incurable usurer.

Now Bade Khan, the policeman, is a representative of the Government, and is a symbol of power and corruption. If Bhatta is "the symbol of usury and false orthodoxy and low cunning," Bade Khan is "the symbol of oppression, the soulless bureaucracy made visibly repulsive."[22] The policeman is prone to bribery, and the outspoken Range Gowda rightly grows indifferent towards him and warns him in advance : "You'd better take care not to warm your hands with other's money. For that would take you straight to the Pipal-tree…" (p. 21). When Bade Khan finds no foothold at Kanthapura, he saunters away to the Skeffington Coffee Estate, where the Red-man looking after the Estate accommodates him in a small tin-roofed hut. Bade Khan calls a neglected pariah woman to clean it and to cook for him and to make his bed warm. The Skeffington Coffee Estate is a symbol of "the impact of industrialization on the traditional community life at Kanthapura."[23] The Red-man and the maistri supervising the coolies of the Coffee Estate also stand for oppression and corruption. If Bade Khan strikes Moorthy on the head (p. 85), the Red-man and the maistri mercilessly whip the poor and innocent coolies. The nephew of the old red-man who joins the Coffee Estate after the retirement of his uncle is though kind-hearted and generous in making advance payments to workers, he is a woman-addict :

> "He is not a bad man, the new Sahib...but he will have this woman and that woman, this daughter and that wife, and every day a new one and never the same two within a week" (p. 79).

Besides these characters, the policemen led by their Inspector are true to their salt and do not hesitate to bang the heads of men and women with their brandishing *lathis*. After they take the *Satyagrahis* to the Police Station, they twist their arms and beat them on their knuckles, and spit into their mouths (pp. 122-23). No doubt, during the British days in India, a red turban was a terror to the whole village, and its atrocities on the general public had become proverbial. Thus, the red turban came to be associated with terror and oppression.

Amongst the other characters in the novel, the robust and dauntless Range Gowda is "the symbol of sense and stolidity, and sort of Sardar Patel to Moorthy — the village Mahatma."[24] The spirit of Revolution is symbolized by Moorthy, Rangamma, and Ratna, and Advocate Sankar. All the *Satyagrahis* and the Congressmen are the soldiers of the Mahatma. The wearing of *khadi* by the political activists denotes the boycott of foreign clothes and goods, which are a token of our slavish mentality.

Raja Rao occasionally established a harmonious rapport between man and the external world of nature. In fact, the Ganga in *The Serpent and the Rope* and the Himavathy in *Kanthapura* are very apt symbols of this kind of harmonious relationship between man and nature. When Ramakrishnayya dies, the river Himavathy pays its homage to the departed holy soul by rising suddenly and sweeping the bones and ashes away, and "no cow would give its milk, and all the night a steady rain kept pattering on the tiles, and the calves pranced about their mothers and groaned…" (p. 145). Similarly, on getting beaten by the policemen, women raise "such a clamour and cry that the crows and bats set up an obsequial wail, and the sparrows join them from the roofs and eaves and the cattle rise up in the byre and the creaking of their bones is heard" (p. 120). Thus, the natural world is in sympathy with the suffering human world. Prof. M.K. Naik characterizes this perfect understanding between the two as "this noble nexus."[25]

There are, then, certain traditional symbols in *Kanthapura* belonging to the female world, such as *kumkum*, bangles and *saris*. A woman adorned with these things is undoubtedly a fortunate married woman, whereas a clean-shaven woman putting on white *dhoti* is the symbol of a widow. These symbols "are woven into the narrative of the novel."[26] The presence of a widow before a marriage procession or in a social and religious function is taken to be inauspicious. That's why Waterfall Venkamma, a widow, threatens to stand before the marriage party of Moorthy in case he marries the daughter of the Coffee-Planter Ramayya. These symbols are also to be found in *The Serpent and the Rope*, where the hero Ramaswamy (abbreviated to 'Rama') puts the toe-ring in the toe of Savithri and applies *kumkum* on her forehead as a token of his acceptance of her as his spouse. Like the use of bangles, *kumkum*, and *saris*, the breaking of coconut and the scattering of rice-grains are also supposed to be auspicious symbols in Indian society.

III

An examination of Raja Rao's *Kanthapura* in the light of its symbolism convinces us that the novelist is more concerned here with the questions of language and style of story-telling and plot-structure (as his Foreword to the novel attests)[27] than with the question of creating an elaborate system of symbols. But since images and symbols have ever been an integral part of art particularly so in case of Raja Rao, they automatically find a berth in the overall structure of the novel. If the premise is accepted that *Kanthapura* originates from Raja Rao's short stories like "Narsiga" and "The Cow of the Barricades" which are themselves impregnated with an enviable wealth of symbolism, then it has to be conceded that the novel is not without its symbolical significance. Its *puranic* texture, its abundant application of the Hindu myths and legends, its recurrent use of certain virtues and vices to create an atmosphere of tension and conflict, and its occasional display of harmony and understanding between the human and natural worlds : all these tend to confirm that the novel employs certain appropriate symbols at appropriate places. *Kanthapura* is admittedly not so rich in symbolism as *The Serpent and the Rope* or *The Cat and Shakespeare*, but it definitely makes use of symbols here and there, adding thereby a wealth of signification and suggestiveness.

NOTES AND REFERENCES

1. Raja Rao "Foreword", *Kanthapura* (Delhi: Hind Pocket Books Pvt. Ltd., 1971), p. 6.
2. *Princeton Encyclopaedia of Poetry & Poetics*, eds. Alex Preminger, F.J. Warnke and O.B. Hardison, Jr. (London & Basingstroke : The Macmillan Press Ltd., 1975), p. 833.
3. René Wellek and Austin Warren, *Theory of Literature* (Middlesex, Essex : Penguin Books; 1980), p. 188.
4. *Ibid*., p. 189.
5. *Ibid.,* pp. 189-90.
6. Edmund Wilson, *Axel's Castle* (London : The Fontana Library, 1959), p. 23.
7. Charles Feidelson, Jr. *Symbolism and American Literature*, 5th impr. (Chicago and London : The University of Chicago Press, 1961), p. 49.
8. C.D. Narasimhaiah, *Raja Rao* (New Delhi and London : Arnold-Heinemann, n.d.), p. 39.
9. Raja Rao, "Foreword," *Kanthapura* (1971 ed.), p. 5.
10. C.D. Narasimhaiah, "Introduction," *Kanthapura* (Madras : Oxford University Press, 1974), p. vii.
11. V.A. Shahane, "Fiction and Reality in Raja Rao," *Perspectives on Indian Fiction in English*, ed. M.K. Naik (New Delhi : Abhinav Publications, 1985), p. 62.
12. P.P. Mehta, *Indo-Anglian Fiction* : *An Assessment* (Bareilly : Prakash Book Depot, 1968), p. 197.

13. Raja Rao, "Books which have Influenced Me," *Aspects of Indian Writing in English*, ed. M.N. Naik (Delhi : the Macmillan Company of India Ltd., 1979), p. 48
14. *Ibid.*, p. 49.
15. Meenakshi Mukherjee, *The Twice-Born Fiction*, 2nd ed. (New Delhi : Arnold-Heinemann, 1974), p. 141.
16. Raja Rao, *Kanthapura*, ed. C.D. Narasimhaiah (1974), p. 176. All the textual quotations are taken from this source only.
17. R.S. Singh, *Raja Rao's Kanthapura : An Analysis* (Delhi : Doaba Houses Pvt. Ltd., 1973), p. 111.
18. *Ibid.,* p. 115.
19. *Idem*.
20. C.D. Narasimhaiah, "Introduction," *Kanthapura* (1974), p. xvii.
21. *Idem*.
22. K.R. Srinivasa Iyengar, *Indian Writing in English* (New Delhi : Sterling Publishers Pvt. Ltd., 1984), p. 392.
23. *Ibid.,* p. 393.
24. *Ibid.,* p. 392.
25. M.K. Naik, "Coils of the Serpent : Raja Rao and the 'Unreal' World," ed. A.N. Dwivedi (Allahabad : Kitab Mahal, 1987), p. 165.
26. R.S. Singh, *op. cit.*, p. 116.
27. Raja Rao, "Foreword," *Kanthapura* (1971 ed.), pp. 5-6.

13

FARRUKH DHONDY'S *BOMBAY DUCK* : A CRITICAL STUDY

Farrukh Dhondy published his first novel entitled *Bombay Duck* in 1990. He was born in Poona in 1944, and was educated in both India and Great Britain. He has published a good number of children's books and has written extensively for the television network. At the moment, he is a commissioning editor for Channel 4. When *Bombay Duck* was released, it was shortlisted for the Whitebread First Novel Award. On its appearance, the novel was greeted with cheers. Neil Berry, the reviewer of *The Times Literary Supplement*, welcomed it as "a serio-comic extravaganza, written with patent relish, a plot of uninhibited zaniness,"[1] and Candice Rodd, reviewing it for *The Independent on Sunday*, commented on it thus : "It is a brave novelist who sails full tilt at the deep cultural waters between the Indian subcontinent and the West. Unabashed, Farrukh Dhondy offers not one, but two dense and energetic narratives which address, among much else, the painfully current issue of religious fundamentalism…never less than lively in an intelligent and ambitious novel."[2] *Bombay Duck* is unquestionably a powerful fiction of hurriedly shifting scenes and moods, and we have to go deep to comprehend its motif, its title, its plot-structure, its narrative technique, and its art of characterization. For one thing, it is a novel of good length and remarkable variety.

Divided into two parts, the novel has Gerald Blossom as the protagonist in the first part and Mr. Xerxes Xavaxa (shortened to Mr. XX) in the second. In the first part, scenes are laid in

London, Edinburgh and Delhi, and in due course Gerald assumes the name of Ali Abdul Rahman and finds both fame and fortune in a way. But in the initial stages, Gerald, who is an unclaimed actor of Caribbean origin, has to struggle a good deal to find a foothold in his profession. While living in London, Gerald gets the chance of singing "the few tracks to the audiences of London and Edinburgh" (4) through the agency of his friend Bawdy, the small-time Director of Blade Star Theatre. The assignment is related to the staging of *Tony and Cleo*, a modern adaptation of Shakespeare's famous play, by the Pakistani writer Jamil Jamal in the Edinburgh Festival. But the show proves to be a flop there in spite of advertisements in local papers and over T.V. The troupe of actors consists of Gerald, the black Zimbabwean Tawanda, and the Negro American George. After the utter failure of the show, Gerald returns to London with the gold tooth of George by catching the night train and loses his wallet while fast asleep. Getting down the tube and being moneyless and cheerless, Gerald goes straight to the apartment of his white wife, Maureen, who has already discarded him. He has a six-year-old daughter from her, whose name is Martha. On the instructions of Maureen, he takes Martha to her school, and has to part with the gold tooth of Gerald in order to provide for her dinner. Later, on the persuasions of his Muslim friend, Ullah, he alters his name and becomes Ali Abdul Rahman for the sake of a better prospect in his profession. Luckily, he is circumcised too.

What follows is decidedly "a serio-comic extravaganza," for instead of a well-knit story we witness 'the David Stream Affair' (as found in Sara Fraser Stuart's papers, diary, and clippings). The whole affair comes to us through the reportings of Sara, mainly to Robin, the editor of the *New Citizen*. Jamil actually wants to write a novel based on her notes and clippings. He meets Ali and seeks his assistance, which Ali offers him with a grumble. Ali starts doing his job and browses through Sara's papers and other related documents. Sara is an integral part of this affair, being a close confidant to David Stream, the big boss director. David persuades Ali and Co. to stage *Anthony and*

Cleopatra in Egypt, and asks Sara to cover up the performance of the troupe. Immediately after, the troupe leaves for India to stage the *Ramayana* there through the Western eyes. Sara's letters and reportings reveal her liaison with Robin. Ali discloses his past to Sara in an interview — that he was a bus conductor first and later became an actor. The Indian girl, Anjali, is imported direct from Paris to join the troupe to act as Sita. She comes with S. Patel, a sparkling actor of her choice. Anjali is the daughter of "a corrupt Indian politician and a businessman," (44) while Patel is a nice boy brought up in Kenya who "blundered into acting through the enthusiasm of some BBC gang that was looking for an Indian boy" (44). The latter has "a heavy Kenyan Asian Gujerati accent" (45).

The labyrinthine story moves through a series of scenes and rehearsals of the *Ramayana.* Ali plays the role of Shri Rama and Anjali that of mother Sita and Kojin (a Chinese) that of Laxman. There are more persons in the cast, and the play is directed and supervised by David Stream himself while Sara looks after the task of reporting and shares in management. In between we have glimpses of the truncated family-life of Gerald, whose wife, though not evil at heart, is all for a Pak weapons-supplier, who is a heavy drunkard yet prosperous enough and who occasionally renders miserable the lives of Maureen and Martha; of the feverish passion of Ali for Anjali and of Sara's deep attachment to Robin. After a good deal of rehearsal, the David Stream Co. flies to New Delhi, with the intention of performing six shows in Bombay, and three each in Calcutta and Madras. Binky, who is now in London and who is a friend of David, has his political connections in India and writes a letter to the then Premier, Rajiv Gandhi, to see the performance for himself. In truth, we get references to many other celebrities of the day like Amitabh Bachchan, Balraj Sahni, Indira Gandhi; also to the Punjab terrorists and the Pak involvement in it. The David Stream Co. comprising some fifty odd men and women stay at the Oberoi in Delhi. The first show is a grand success, but the second one proves an utter failure. The racial and communal frenzy rises to spoil the whole game.

The players get stranded at the end of the second show, and Tilak has to go out to fetch taxis to enable them to return to their place of stay. On the way, however, Ali and Anjali are attacked mercilessly. Someone in the crowd attacks Anjali with a heavy iron rod and she dies then and there. Ali is also knifed to the point of death, but he somehow survives at the cost of his speech. Maureen phones to him from London to enquire about his well-being, without knowing that he can't speak. It is a very touching and pathetic scene indeed! David manages to get back to London in a mood of total dejection and desperation, having no desire to "revive the *Ramayana*" (150). Ali is left behind to the care of Binky. In passing this is to be noted that Ali and Anjali make hectic love to each other just one night before their tragedy while staying at the grand hotel.

The second part of the novel brings before us the life-story of Mr. Xerxes Xavaxa, a hoax extraordinary. By birth he is an Indian, precisely a Parsee of Poona in Maharashtra, who goes to England for his education, obtains the Bachelor's Degree in religion and ethics from the University of Cambridge, but finds no suitable job and runs from pillar to post for it. At the opening of this part, Mr. Xerxes is seen writing letters to Sara from his London flat, and Sara is still travelling around India and gaining experience of life. He informs her that he has been arrested by the British police for being "a dealer in the international traffic in babies" (154). After his arrest, he hands over the keys of Sara's house to Leslie de Freitas, Sonya's dad, who in turn offers them to Ali to move back in to feed her domestic cats. Mr. Xerxes (or Mr. XX) is being prosecuted and is awaiting an extradition hearing soon. Lesile has engaged a solicitor named Mira, an Indian girl-advocate, to defend him. He is offered assistance by Robin at the request of Sara. The hearing is to come up in a month or so, and Mr. XX has time enough to tell his whole story for the sake of Leslie, who is on the staff of a large London-based publishing house. The story of Mr. XX is narrated in an absorbing manner. First we are told about his interest in Science, which later shifts to Oriental languages and religions. For a while, he does this or that, selling ladies' umbrellas and battery-operated torches at the Earls Court, where he resides. On the expiry of the Sri Lankan guy, who is his close neighbour and who worked with BBC at times, Mr. XX sees a chance to step in his shoes as a translator of Indian languages. The two BBC men, Mr. Dexter and Mr. Khan, approach him for doing research on Zoroastrianism in Bombay. He accepts the offer and goes out in search of "the whole Parsee religious ceremonies, philosophy, etc" (159). Reaching Bombay, he first meets Tilak, a person of some artistic taste, and stays with him. In one of his outings with Tilak, he finds an abandoned baby (a fresh-born girl), picks it up, brings it home, and gets it cleaned. He also visits a few fire-temples in the city, observes the Parsee way of worship, and contacts one or two Parsees. Having collected some relevant material, he decides to return to England along with the baby, whom he christens Fara. At the Heathrow airport, he is closely scrutinized and is eventually let out along with the baby. He comes to Brixton, and sends a brief report to the BBC men who do not accept it. Mr. XX now runs out of money and is unable to pay his rent for months together. So, he goes to Jam and his wife Cress — the childless couple — to demand of them a loan. Jam has become rich by now, for his wife had brought fabulous wealth to him by way of dowry. Mr. XX gets a hundred pounds for his upkeep.

Meanwhile, Mr. XX's grandad (from the mother's side) expires, leaving behind some papers and money for him, and he hurries back to Bombay and thence to Poona after entrusting the small baby to Cress and taking some more money from her for his journey. He attends the funeral of his grandad, stays for four days at Poona, collecting his papers and money, and flies back to London. But to his great dismay, he discovers that Jam has left Brixton along with his wife and the baby, and that his flat is slated for sale. Mr. XX tries to contact the agents of the flat for Jam's address or phone number, but they are of no help. He makes a big hole in the flat and enters it, but the rattling sound invites the attention of the police and he is caught and sent to jail. When Jam and his wife come to know of his predicament, they sympathize with him and offer to withdraw the police case provided he gives up his claim on Fara. Devoid of money and resources, he forsakes his claim on the child and gets a hundred pounds in return plus the status of an uncle (175). Mr. XX turns a writer of a sort on the Parsee religion and community, but money still plays hide and seek with him. This is how he describes his condition at the moment : "Mr. XX, supply teacher extraordinaire, Gandoo and lund fakir. Useless to the world of wealth making" (179). To eke out a living for himself, he becomes a school-teacher for the third time. He is asked by the Headmaster to take some thirty small kids to the theatre to watch *Romeo and Juliet* by Shakespeare, a task in which he will be assisted by Sonya and two more sixth formers. The picnic, however, fails due to the unruly behaviour of some nasty children of the fifth year. The school-service provides him opportunities to draw closer to Penny, a school teacher herself, and to Sonya, his erstwhile pupil. Penny's flat-mate, Eileen, is a lesbian and hates men, and she goes distracted at long last. And Sonya drifts towards Tilak, a married man with children, who is in England in connection with an exhibition of his paintings and later with the staging of his *Ramayana*. Tilak is verily a counterpart of David Stream and tries to present the *Ramayana* in its true Oriental colour.

Mr. XX pursues his business of baby-theft or baby-trade, and he lifts a girl for the second time from Calcutta at the instigation of Ullah and Tilak in order to fulfil the desires of his Muslim friend, whose wife is terribly upset over the loss of an adopted son and refuses to have sex with him. In the meantime, Mr. XX becomes very friendly with Sonya's parents. Leslie de Freitas and Lyla talk spiritedly before them about Zoroastrianism and Hinduism and about the present Indian Government's policy of Secularism. The third time Mr. XX smuggles an Indian child to Britain is for Penny and Eileen for their adoption with mutual consent. She is given the name of Ghazal II (the first Ghazal being the baby adopted by Jam and Cressida). The task is accomplished with the active co-operation of Sonya by scaling over the wall of a hospital. Mr. XX has to leave the house of Firdaus and Naomi forthwith, and has to take shelter in a hotel for a night before he flies back to London. For a few months, the child is reared up by "joint motherhood" (307), but one day Eileen goes out of her flat in a huff and does not return at night. Later the police knock at the door of Penny and inform her that Eileen has been arrested at Heathrow for snatching a baby outside the local supermarket, and that she is 'very disturbed' at the moment. During the interrogation by the police, Eileen reveals the name of Mr. XX as a procurer of children. Penny also confirms it in a prolonged six-hour interrogation. Mr. XX is therefore arrested and remanded to police custody till the disposal of his trial. Mr. Leslie makes arrangements for a solicitor for him, and Mira is engaged to plead his case. The editor Robin also extends his helping hand to him at this hour of crisis at the request of Sara.

Towards the close of the novel, Mr. XX shows his preference for Penny and proposes that, when she gets married, she should write on the application form : "Adoptive father's profession: convicted child-thief" (311). But Roshni, a Parsee girl of independent career, keeps in constant touch with him even when she is in America. The novel ends with a dream of Mr. XX in detention awaiting his trial: Sara is seen riding on a horse with a scythe in her hand; the urchins are tumbling over each other on the waterfront; the city of Bombay is astir with its clear salt-air and its milling crowd of people, and Songya is prosecuted here along with many other pedlars of drugs and injections, and Mr. XX himself wandering here in handcuffs to be taken to guillotine in a tumbril. Sara, the avenging angel, reappears in a masked attire, cutting the rope with her weapon and carrying Mr. XX through the crowd on her galloping horse; a massive machine-gun booms, signalling his death; and finally, he is walking home to Firdaus' late at night. The swishing Arabian sea is ceaselessly beating against the shore, letting the breezes in from the gloomy Africa and carrying "the corrupt smell of

Bombay Duck drying on the sands" (316). The dream-sequence indicates the possible course of events in the near future for the protagonist.

The title of the novel calls for our immediate attention, and luckily the novelist has thrown sufficient light on it for our enlightenment. 'Bombay Duck' is actually 'Bombay Dak' or 'Bombay Mail,' by means of which the plenty of dried fish of Bombay was supplied to other parts of India during the British Raj (which had just introduced railways for public use). Clarifying the source of the title, the novelist writes :

> Bombay Duck is not a duck at all. In fact it should be spelt Bombay Dak. What it is, is dried fish (known in Bombay as Bombil) and when the British introduced the railway system to western India under their Raj, it started going in wagonloads to interior from Bombay. The crates stank of dried fish, like stale penises. They were marked 'Bombay Dak,' literally 'Bombay Mail.' At the time the railway was run by whites. The English may call a spade a spade, but they don't call 'stinking fish' by that name. They referred to it euphemistically as 'Bombay Dak,' the Bombay Mail (241).

The novelist further informs us that a famous food-store, later on, begins to sell a packet of mixture labelled 'Onion Bajee', and changes the spelling of 'Dak' to 'Duck' (242). In fact, Penny inspires Mr. XX to write a book on British-Indian etymology called *Bombay Dak* when his other writing ventures and his work with the BBC fail (244). At the very close of this novel, when Mr. XX is almost lost in his dream of future visions, he confronts the sea-breezes carrying with them "the corrupt smell of Bombay Duck drying on the sands, just a few hundred yards away" (316).

Now, having examined the story and the title of the novel, we shall look into its artistic aspects. First, about its plot-construction. It is executed in a meticulous manner and through calculated steps. The movement is apparently backward, *i.e.*, the ending of the story is reported first and then takes place a recordation of incidents and situations leading on to that ending. This is particularly true of the second part of the novel dealing with the life story of Mr. Xerxes Xevaxa, a Parsee scholar historian based in England and helping others in acquiring babies in questionable ways. The novel is conceived in a serio-comic vein and has "a plot of uninhibited zaniness," as Neil Berry has rightly pointed out. It is a fantastic composition with a sound command of language and technique. As for the first part, it is largely occupied with the narration of the fluctuating fortunes of a Caribbean actor called Gerald Blossom, who later assumes the name of Ali Abdul Rahman. In the writing of this work, Dhondy employs the devices of masks, impersonations and deceptions at times. Both the protagonists — Ali and Mr. XX — are the living examples of it. Even forgery is not altogether ruled out, and many a time Mr. XX is seen tempering with his visa and trying to obtain false birth-certificates of the babies he has picked up or stolen from various places. The following statement of Cressida, Jam's wife, will bear it out :

> When we're out she says, "I haven't forgotten my threat about the police. And if you think you've got documentary proof. My dad can also get a birth certificate and besides it's a country doctor's certificate, British, so who will they believe?"(175).

In truth, the business of child-trading in which Mr. XX specializes instigates him to improvise things and persons, and this definitely smacks of criminal stories of great suspense. After accepting the 'uncle status' and some money from Jam and his wife (which is nothing short of bribery), Mr. XX reacts thus : "Yet her (Fara's) name is still in my passport and I did it again. I transferred a child between continents. I passed off another girl as Fara Xavaxa. But that comes later" (175). In a different situation, Gerald takes to impersonation when success eludes him. He curses his father for the kind of mess he is in : "Gerald, my dad wasn't thinking.... One easy leap to boot polish. I called myself Ali Abdul Rahman.

My daughter should now be called Martha Rahman" (18). One peculiar feature of Dhondy's plot-construction is that it often leaps back and forth and thereby keeps the reader on tenterhooks. It is very intriguing to note that instead of one single compact and continuous story, we get two stories and both are of an independent nature, barring the overlapping of a few characters. One has to be watchful in establishing links and contexts in such a novel. The blurb-matter is hardly of much help in this regard; for instance, it reports that Rahman "finds fame and a kind of fortune," but to the reader it is somewhat a misleading statement because at the close of the first part Rahman is left completely broken and bruised, dumb and shocked, by the ruthless assault of rioters in Delhi, and his Sita — Anjali Patnaik — is killed under his nose.

The technique of narration of the tale is undoubtedly gripping and arresting. Both the stories are told by the protagonists. Gerald Blossom is the narrator in the first part, while Mr. Xerxes Xavaxa in the second. Both narrate the stories of their lives, and so we get first-person narrations in them. This certainly enhances their credibility and authenticity. The novelist employs the flashback technique for the revelation of the protagonists. He pushes forth the narration in a mixed way — through direct statement as well as through dialogues. His dialogues are usually short and crisp, witty and meaningful, as the following example shows :

> 'You had something to do with the Sara woman, David Stream's Sara?'
> 'Sure,' I say, 'I did. I've got her flat in London. I've left it to her friend Ali while I'm here. He's feeding her cats.'
> 'More than having her flat, I mean. You didn't just move in there. You were screwing her.'
> 'So?'
> 'You know she stayed in Tilak's village?'
> 'Your dad told me.'
> 'Well, I think it's her writing — all this shit.'

> 'It's not her style, is it? So you came to tell me because we're both aggrieved lovers?'
> 'Of course, it is Sara'a style.'
> 'Don't be ridiculous, Xerxes, I don't own Tilak. I didn't even ask him. His wife owns him, anyway' (270).

This is a trenchant conversation between Sonya and Mr. XX, the two old lovers, about a fiery journalist called Sara Fraser Stuart, who plays a very crucial role in the first part of the novel. The extract given above helps to further the story of Sonya and Tilak as well as it reveals the existing friendly bond between Sonya and Mr. XX. The direct-method narration is to be found when the novelist speaks of various religions and traditional customs, such as Zoroastrianism, Hinduism, Mohammedanism, and the Parsee customs of marriage and worship in particular. But when he has to reveal the passionate feelings of lovers, he invariably resorts to short and sententious dialogues. This is how the two fond lovers, Perry and Mr. XX, are ȩngaged in a *tete-a-tete* :

> 'You'll have to get rid of Eileen.'
> 'You're still seeing Sonya, aren't you?'
> 'What's that got to do with it?'
> 'My theory of relationship.'
> 'I've got a class, bloody 3M, but I'll catch up with your theory of relationship over a pint at the Maple, OK?'
> 'Eileen bursts in and we die of stab wounds in a pub in the nethers of London : "School-teachers stabbed in lesbian triangle" (192).

This passage reveals a good deal about the emotional life of Mr. XX, Perry and Eileen — that Mr. XX does not like Perry's lesbian relationship with Eileen, that Perry also chides him for his continued contact with Sonya, and that Eileen is a hardcore 'feminist' and anti-male. Occasionally, Dhondy also employs the epistolary method of narration in this novel. The first part and the opening of the second part are cast in this method.

Dhondy is quite at home in the handling of the English language. He shows his unerring sense of this powerful language, of its various shades and nuances, of its timely twists and turns.

His education and stay in Britain has enabled him to capture the nuances of this living language. Even the dialect is not beyond his reach; for example, the very opening paragraph in the novel offers us this : "Backyard, them woulda ask her, 'Whey 'tis yuh smile at girl? Yuh have a date with a Yankee sailor? Maybe sometime she frown, but she don't wail and bawl and call on her mother and God's mother and the mother of the devil to rescue her" (3). This is definitely the living language of a class of the British people, not the kind of language we Indians generally use. The commendable command of English displayed by Dhondy does not warrant us to deduce, as K.R. Srinivasa Iyengar does, that the Indian English novelist "is actually recording a kind of half-conscious translation (from mother tongue into English) that has taken place in the mind."[3] That's not the case with Dhondy. Perhaps it would be more appropriate to state, as Iyengar himself does, that "some writers, in their choice of themes and their handling of the English medium, have a foreign audience in mind."[4] Obviously, Dhondy has an international audience in mind in the choice of his locale, subject-matter, and language. Accordingly, he places his scenes in London, Edinburgh, Delhi and Bombay, and keeps them shifting swiftly like the lenses of a cameraman. And he is certainly international when he writes English like this : "What country, mate. Don't give me that 'this country' shit. I'm fucking British" (32). Or, like this : "The money for the last production in New York was by subscription from rich Americans. Yes, he's had British money, French money, roubles, baubles, noodles, the lot. Robbed every nation for art" (24). The language tends to be highly rhythmical here. Occasionally, it becomes bawdy and lewd, and words like 'fuck' or 'fucking,' 'bullshit' and 'arsehole' are used in this novel a number of times. This is George, the Yank, speaking to the Zimbabwean nigger Tawanda on the stage while performing *Tony and Cleo* : "OK, come on, man. I spat in your face, mother-fucher. I'm here. Defend what you do, nigger!" (10). At his daughter's school, Gerald Blossom is rebuked by one of the black women thus : "Eh, don't fuck me with your eyes, black boy" (17). Of Sara, Gerald says, "I thought she was serious even though the article rebound on her arse" (33). In describing the scenes of actual sexual intercourse, the novelist appears to be a romantic. Here is one such description :

> I get in with her and like a boy I'm shivering with anticipation. She gets hold of me with a sweaty hand and crudely pulls it to and fro. No arts of the Kama Sutra here. The girl is like a nervous bird and I was so greedy to look at every inch of her, the colour of her skin, the exact shape of her back, her legs.... But faced with it my greed disappears. I look into her eyes. She shuts them and when she looks at me it is to kiss and then she drowns her lips in mine. She wants to lose herself somewhere in the kiss, so she doesn't admit what we are doing.
>
> Her nipples are small and brown and the hair in her crotch is thick and her cunt is tiny, a fish's mouth. She lets out a little cry and closes her eyes when I enter her and she puts both hands on my hips and shoves me out (133).

And thus the sensuous description goes on while Ali and Anjali are involved in sex-act. What is to be marked is that the writer gives details of such things with gay abandon whether he is describing the indulgence of Penny and Mr. XX or that of Sonya and Mr. XX or that of anyone else. This is how he presents the sex-involvement of Penny and Mr. XX :

> "Don't stop, nothing's wrong"...and her hips moved so that her thumb of a clitoris scraped the base of my prick, the line where hair stops (292).

Penny is the speaker here. And this is how Dhondy goes along the frantic love-scene between Sonya and Mr. XX :

> 'I was going to read, maybe, write.'
> 'Don't then. Smoke this.'
> She smiles. Then she takes her clothes off. All of them.
> 'I'm noisy,' she says huskily as I get into bed with her.
> 'Put a pillow on your mouth'....

> She screams, 'Fuck me, you horny bastard, you animal, there, there, there, you've got it, there, just there, oh God! There, there, there!' (195).

Clearly, the passage like the ones quoted above tend to be highly sensual and erotic, capturing the enactment of real sex-drama, and eroticism and eloquent sensuousness are writ large.

One of the fascinating attributes of Dhondy's prose is its wit and humour. David Stream is spoken of as "street-wise" and "house-foolish" (9). Maureen is mentioned as one who "uses all that woman-together thing, the feeling how bad men are, especially black men" (16). Sara "had her Stream year too" (21). Claude the Frenchy is mimicked thus :

> 'I tell you ze sto-wy of ze man K.'
> So it go on.
> Ze sto-wy of ze man K is quite good. You see zere waz zis man whom Claude knew who has gone to the Himalayas and zat was why Claude applied to come with David on ze great quest of *ze Ramayana* (39).

Ali becomes an actor not so much by "the pull of the stage" but by "the push of the bus' (41). S. Patel always says "ko-fee instead of coffee" and he "calls it 'pope' music" (43). Tilak informs Mr. XX : '"Bullshit is only an abuse in the West. Here it is a God-given blessing. So much you can do with shit of bulls" (161). Jam, the third-rate playwright, is a person who never remembers owing money to anyone, and hence "A tenner taken" is "a tenner gone" (69). Mr. XX's grandad advises the Parsee historian to collect "all my best thoughts," for "the West can pay you for the wisdom of the East" (172). How witty it is! Mr. XX has become a collector of shamelessness, and as such he receives "rejection slips…from thirty-two publishing houses for my projected book" and makes "a study of his own shades of shamelessness in salesmanship" (177). The humorous vein is unmistakable when the novelist starts describing Mr. XX : "I sign myself Xerxes Xavaxa. The Parsee from Poona. Girls behind tills in banks look at me. They think the signature is an affectation. Such is the power of the X" (178). And again :

> X. The syllable haunts. X : he shaves his beard when the crime is discovered. X : he is caught, plain old Mr. Botany B in the deserts of Guyana, hunted down by primitive police helicopters. Xed : he was hanged and his mamma cried. But my XXX, it's real, for real, that's what I inherited, Xerxes Xavaxa. Good day to you too, Sir! (179).

A little onward, Mr. XX is presented as a worthless fellow — as a "Gandoo and lund fakir." Dhondy's wit is incisive, and his humour spares none, including the narrator of the story.

Dhondy has raised the thorny issue of religious fundamentalism in the Indian context. He seems to be all for harmony and peace in the Indian sub-continent, and does not favour a dogfight between the Muslims and the Hindus, or between the Sikhs and the Hindus, or between the Christians and the Muslims. Any unwanted fight is bound to bring about national disintegration and fragmentation. To avoid this, we the Indians have to shun extremes in religious matters and to follow the path of truth and *ahimsa* (non-violence) as visualized by our national leaders like Gandhi, Nehru, Subhash and Patel. This is what we gather after taking into account the mixed lot of actors in the first part (wherein the three communities — Hindu, Muslim, and Christian — figure) as well as the cross-section of people in the second part (where, again, all the religious sects and creeds are nicely represented). The novel also contains details about Hinduism, Christianity, and Zoroastrianism (though it has very little about Mohammedanism). In an informal chit-chat with Mr. XX, Mrs. De F (who is a Hindu by birth and whose proper name is Lyla) asks :

> 'What do you feel, Mr. Xavaxa, or Xerxes? As a Parsee.'
> 'Parsees. We don't feel threatened, I don't think.'
> 'Sikhs do and Muslims certainly do and there's been slaughter these last forty years, says an actress girl (199).

And to tone off the intensity of the talk, Mr. XX casually suggests : "The only solution is for India to declare itself a non-secular Hindu state. Iran burns with fervour, Pakistan is going that way and Bangladesh and China have religions of their own" (199). And the explicit reason that Mr. XX offers for his viewpoint is that Hinduism "has never been codified" and that "its political development has always been interrupted" (199). Mr. XX also points out that the need of the hour is to "codify" Hinduism, and then one will discover that "Secularism is part of Hinduism, because it isn't a religion at all in the normal sense" and that "the constitution would say that Muslims, Parsees, Sikhs, Buddhists, Christians, Jews all have to be free to practise their religions and have equal political rights" (200).

Dhondy has also given attention to the development of characters, at least to some of them, and to the finesse of the art of characterization. He has made Gerald Blossom (later Ali Abdul Rahman), David Stream, Sara and Anjali living characters of flesh and blood in the first part of the novel, while in the second part he has created some full-blooded and rounded characters like Mr. Xerxes Xavaxa, Leslie de Freitas, Sonya, Penny, and Tilak. These characters crowd the pages of the novel and render it 'a strange medley', reminding us of what Dryden has remarked in another context — "Here's God's plenty". All ranks, all creeds, all countries, all climes are remarkably represented here. Both the sexes — men and women — are properly sketched. At places, Dhondy evidently becomes vulgar and smelly in drawing his characters, as though there is no life beyond sex — but, on the whole, he sounds convincing in giving minute details about them. Of course, the overlapping of characters from one part of the novel to the other is somewhat confusing, requiring extra vigilance on the part of the reader, but that is how he could possibly create the impression of continuity between the two parts.

Finally, Farrukh Dhondy has produced a serio-comic novel of good length and merit. It is felt that he should have reduced its size and shape by curtailing the David Stream affair and reporting it through the mouth of the first-person narrator and not through the epistolary method. Going through the newspaper reports, clippings and diary of Sara is not a very happy experience, and at the top of it the staging of the *Ramayana* in Delhi by David Stream & Co. ultimately fizzles out, leaving the actress Anjali slaughtered and the main actor Ali mortally wounded. The first part of the novel has nothing to do with its title; it is only the second part that has a relevance to it. It would have been better if the novelist had concentrated on the second part only with greater fire and force. No doubt, there are some links and associations of characters and situations between the two parts, but more often than not they turn out to be feeble and pale. For the sake of quality, the novelist must avoid the temptation of quantity or bulk, and he must give up the habit of falling into the trap of the epistolary technique of Smollett. Barring these few lapses, *Bombay Duck* does not fall short of our expectations, and as Francis King has rightly remarked in the *Daily Telegraph* it is "a delightful book — astute, disturbing and funny."[5] There is "enough in bulk and variety"[6] here to please and tease us and to make us think. This is certainly no mean achievement for a writer who has ventured in the domain of fiction for the first time.

NOTES AND REFERENCES

1. Quoted from the back cover of *Bombay Duck* by Farrukh Dhondy (Calcutta : Rupa, 1991).
2. *Idem.*
3. K.R. Srinivasa Iyengar, *Indian Writing in English* (New Delhi : Sterling, 1984), p. 708.
4. *Ibid.*, p. 776.
5. Quoted from the front cover of *Bombay Duck.*
6. Meenakshi Mukherjee, *The Twice Born Fiction* (New Delhi : Arnold-Heinemann, 1974), p. 198.

14

THE HUB OF THE WHEEL : RECURRING METAPHORS IN SHASHI DESHPANDE'S NOVELS

I

Through analogies, similes and metaphors, an author renders his expressions concise, concrete and condensed. Of all the literary devices employed by an author, metaphors speak volumes of his or her mental attitude and concentration of vision. That is why Aristotle allotted the pride of place to 'metaphor' in an artistic creation. He remarked :

> But the greatest thing by far is to be a master of metaphor. It is the one thing that cannot be learnt from others; and it is also a sign of genius....[1]

Obviously, a metaphor is very helpful in image-making, in concretizing emotions, and in crystallizing moods. As C. Day Lewis maintains. "An epithet, a metaphor, a simile may create an image...."[2] A metaphor is, thus, a recognized literary device to capture the intensity of an artist's creative vision and the fertility of his imagination. In a brilliant essay, Middleton Murry attributes the qualities of 'intensity' and 'fertility' in artistic matters to 'the non-measurable world' created with the help of metaphors :

> All metaphor and simile can be described as the analogy by which the human mind explores the universe of quality and charts the non-measurable world.[3]

In other words, metaphor is closely related to 'the universe of quality' in artistic creations.

The present paper endeavours to explore some of the recurring metaphors in the fictional works of Shashi Deshpande. These metaphors include 'the dark' and 'the sunlight,' 'death' and 'life,' 'silence' and 'the binding vine.' They tend to neatly summarize the fluctuating moods and the mysterious emotions of a sensitive woman. Though these metaphors are not too many in number, they put on the track the running wheel of her fictional world. They clearly reveal the inner workings of the protagonists' minds and the emotional ripples in their hearts.

II

The very first novel, *The Dark Holds No Terrors* (1980), is built around the metaphors of 'the dark' and 'the light.' There was a time when Sarita (or Saru), the protagonist, was afraid of 'the dark' at night fearing that a man would invade her body and commit monstrosities upon her. The woman, who had been so defiant in her childhood and adulthood,[4] felt utterly helpless and panic-stricken with the approach of the terrible dark. She described her none-too-happy condition in the following manner :

> Panic and terror mounted in me as the hands, deliberately, with a kind of casual cruelty, gradually tightened round my throat. Oh God, I was going to die.[5]

The suffocating dark, the heavy weight, the pain and the hurt associated with the sexual act made her life a hell, and she longed to see the light, to have relaxation, and to emerge out of a sickening state of *ennui*, boredom and exhaustion. In this novel, the metaphor of 'the dark' is inseparably linked with "panic and sensation" simultaneously (12).

As the novel opens, Sarita is already in the grip of "the familiar irritation, the familiar exasperation" (17) owing to an unbridgeable gulf between herself and her husband even after their companionship of fifteen long years. She is a medical doctor by profession and self-reliant woman by all means, yet her marriage with Manohar (or Manu) has not proceeded smoothly. So, she turns back to her parental home, leaving behind her children. She is seized with a "strange new fear of disintegration" and a "terrified consciousness of not existing" (22). The real cause of the disintegration of the family is a searching interview of Manohar by a lady reporter for a women's magazine : "How does it feel when your wife earns not only the butter but bread as well?" (35-36). Since than, Manohar becomes a sadist, torturing Saru in bed at night. Her dreams of a happy home with children twittering about and a loving husband to prop her up in the struggle of life are now totally shattered. She wants to "sleep peacefully the night through. To wake up without pain. To go through tomorrow without apprehension" (27), but she does not find the congenial atmosphere of her parental house and its peaceful surroundings :

> Saru's parental home is in contrast to her spousal home, where, in her own words, "Terror waited for me in our room. I could not escape it" (79).

Her desire to disclose the tortures and terrors of the night to Manu evaporates into thin air with the appearance of the sun on the eastern horizon. But when Manu goes on repeating his actions at night, Saru goes away, leaving behind her family and associations and also aches and bruises and apprehensions. To her father she confesses her tortures and terrors caused by Manu, reducing her to a "two-in-one woman" and a "a terrified, trapped animal" (134). She has certainly suffered unspeakably and at times she thinks that her sufferings are a return of her own misdeeds in the past connected with the drowning of Dhruva in a deep pond in early childhood, of the miserable death of her disgruntled mother, and of her improper conduct as a housewife (deriving undue favours from an ambitious man like Boozie). Her terror persists with her like a canker : "When the light comes on, it goes away. When the dark comes, it returns" (205). At moments she feels like "a trapped animal" (215) full of desperation, loneliness and failure. The 'dark' engulfs her completely, and she yearns for the 'light.' In *The Dark Holds No*

Terrors, 'the dark' and 'the light' are frequently used as the contrastive metaphors. While the former denotes fear and sorrow, dejection and estrangement, the latter signals joy and fearlessness, company and compassion.

The metaphor of 'the dark', with the same signification, is also used in one of the short stories of Shashi Deshpande. The story "It Was Dark" brings out the miserable lot of an unmarried girl having been molested by an unknown young man, resulting in an unspeakable shock to her owing to an illegal pregnancy. In the story the man is identified with 'the dark' or with 'the evil.' The unfortunate girl of the story eventually veers round the idea that the 'dark' represents the engines of tyranny and forced submission : "There was no enemy by the dark, no fear but the fear of being alone."[6] The metaphor of 'the dark' is here associated with fearfulness and tyranny.

Another dominant metaphor operating in Shashi Deshpande's fiction is 'death,' which remains in sheer contradiction to 'life.' In two of her earlier novels — *If I Die Today* (1982) and *Come Up and Be Dead* (1983) — this metaphor comes out clearly, though in later novels, too, the idea of 'death' is not altogether absent. In *If I Die Today* and *Come Up and Be Dead,* the metaphor of 'death' becomes powerfully evocative and assertive.

As *If I Die Today* begins, we are introduced to Guru coming from his village to get admitted to a modern medical college and hospital set up by Sethji for the treatment of cancer. A disappointed Meera states the following about the pitiable condition of Guru :

> ....Ashoka tells me there's no hope for him at all.
> He's going to die. I mean, they're going to operate
> on him, ...He'll die in any case.[7]

Though others are scared of Guru's impending death, he himself is not. Philosophically he remarks : "If I die today, you die tomorrow" (7). Clearly, Guru has "risen above all human weaknesses and crossed that dreadful barrier...the eternal human fear of death" (9). According to Manju, Guru is a detached 'spectator,' and Meera also thinks of him in the same way.

Manju and her husband Vijay, however, live in a world of make-beliefs and speculations. Manju even laughs at Guru's matter-of-fact approach to life. The Dean, his sister Dr. Vidya Agarwal, and Dr. Kulkarni seem to be very serious about their medical profession. Dr. Vidya is an abnormal woman — a case fit for the psychiatrist. She leads a secluded life with her brother, while her sister-in-law, Rani, lives far away in a flat in Bombay. Rani joins the Dean only when her two children return home from the boarding schools. Dr. Vidya's occasional derangements are so fierce that she first kills Guru, then Tony, and finally makes an unsuccessful bid on Vijay. She appears to be always disarrayed and jittery, always fear-ridden and shame-faced. At the dinner hosted by Rani, Guru and Manju speak of a convict who has slain "more than forty people (27). The medical campus is also agog with deaths and murders, including that of a labour leader Prabhakaran Tambe. Thereafter, Guru dies "in his sleep" (53), and it is whispered around that he was murdered by one of the medical staff. Then the death of Sumanta's wife is reported, and an erstwhile nurse Vimala is implicated in it. Tony is also killed for his quarrelsome outspokenness. As sensitive Mriga, Dr. Kulkarni's daughter, informs : "Tony uncle...he's dead. He's floating in the tank near the temple" (88). This very girl once dreams of her imaginary accident and her admission to a hospital where her rude father would come rushing, and then she would console him : "Don't cry, daddy. And then I would die with a smile on my face and he would be heart-broken for ever after" (91). The girl wishes that her parents were dead, particularly her hard-hearted father. Towards the close of the novel, Dr. Vidya, behaving like an "insane animal" (133) in one of her fits, makes a murderous assault on Vijay in the dark of night. The metaphor of 'death,' as stated earlier, works as a contrast to that of 'life,'[8] about which the narrator remarks : "Every human being has the right to live out his full span of life" (137).

The metaphor of 'death' is emphatically employed in *Come UP and Be Dead* (1983). The novel opens with the premature death of Mridula Dutta of the 10th standard. Some think that she died of "brief illness" caused by a terminated pregnancy, while others believe that it was a case of suicide (23). Though the novel briefly mentions the "peaceful, tranquil death" (98) of Devajani's (or Devi's) father, it is largely preoccupied with the mysterious death of Mridula. First, they suspect Pratap, the nutty brother of the school Head Mistress working as a peon-gardener there, to be the cause of her sad death, and the Head Mistress is also implicated in the case. In the midst of rumours afloat, Pratap is called out of his room and killed in cold-blood. According to the narrator Devi, "Pratap's death had been no accident. He had not died because of a fall from a ladder. Someone had killed him" (144-45). Thereafter, Mrs. Jyoti Raman, the weak-eyed and specter-thin mother of Sonali (or Sona) is "strangulated with her own scarf" (172) on the occasion of the Annual Festival. Last of all, the seventeen-year-old Sharmila is stabbed by her own lover, Sanjay. The last few pages of the novel inform us that Dr. Girish, who is ever in need of ample money for his demanding, smart and spendthrift wife, and Mr. Varma, who is "a sorrowful widower" (264), are the real villains of the piece. Of the two, Mr. Varma is worse for having run a call-girl racket at the hotel Open Sesame.

The two novels *If I Die Today* and *Come Up and Be Dead* contain a lot of thrill and suspense in them, and they clearly betray Shashi Deshpande's readings in Agatha Christie and Sherlock Holmes. The same sort of atmosphere also pervades *The Binding Vine* (1993). The narrator, a clever and sharp-tongued woman called Urmi (or Urmila), is seen grieving over the untimely death of her young daughter Anu. Her sailor-husband lives far off, and is a rude and rough person. The narrator does not want to die in any situation; instead, she says, "...I would feel life tingling through me. I was alive, I could not be dead, I would never know what it felt like to be dead."[9] Urmi busies herself for a while in the poetry of her long-dead mother-in-law, Mira, whose poetry, like her life, was full of pity, rage and anguish (67). Mira bled to death after her child, Kishore (Urmi's husband), was born (136). The heart-rending story of

Mira runs parallel to the equally, or even more, disgusting story of Kalpana, a young and beautiful girl hanging between life and death, scuttling between home and hospital. Kalpana is also a victim of rape and torture, and her helpless mother, Shakuntala (or Sakutai), is terribly upset and shocked over the cruel incident. Commenting on the deteriorating condition of Kalpana, the narrator says :

> ...I notice how the contours of her face have changed, the bones pushing themselves against the parchment like skin. There is a kind of deathly stillness about the body, the face almost a mask in its rigidity (109).

Sakutai wants her own death as well as that of her daughter (177). The title of the novel, in fact, comes from the last poem of Mira's on the theme of love. The 'binding vines' for Urmi are her son Kartik and her mother Inni; for Akka it is Bhaskar; for Shakutai, her daughter Sandhya and her sister Sulu; and for Vanaa, her man Harish. In the course of the story, however, Shakutai's kind and loving sister ends her life by setting herself aflame after sprinkling "a whole bottle of kerosene" (188). Somehow, Sulu comes to know that her own husband has wrecked the life of Kalpana to satiate his wolfish desires, and she is left with no option but to commit suicide. However, the novel ends on an optimistic note, and in the midst of deaths, rapes, and tortures, the narrator is seen searching for "the spring of life" (203).

The metaphor of 'death' is also operative, though on a much smaller scale, in Shashi Deshpande's short story entitled "Death of a Child." This story deals with the problem of a woman's unwanted pregnancy and her subsequent decision to get it terminated. The woman is always obsessed with the question of her own survival : "I don't want it; I can't."[10] She heaves a sigh of relief when the child is finished, and yet remarks : "I feel as we walk away, that I am not alone. I feel that the ghost of my dead child walks with me.'[11]

In Shashi Deshpande's novels 'silence' recurs insistently. Saru says in *The Dark Holds No Terrors* : "Silence had been a habit for us" (199); Indu in *Roots and Shadows* (1983) says about her cold relationship with Jayanta that "I am passive. And unresponsive. I'm still and dead;"[12] and in *The Binding Vine*, Urmi adopts a posture of 'silence' on being asked by Bhaskar, her lover, about her none-too-happy marriage with Kishore. "I can say nothing. The silence stretches between us" (161). But it is in the Sahitya Akademi award-winning novel *That Long Silence* (1988) that the metaphor of 'silence' is worked out majestically. In this work, the narrator-heroine's dreams of having a happy home with her husband Mohan and children prove to be a chimera at long last. The corrupt practices of her husband in his office and his overgrowing jealousy towards her literary career create a wide chasm between them, and they adopt an unbreakable yet unnerving silence towards each other. As elsewhere, here too 'silence' denotes lack of communication, frigidity of feeling, and want of understanding and compassion. Being devoid of emotions in real life, Jaya's short stories become emotionless and puerile. As Sarabjit K. Sandhu remarks :

> This unhappiness is reflected not only in her [Jaya's] conjugal life, but also in social life. Her books, her stories lack anger and emotion.[13]

The result is that Jaya loses her "personal vision,"[14] her individuality, and her identifiable features, and that she miserably fails in her writings. A strained relationship with her husband creates a void in her married life, which ultimately results in failure and frustration in her creative activity. There is a complete communication-gap between the couple, and they drift apart. Jaya finds a good companion for herself in her neighbour Kamat, and she discusses with him her personal problems in an uninhibited way. In due course, they become so intimate with, and fond of, each other that they start making physical advances. After his sudden death, Jaya continues to live with Mohan but in a mood of "emptiness" (185). When the mood of loneliness and truncation overpowers her, she realizes the mistake of leading a marooned and cocooned life, and finally, resolves to "erase the silence" between herself and Mohan (192). Her resolve to speak to her husband and to listen to him intently cuts the ice. Both Jaya and Mohan realize that they are complementary to each other in real life. They begin to speak the human tongue and express human emotions, and thus usher in a new kind of life based on understanding and harmony. To the relief of readers, the wall of 'silence' is broken asunder at the close of the novel.

III

All the novels examined above combinedly enforce the idea that the novelist has all along been striving towards self-discovery or quest for identity. In them she makes a powerful study of female psyche and its problems. She unmistakably highlights women's helpless and hapless situation, their existential dilemma, their want of understanding or compatibility with their husbands. Even a cursory glance at her novels like *The Dark Holds No Terrors* and *That Long Silence* corroborates it. In *The Dark Holds No Terrors*, Saru is riven between two selves; in other words, she is a "two-in-one woman" and "a terrified trapped animal" (134). She marries an educated boy out of her caste and against the wishes of her parents, but after a few years of happy married life she feels suffocated and estranged from him and drifts apart. Saru is a successful doctor, and earns the bread and butter for her family, while her husband is a poor college teacher depending largely upon his wife in financial matters. An unexpected interview by a lady reporter for a women's magazine turns Manu a 'sadist,' who adopts all sorts of tricks to torture his wife at night. As a result, she becomes totally terror-stricken and tension-ridden. Her helplessness in the given situation is pathetic :

> The dream, the nightmare, whatever it was, continued. Changing now, like some protean monster, into the horror of rape. This was not to be death by strangulation; it was a monstrous invasion of my body, wriggling under the weight that pinned it down. It was impossible. I was

> pinioned to a position of an abject surrender of my self. I began, in sheer helplessness, to make small whimpering sounds, piteous cries (11-12).

Getting no respite form her nocturnal tortures and terrors, Saru decides to leave for her parental house, leaving behind her two children and husband, only to return at the end of the novel. The message seems to be that a married woman has no other place to live and be happy than her husband's. No proper remedy is offered to Saru's terrors and tortures, to her emotional and mental hurts. Her pitiable conditions remind us of those of Sita in Anita Desai's novel, *Where Shall We Go This Summer*? (1975). Both Sita and Saru are faced with an identical dilemma in their lives. They are not their normal selves by any means. Their existential problems do not allow them rest or relief, and in utter helplessness they run away to their parent's homes, hoping against all hopes to get over the sense of frustration and alienation. Surely, both of them go out in search of 'self' or in quest of identity.

That Long Silence depicts Jaya as a torn 'self' or a split personality. Jaya is shown reflecting on what she was before her marriage and what she has become after it. Hers is a peculiar dilemma — 'to be or not to be.' In the span of seventeen long years of married life, she is blessed with a son and a daughter. But her husband's corrupt practices at his Bombay office and the ensuing inquiries and Jaya's unredeemed domestic drudgery and tortuous confinement to the Dadar flat wreck her conjugal life. Adle King characterises these unfortunate developments as "odd misfits" and "petty bickerings over money" and "jealousy over affections."[15] Jaya's relations, as a consequence, with her man run into a rough weather, and they become cold towards each other, observing an unbreakable 'long silence.' The trouble arises from Jaya's fitful anger, and she calls Mohan's mother a 'cook' (which she certainly was). Mohan has never expected this from his well-educated and well-cultured English-speaking wife, and he has always thought that anger makes "a woman unwomanly" (83). His dreams are now shattered, and he slumps into a long-drawn silence. This worries too much, and she starts wondering whether "there is such a thing as one's self, intact and whole, waiting to be discovered" (69). Jaya is actually a victim of circumstances, of "an atmosphere of apathy and boredom."[16] She is an alienated 'self,' longing for love and companionship. It is at the close of the novel that she moves towards the realizing of her true 'self.' Thus, the search for self-discovery or the quest for identity forms a recurrent motif in Deshpande's fiction, and the dominant metaphors used in it strengthen the motif.

This is further borne out by the short story entitled "I Want..." wherein a good deal of self-searching or self-exploration is carried on. The story has a twenty-seven-year-old Alka as its protagonist. She is young and unmarried and subjected to "the insolent stares, and the impertinent questions"[17] by the groom's party. She feels uneasiness, consternation and hopelessness, and broods : "The woman in me was outraged and protested. I crushed her. She had no place there. None at all."[18] She is terribly upset within, and remarks : "Sometimes I feel we are all doomed to be strangers to one another, forever sealed in separate glass jars we call 'self.'"[19] What keeps Alka apart from the commonality of women is her strong sense of 'self' which she wants to preserve at all cost. In a mood of self-preservation, she says : "I had a shape and form I had to preserve. A self I had to treasure."[20] Evidently, she is a woman of self-consciousness, and wants to discover her integral personality. As for her marriage, she has little choice of her own; moreover, her parents are there to safeguard her interests. But being a thoughtful woman, she has her own desire to fulfil. Though she does not desire a husband having a four-figure salary or a car, she still wants a man who 'hears my voice when I speak, who understands me even when I don't....'[21] At the close of the story, she accepts the reassurances of her Baba (who immediately reminds us of Sarita's Baba in *The Dark Holds No Terrors*). Clearly, Alka wishes to shed off the slough of despair and darkness and to emerge in a world of companionship and sunlight.

Thus, Shashi Deshpande has woven a delicate and subtle texture of her fictional world with a good deal of thought and dexterity. Though the metaphors used in her novels are not many, they powerfully highlight the dichotomy of human life, characterized by sorrow and joy, failure and success, death and life, alienation and attraction, thereby setting the scale of existence balanced and reasonable, though the scale sometimes does swing towards misery and anguish, death and destruction, hopelessness and helplessness. These metaphors also reveal that Shashi Deshpande's world, like Jane Austen's, is a small and closed one, where the novelist is definitely at home.

NOTES AND REFERENCES

1. Ingram Bywater, *Aristotle : On the Art of Poetry*. Oxford : Clarendon Press, 1967, p. 78.
2. C. Day Lewis, *The Poetic Image*. Cambridge University Press, 1955, p. 4.
3. J. Middleton Murry, "Metaphor," *Twentieth Century Poetry*, eds. G. Martin & P.N. Furbank. Walton Hall, Milton Keynes : The Open University Press, 1975, p. 28.
4. K.R. Srinivasa Iyengar describes Saru as "an unusual character... who defies her mother to become a doctor, defies her caste to marry outside, and defies social conventions by using Boozie to advance her career." *Indian Writing in English*. New Delhi : Sterling Publishers, 1984, p. 759.
5. Shashi Deshpande, *The Dark Holds No Terrors*. 1980; Delhi : Penguin India, 1990, p. 11. Textual references to Shashi Deshpande's novels, except their first occurrence, have been given parenthetically.
6. Shashi Deshpande, *It Was Dark*. Calcutta : Writers Workshop, 1986, p. 23.
7. Shashi Deshpande, *If I Die Today*. New Delhi : Vikas Publishing House, 1982, p. 5.
8. Shashi Deshpande, *Come Up and Be Dead*. New Delhi : Vikas Publishing House, 1983, p. 8.
9. Shashi Deshpande, *The Binding Vine*. Delhi : Penguin India, 1993, p. 20.
10. Shashi Deshpande, *The Legacy*. Calcutta : Writers Workshop, 1977, p. 87.
11. *Ibid.*, p. 95.
12. Shashi Deshpande, *Roots and Shadows*. New Delhi : Orient Longman (Disha Books), 1983, p. 83.

13. Sarabjit Sandhu, *The Novels of Shashi Deshpande*. New Delhi : Prestige Books, 1990, p. 41.
14. Shashi Deshpande, *That Long Silence*. Delhi : Penguin India, 1989, p. 147.
15. Adle King, "Shashi Deshpande, : Portraits of an Indian Woman," in *The New Indian Novel In English*, ed. Viney Kirpal, Delhi : Allied Publishers, 1990, pp. 165-66.
16. Madhu Singh, "Intimate and Soul-Searching Portrayals of Marriage," *Indian Book Chronicle* (July 1993), p. 22.
17. Shashi Deshpande, *The Miracle*. Calcutta : Writers Workshop, 1986, p. 36.
18. *Ibid.,* p. 37.
19. *Ibid.,* p. 36.
20. *Ibid.,* p. 37.
21. *Ibid.*, p. 42.

15

SHASHI DESHPANDE'S *THAT LONG SILENCE* ('88) : A FEMINIST READING

Shashi Deshpande (born 1938) occupies a distinctive place in contemporary Indian English fiction because of her unequivocal feminist stance. As a writer, she has imbibed influences from various quarters — from her parental family, particularly her father (who was a dramatist of ideas), Jane Austen, Charles Dickens and George Bernard Shaw. She has also been influenced by some of the Western feminists like Simone de Beauvoir, Betty Friedan and Germaine Greer. In her interview with Vanamala Vishwanth, Deshpande informs us that these feminists have not influenced her directly, but they have "helped to place... confusions and put them in order."[1] These 'confusions' should have presumably been about the choice of her subject-matter, its small or large canvas, and about the leading role, and through her practice in short stories she took no time in deciding these vital issues. She made her novels, including *That Long Silence* (1988), women-oriented, opting for the 'two inches of ivory' like Jane Austen and allowing the domineering role to her female protagonists. She confesses that "only a woman could write my books — they are written from the inside, as it were."[2] Thus, Deshpande writes from her own experiences of the educated middle-class Indian woman's predicament, and her novels and short stories tend to be gender-specific. She minutely analyses the unwholesome situation in which a sensitive woman has to live and move about, caught between the powerful currents of tradition and patriarchy, of terror and suppression. Such a woman is inescapably subjected to physical tortures and sexual assaults in society. Consequently, her personality is crushed, her voice is hushed up, and her instinct of self-assertion gets catapulted. The loss of personality, voice or self-assertion leads her to confusion and tormentation, to loss of self-identity and even prestige. Madame Deshpande understands it very well, and hence she makes her female protagonists search for 'self' or discover her identity.

Here in this paper I have chosen to analyze and interpret the text of *That Long Silence*, a Sahitya Akademi award-winning novel, from the feminist angle. If occasionally I mention Deshpande's other novels, it will be only for illustration and elucidation. In *That Long Silence*, as elsewhere too, Deshpande raises her strong voice of protest against the male-dominated Indian society and against man-made rules and conventions.

I

That Long Silence is the story of Jaya, the protagonist, who remains a sufferer in her childhood and adulthood. As a young girl, she is chided by her grandmother for her inquisitive and witty nature. The grandmother cautions this girl thus : "For everything, a question, for everything a retort. What husband can be comfortable with that?"[3] The girl is thus being conditioned toward the comforts of her future life-partner. Jaya is reminded repeatedly that "a husband is like a sheltering tree" (p. 137), and that "the happiness of your husband and home depends entirely on you" (p. 138). With the possible exception of Urmila in *The Binding Vine* (1993), all other female protagonists — Jaya, Sarita shortened to Saru, and Indu — are brought up in traditional Hindu families where the girls are tutored to direct all their prayers, penances and rituals to the procurement of proper husbands, to their welfare and longevity, and to the propagation of their lineage through the birth of male children in their families. In *The Dark Holds No Terrors* (1980), we come across the dilemma and crisis in the life of Sarita, a successful medical practitioner by all means. Her nocturnal experiences with her husband, Manu, have been so exasperating and terrifying. Manu abuses her body at night but plays the normal husband in daytime. Every night he monstrously invades her body as a cruel rapist :

> ...it was a monstrous invasion of my body. I tried to move, twisting my body, wriggling under the weight that pinned it down. It was impossible. I was pinioned to a position of an abject surrender of my self.[4]

Sarita gets fed up with her life and runs away to her parental home for relief and respite on hearing the news of her mother's death. Manu has become a sadist because of the callous and careless remark of an interviewer like this : "...wife earns not only the butter but most of the bread as well" (p. 200). This remark has hurt Manu deeply, but Sarita is made to suffer for no fault of hers. A similar critical situation is created for Indu too in *Roots and Shadows* (1983). Like Sarita, Indu is also educated, modern, self-reliant, and married to a man of her choice. By marrying Jayant, she subdues her own hobby of writing and alters her life-style to please him. She eventually becomes a submissive wife to a domineering husband, letting herself to be swayed by the patriarchal notion that a man is superior to a woman. She says, "He chooses his level. And I try to choose the one he would like me to be on."[5] Jayant finds Indu's passionate nature quite shocking, and this generates a peculiar tension between them, compelling her to hide her true 'self' from him :

> I had learnt to reveal to Jayant nothing but what he wanted to hear. I hid my responses and emotions as if they were bits of garbage (p. 41).

Fortunately, Indu is summoned by her grand aunt Akka who is now lying on her death-bed. At her natal home, Indu reflects on the cause of her discontentment and discovers it to her unassertiveness resulting in the loss of her self-respect and freedom. For the first time in her life, she asserts herself by financing Mini's marriage with Akka's money. She also avenges herself on Jayant by making love to her friend Naren.

Jaya's condition in *That Long Silence* is none-too-happy, but to her we shall revert after dealing with Urmila (shortened to 'Urm') in *The Binding Vine* (1993). Urmila stands apart from the rest of Deshpande's female protagonists, as she is a liberated woman. She is well-educated and self-dependent, and serves as a Lecturer in a Bombay College and lives with her mother Yamini (or Inni) and her six-year-old son Kartik. She chooses Kishore for her husband who is her close neighbour and who now works with the Merchant Navy away from his home. Urm is a strong-willed woman, being sometimes novel and startling in her ideas. Here is the stance of a staunch feminist who remains assertive and aggressive throughout. She takes decisions on her own, and the crisis in her life is not caused by Kishore but by the sudden demise of their one-year-old baby Anu. The demise upsets Urm completely and she cannot reconcile with it easily :

> I am running along the sea. There's someone else with me ...I can hear the footsteps. I can hear too heavy breathing, but I cannot see whoever it is...I have to keep running....[6]

In fact, Urm is passing through a state of psychological tension. As regards her relationship with Kishore, it is based on mutual love and trust. But sometimes she becomes apprehensive of the safe return of her husband :

> Now there is — the fear of Kishore never returning home ... the fear of his not wanting to come back to me. Yes, that's the thing, that's what I am most afraid of (p. 82).

She, however, controls her feelings and thoughts and does not ask Kishore, even once, to leave his job and do some other work. She does not want to hurt him in any way, and hence feels incessantly sad and disappointed inwardly. At such moments, she is no better than an ordinary unlettered woman. If she does not interfere with her husband's (or anyone else's) affairs, she does not allow anyone to meddle with hers. So, she continues her friendship with Bhaskar Jain despite the family protests. Her role as a liberated woman comes out vividly in the novel when she extends her unstinted support to the raped young woman, Kalpana, and her anguished mother, and to Shakutai, a domestic servant. By indulging in such social works, Urmila finally overcomes her sense of suffering and shock caused by the death of Anu.

II

Like other female protagonists, Jaya also finds herself in the midst of a domestic tension when she tries to know about her husband's (Mohan's) corrupt practices at office. In order to avoid exposure in public, Mohan shifts from his posh Churchgate flat to a small apartment in Dadar, where they had once lived soon after their marriage. Here the couple sinks into utter silence in a mood of frustration and depression, without talking to each other and without sharing their ideas. Jaya is terribly disturbed by the prevailing circumstances in the family, and she starts questioning herself. Consequently, her husband loses his status, and she her identity, her selfhood. She comes to realize as follows :

> The real picture, the real 'you' never emerges, looking for it is as bewildering as trying to know how you really look. Ten different mirrors show you ten different faces (p. 1).

From the above text it is clear that Jaya is a fragmented self with a tormented consciousness. Evidently, she does not know her identity and does not enjoy individuality of her own. She sees herself as someone's daughter, wife and mother, having no status of her own. She therefore says : "I was born. My father died when I was fifteen. I got married to Mohan. I have two children and I did not let a third live" (p. 2). The last clause of the last sentence clearly hints at an abortion undertaken by Jaya without consulting her husband. The abortion is another name of infanticide, and unquestionably suggests the unethical practice on the part of a wife especially when she maintains perfect secrecy about it. If we read between the lines, the secrecy is a pointer to the lack of freedom for the wife.

Up to this point, Jaya accepts a life of passivity for herself. Whatever she practises or whatever she follows is dictated by only one consideration — and that is what her husband will think of it. So, the role-model for her up to this stage is that of a dedicated wife, even at the cost of losing her own identity. This is how she reminisces her relationship with her husband later on : "I'm Mohan's wife, I had thought, and cut off the bits of me that had refused to be Mohan's wife" (p. 191). Jaya's review of her relationship with her husband points to an unhappy past. To her, married life becomes unbearable and monotonous, as it moved in a fixed pattern. Thus we have the following :

> Worse than anything else had been the boredom of the unchanging pattern, the unending monotony (p. 4).

Jaya and Mohan are leading the life of 'a pair of bullocks yoked together'. They have nothing better to do but to pretend 'the illusion of happiness', as most couples generally do. But there is no place for hypocrisy and pretentions in a really happy married life. In fact, Deshpande is out to explode the myth of perfectly happy wife and mother.

In her traditional role-model, Jaya had upheld the maxim that 'a husband is like a sheltering tree', and she has hardly ever stepped out of his shadow. She has reduced her wants and desires to the bare minimum. Trying to be an 'ideal' wife, and mother, Jaya always thinks of the comforts of her man — of his breakfast, lunch, tea and dinner. Mohan also expects these things from her. Mohan had named her Suhasini after their marriage. To Jaya, Suhasini has become a symbol of the painstaking and fastidious house-wife, who looks after children very well and who maintains the house in order. She regards herself as a mere travesty of the noble Gandhari who had wrapped her eyes with a piece of cloth in a supportive gesture towards her blind husband, Dhritasashtra, king of Hastinapur. Though Jaya is gifted with talent, and she can write perceptively, she has given up her hobby of writing just because Mohan does not like it. Thus, Jaya has faithfully practised the traditional role of an 'ideal' wife, allowing her talent to 'rust in unuse' (as Lord Tennyson would express it). She even turns a blind eye towards her husband's illegal means of earning and corrupt practices.

Jaya's supportive and submissive role proves detrimental to her creative talent. She stops writing about the oppressed women, — a subject in which her imagination soared high. So much so that she compromises on the quality of her writing, and now writes about silly and nonsense things for a magazine which do not satisfy her intellectual requirements. She writes the Seeta column for this magazine, and comes to believe that everyone likes it. It caters to the taste of Mohan, editors and readers. But later on, in her moments of self-analysis and self-scrutiny, she realizes that the Seeta column — a patriarchal construct, no doubt — is :

> The means through which I had shut the door, firmly, on all those women who invaded my being, screaming for my attention; women.... I could not write about, because they might resemble Mohan's mother, or aunt, or my mother, or aunt. Seeta was safer (p. 149).

Thus, Jaya has deliberately annihilated the creative aspect of her personality by ignoring the subject of women's suffering which is so close to her heart. In accepting the role of a traditional housewife, she has actually negated her own 'self,' her own identity. Definitely she is not another Urmila, but she can easily be another Indu (who is also a writer of a sort). Jaya, as we find her in the novel, finally decides to come out of the cocoon when life becomes intolerable to her. Her stay at the Dadar flat makes her realize that she has really distanced herself from her true inner self and that this distancing is due to her desire to act according to the wishes and patterns of others. So long she has acted as her father's daughter, as Mohan's wife, and as her children's mother, without realizing that she has a personality too and that she has an independent existence of her own. Hence, she firmly resolves to break the icy silence which has plagued her family since long. She wants to get back to her old, happy days by setting the present situation on a right track. Now she decides to "...plug that 'hole in the heart' ...I will have to speak, to listen, I will have to ease that long silence between us." (p. 192). This decision is her own and she now moves towards 'setting limits.' This decision may not be so drastic or so startling, but it is of far-reaching significance in the conjugal life of Jaya and Mohan. Clearly, it will break the ice in the relationship of wife and husband. It is to the credit of Jaya that she takes the initiative in this matter. No one's pride is at stake. Moreover, it promises a happy life of understanding between the two, and if they have learnt the right lesson out of the present imbroglio they will not create such a situation again. Jaya's initiative in breaking 'that long silence' is decidedly a welcome step towards restoring normalcy and happiness in the family. Through her the novelist wants to send a message to the entire humanity as to where lie the roots of domestic joy and bliss.

III

A feminist reading of *That Long Silence* leads us to believe that it is primarily a domestic novel, like the fictional works of Jane Austen. The novel does not strive towards match-hunting or match-making, as in the novels of Austen, but towards peace-making between the stung, sensitive wife and the pompous and self-centred husband. Broadly speaking, Jaya's predicament is caused by lack of communication between the couple. The moment she decides to override the false sense of pride in her — as the heroine Elizabeth does in Austen's novel, *Pride and Prejudice* — and to communicate with Mohan, a perceptible change in their behaviour is observed and the icy 'silence' creating a chasm between them is broken. Deshpande visualises a situation here which is not conducive to a harmonious relationship between man and woman. Deshpande's feminism is not so aggressive and tempestuous as that of the Western writers. The French theorists of feminism like Julia Kristeva, Helene Cixous, Luce Irigaray, and Monique Witting apply Derrida's method of deconstruction and look upon the language as a means of subjugation; they treat the structure of language as phallocentric (or phallus-dominated) and hence reject all language and literature. In their over-enthusiasm, they even call for a feminine language (*parler femme*). The Anglo-American exponents of feminism like Showalter, Gilbert, Gubar and Cheri Register also opine that woman's consciousness is much different from that of man's, and so women writers ought to be studied by their own standards and ought not be relegated to a secondary position. Combinedly, the French and Anglo-American feminists channelise their energy toward exposing the sexist modes of male authors and patriarchal practices in society and assigning an honourable place to the literary works of women writers. But Indian feminists do not adopt so stiff an attitude towards the males as their Western counterparts, though they are also culture-oriented and gender-oriented. An Indian feminist, Susie Tharu, in one of her recent articles,[7] is of the view that woman's writing in India needs resurrection and that it should be examined in a proper perspective and in a relevant literary tradition. The Indian feminist movement has arisen in the form of a pointed protest against certain social customs, like *purdah-system*, child-marriage, dowry, polygamy and *sati* (the practice of woman-burning on the husband's pyre). It is largely inspired by the spirit of 'activism' and seeks equal rights and status for women in our society. It aims at the redressal of their grievances and sufferings, such as rape, physical torture and assault, dowry-system, and divorce and desertion for whatever reasons. But Indian feminism, unlike its Western counterpart, is not bothered with problems like lesbianism or single motherhood because such things have no scope in our society. As a feminist writer, Shashi Deshpande often concentrates on the tortures and sufferings of middle-class Indian women who happen to be educated and sensitive and who are conscious of their legal, social and conjugal rights. More often than not, Deshpande highlights the household conflict between wife and husband, and this conflict operates at the emotional, intellectual and sexual levels. Deshpande is fully aware of the patriarchal set-up of Indian society, and she does not plead for any kind of confrontation or militancy between man and woman, between husband and wife. Though *That Long Silence* is cast in the feminist framework, Deshpande does not transgress the limits of Indian socio-cultural reality. As such, the novel is of immense relevance to us in the present-day socio-cultural context.

NOTES AND REFERENCES

1. Vanamala Vishwanath's interview with Shashi Deshpande, "A Woman's World.... All the Way!" *Literature Alive*, 1 : 3 (1987), p. 9.
2. Veena Mathews talking to Shashi Deshpande, "Demythfying Womanhood," *The Times of India*, dated 25th September 1995, p. 8.
3. Shashi Deshpande, *That Long Silence*; 1988 (New Delhi : Penguin India Ltd., 1989), p. 27.
   — Subsequent reference to this text are absorbed in the body of the paper.
4. ——, *The Dark Holds No Terrors*; 1980 (New Delhi : Penguin Books, 1990), p. 10.
   — Subsequent reference to this text are given in the paper itself.
5. ——, *Roots and Shadows*; 1983, (New Delhi : Disha Books, 1992), p. 90.
   — Subsequent reference to this text are absorbed in the body of the paper.
6. ——, *The Binding Vine* (New Delhi : Penguin Books, 1993).
   — Subsequent references to this text are given in the paper itself.
7. See Susie Tharu's article, "Is There a Tradition of Women's Literature?" *The Literary Criterion*, XXI, 1 and 2 (1986), pp. 103–114.

16

REVERSING THE GEAR : A CRITIQUE OF *THE GOD OF SMALL THINGS*

The phenomenal popularity of Arundhati Roy's *The God of Small Things* compels our attention in a serious way. The fact that it has sold about nine million copies the world over and has been translated into as many as twenty-nine languages puts a stamp on its unprecedented popularity. The winning of the coveted Booker Prize in 1997 simply confirms this enviable popularity in 'the realms of gold' (to use a Keatsian expression). This kind of popularity prompts us all the more to critically examine this novel thoroughly, without being swept away by extraneous — non-academic and non-literary — considerations.

In the first instance, a literary star ascending the sky with a single shot arouses doubts and distrusts in the reader's mind. Whether Arundhati Roy will be able to come out of the circle of doubts with her worthwhile future works is a difficult proposition. In fact, she has confessed in one of her interviews that she is not sure to bring out another novel of the same popularity and recognition. This statement creates a situation of uncertainty about her future writing programme. No doubt, Roy has surpassed several writers with a single lucky stroke, but it is likely that the springs of her imagination go dry and she may never attain that height again. To make a hasty judgment at this juncture will merely weaken her case. This will help her in moving about freely with an inflated ego and a false aura, which is dangerous to a creative writer. I therefore suggest that we should allow the euphoria to settle down, and then make a cool-headed and calculated assessment of her literary work and worth.

I am convinced that Arundhati Roy has written her novel with the Western readership in mind. I say so because there are certain things — what she calls 'small things' — in it that do not promote the cause of Indian aesthetics which propagates the principles of 'Satyam, Shivam, Sundaram' (Truth, Goodness and Beauty). Though there is no harm if a writer keeps the Western markets in mind, which guarantees a handsome earning, but it is a little painful and disquieting to see an Indian writer making a work of literature a mere saleable commodity. I shall cite here one or two examples to carry my point home. It is really distasteful to watch twins — a brother and a sister — to get involved in incestuous relationship :

> There is very little that anyone could say to clarify what happened next. Nothing that (in Mammachi's book) would separate Sex from Love. Or Needs from Feelings.[1]

This kind of physical contact, even if it was the twins' need, is uncalled for and totally spoils the artistic taste. It is nothing short of morbidity and vulgarity. Up to this point, the twins had maintained a spiritual bond, but now suddenly they break 'the Love Laws,' as the writer puts it. This breaking of 'the Love Laws' is quite irrelevant and undesirable.

Similarly, the entire fourth chapter titled "Abhilash Talkies" is like a cancer in the body of the novel. It is completely useless and purposeless, and does not add in any way to the progression of the plot. After reading this chapter, it is evident that the writer has set her eye either on swelling the size of the novel or on catching the attention of foreign readers. The chapter renders one tired and bored. The behaviour of the Orange-drink Lemon drink Man towards an innocent boy, Estha, at the Refreshment Counter during the film-interval is unquestionably objectionable. But it is in the nature of Arundhati Roy to exult in lewd and lecherous scenes. This is how he writes about the man-boy encounter :

> 'New if you'll kindly hold this for me; the Orange-drink Lemon-drink Man said, handing Estha his penis through his soft white muslin dhoti. 'I'll get you your drink. Orange? Lemon?' (p. 103).

And she does not stop here and moves forward :

> Then the gristly-bristly face of the Man contorted, and Estha's hand was wet and hot and sticky. It had egg white on it. White egg white. Quarter-boiled (p. 104).

The beastly act of the man causes headache and vomiting for Estha. All this is useless and serves no purpose in the text. The entire episode is smelly, stinky, and un-aesthetic, and it would have been much better if she avoided it.

Elsewhere also Arundhati Roy shows her expertise in depicting erotic and passionate scenes, as in the last chapter titled "The Cost of Living" where man-woman relationship reaches full consummation. But there is a reason for it — Ammu (the mother of the twins) has been a day-dreamer having afternoon-mares, and as an abandoned woman she remains unrequited physically. Roy, in portraying the restless feelings and passions of Ammu, is more womanlike, more earthy, more natural. She is not so perverted and unnatural here as in "Abhilash Talkies" (pp. 94-123). Ammu's divorced and lonely life pays its full price in the last chapter. She always longs to get united to Velutha, a Paravan. Being highly dreamy by nature, presumably through her dreams she fulfils her unsatisfied desires. The writer paints her consummation in unequivocal terms :

> Ammu, naked now, crouched over Velutha, her mouth on his. He drew her hair around them like a tent. She slid further down, introducing herself to the rest of him. His neck. His nipples. His chocolate stomach. She sipped the last of the river from the hollow of his navel. She pressed the heat of his erection against her eyelids. She tasted him, salty, in her mouth.... She felt his belly tighten under her, hard as a board. She felt her wetness

> slipping on his skin. He took her nipple in his mouth and cradled her other breast in his callused palm. Velvet gloved in sandpaper.
>
> At the moment that she guided him into her, she caught a passing glimpse of his youth, his *youngness*, the wonder in his eyes at the secret he had unearthed and she smiled down at him as though he was her child (p. 336).

And Further :

> Once he was inside her, fear was derailed and biology took over. The cost of living climbed to unaffordable heights; though later, Baby Kochamma would say it was a Small Price to Pay....
>
> She was as wide and deep as a river in spate. He sailed on her waters. She could feel him moving deeper and deeper into her. Frantic. Frenzied. Asking to be let in further. Further. Stopped only by the shape of her. The shape of him. And when he was refused, when he had touched the deepest depths of her, with a sobbing, shuddering sigh, he drowned (pp. 336-37).

This intense — highly intense, almost volcanic — relationship between a man and a woman is quite understandable, but not the one we come across in "Abhilash Talkies."

Artistically speaking, Arundhati Roy employs crisp and racy language in her novel, and her similes and metaphors are very accurate and arresting. For instance, "Rahel's new teeth were waiting inside her gums, like words in a pen" (p. 37), and "She put her rosary back into her blouse where she kept it with her melons" (p. 81). Obviously, her spicy and racy style is her *forte*. Her language is littered with South Indian names and nuances, which call for a suitable glossary to explain them to her readers, especially the Western ones. Her prose is appealing, having the hurried motion of a swiftly flowing stream, but at times it becomes wordy and rhetorical. Here is an example of it :

> So old a boat that it had taken root. Almost. A grey old *boat* plant with *boatflowers* and *boatfruit*. And underneath, a *boat-shaped* patch of withered grass. A scurrying, hurrying *boatworld* (p. 202).

The 'boat' being described here assumes the shape and significance of the earth on which plants, flowers and fruits grow. This happens due to the twisting capacity of the novelist — twisting the word (or words) in such a fashion that it loses its place and identity. Commenting on this capacity of Arundhati Roy, C.D. Narasimhaiah writes :

> We soon become aware the novelist has a palpable design — to create an effect, not by her keenness of observation of what is *there* but by the manipulation of words — the words don't mediate experience as she is busy peddling them. Consequently what started as a place in the first two sentences [of Chapter One] becomes *any place*, *with her* seeking in vain to invest airy nothing with a local habitation and a name. This is so in both the paragraphs. 'Mental bombasts,' as Coleridge would have called it, with a feeling *for words*, not *into* them.[2]

Very clearly, Narasimhaiah is not happy with Roy's verbosity and longwindedness, her use of lines and colours and particularly her words. To quote Narasimhaiah once more :

> To invoke the Sanskrit concepts, her *atyukti* [verbal excess] offends against *auchitya* [propriety, authenticity]. In fact this may be said pervasive through the whole book. The reader can see how the narrative is made to halt frequently for pictorial display. *Chitrakavya* long ago brought upon itself an inferior status in Indian Poetics.[3]

Being an architect by profession. Arundhati Roy draws pictures in her work by means of words, and occasionally she overdoes it.

Though Roy displays her dexterity in coining and compounding words (for example, 'thiswayandthat,' p. 101; 'stop it' becomes 'stoppited,' p. 141), greater is her propensity for word-distortion (for example, 'Locusts Stand I' for "Locus Standi,' p. 57; and 'Myooezick' for 'music; p. 95). Frequently she slips into the fault of carelessly using punctuation marks and capital letters. For instance,

> She used her windows for specific purposes. For a *Breath of Fresh Air*. To *Pay* for the *Milk. To Let Out a Trapped Wasp*... (p. 28) Italics mine.

And :

> She deemed them *Capable of Anything* (p. 29). Italics mine;

I imagine, this has been done to emphasise a point. Roy also takes the liberty of truncating words at times (*e.g.,* 'Never. The. Less' for 'Neverthelss'). There are also truncated expressions in the novel; for example, "Rahel followed Estha to his room. Ammu's room. Once" (p. 91). But it is to the credit of Roy that she has made witty and humorous-occasionally ironical-remarks at many places in it :

> History's smell.
> Like old roses on a breeze (p. 55).

And again :

> When the gurgling, bubbling sound came, she [Baby Kochamma] listened with her eyes. A yellow brook burbled through a mountain pass (p. 95).

The first passage contains brilliant imagery in it. And the second one presents a graphic picture of a fatty woman urinating and watching the 'yellow water' jetting forth. The second one is free from inhibitions and becomes somewhat modernistic in details. The woman writer tends to be a little vulgar and ironical in imagery. In fact, nothing is sacrosanct for this perennial joker, this master blaster.

In an on-stage interview by Alice Traux, the editor of the *New Yorker*, Arundhati Roy was asked certain questions after her reading of the excerpts from *The God of Small Things* at the Asia Society in New York. One of the questions related to her employment of the unexpected full stops, rogue capital letters and unpredictable punctuation, and she answered with her usual gusto that "it was because she hadn't studied grammar."[4] This is certainly a cryptic reply to unarm the critics, but she has certainly derailed from the accepted norms of grammar.

Scholars like C.D. Narasimhaiah have found fault with Arundhati Roy's locale. Narasimhaiah remarks : "No, it isn't Kerala, it is Roy's fanciful picture, with remote resemblance to Kerala…"[5] Roy's portrayal of Ayemenem, of the History House, of the Pickles & Preserves Factory and of the 'Chi…Chi…Chi…' people living there, is enveloped in vagueness and darkness. A 'fanciful picture' of a locale is tolerable; even Shakespeare gave 'airy nothing' a local habitation and a name — but the labyrinthine story moving indistinctly in a linear way, the weak characterization, and the over-all vague atmosphere are some of the unpardonable blemishes in a novel. When Hardy created his Egdon Heath or R.K. Narayan his Malgudi, they did not present vague outlines merely, and this is what Roy should have remembered.

Perhaps 'smallness' is the watchword for the novelist here. The title of the novel is a pointer to this fact. Who is this 'God of Small Things?' As the text clarifies, he is :

> The God of Loss? The God of Small Things? The God of Goose Bumps and Sudden Smiles? Of Sourmetal Smells — like steel bus-rails and the smell of the bus conductor's hands from holding them? (p. 217).

This 'God' is undeniably related to Ammu's dreamworld. Many a time the hint is thrown in the text that Ammu, the frustrated and sex-hungry mother of the twins, is a great dreamer. In one place, we find : "There are big dreams and little ones" (p. 89). The 'little dreams' constitute an integral part of 'Small Things.' Hence Ammu's dreams of 'the one-armed man' are directly linked with 'the God of Small Things.' Ammu is such a great dreamer that her children are afraid of disturbing her in her dreams. Speaking of her mother, Rahel remarks : 'She says you should never wake dreaming people suddenly... She says they could easily have a Heart Attack" (p. 217). Ammu often dreamt of "a cheerful man with one arm [holding] her close by the light of an oil lamp. He had no other arm with which to fight the shadows that flickered around him on the floor" (p. 215). This is precisely what we discover in the chapter titled "The God of Small Things." In Chapter 20 also Ammu is leaning against the bedroom door in the dark, neglected. She slips into her afternoon-mare (day-dream), and the "cheerful one-armed man with salty skin and a shoulder" emerges from the shadows of the jagged beach and walks towards her. Who is this man?

> The God of Loss.
> The God of Small Things.
> The God of Goose Bumps and Sudden Smiles (p. 330).

He could do only one thing at a time, as the writer informs us :

> If he touched her, he couldn't talk to her, if he loved her he couldn't leave, If he spoke he couldn't listen, if he fought he couldn't win.

Earlier in Chapter 11, the same sort of information is given about this one-armed man :

> If he held her [Ammu], he couldn't kiss her. If he kissed her, he couldn't see her. If he saw her, he couldn't feel her (p. 215).

Ammu longed for this man feverishly and ached for him with the whole of her biology. And this need of her biology is fulfilled in Chapter 21 through her dream. Evidently, the title indicates that these two lovers in life practised 'small things' clandestinely because society would not permit them to practise them openly. The following extract corroborates this truth :

> ...they stuck to the Small Things. The Big Things ever lurked inside. They knew that there was nowhere for them to go. They had nothing. No future. So they stuck to the small things (p. 338).

Thus, 'the Small Things' in the title of the novel suggests the fulfilment of sexual hunger. Hence the title is a pointer to the unrequited love of Ammu and Velutha.

This 'smallness' in living conditions necessarily leads to despair and frustrations (as clearly witnessed in the case of Mammachi, Baby Kochamma, Ammu, and the twins), to death and destruction (as seen in the case of Velutha and his family). Even Chacko and Margaret are unhappy, especially after the sad demise of their daughter, Sophie Mol, who got drowned in the river Meenachal. The financial constraints add to the misery of the Mamachi's family.

To win a Booker Prize is a great occasion for a writer to be happy and proud. And for Roy it is all the more so because it is her first attempt. But whether it is V.S. Naipaul or Salman Rushdie or Arundhati Roy, he/she knows the tricks of the trade. The writer knows *how* to make the work alluring for the Western readers, even to the grand juries sitting on judgment seats. In the case of Roy, the five-member panel of jury was presided over by a female professor, and they found *The God of Small Things* to be 'spell-binding' and 'wonderful.' The reaction of Arundhati Roy on winning the Booker Prize is contained in the following extract :

> About the success of the book and it being nominated for the Booker, I felt I was being coopted into a place where I didn't want to go or where I didn't want to be. True, it was a tremendous honour. But with all that betting going on, I felt humiliated. And yet, with all the ups and downs and the antics of the bookies, I began to hanker to win.... It was a complicated feeling.

The above reaction of the novelist is contradictory in nature — "...where I didn't want to go or where I didn't want to be" and "...I began to hanker to win it..."

As a writer of the Nineties, Roy is a representative of the current Indian Writing in English. She seems to be a harsh critic of the traditional way of Indian life, especially the one that Indian women have been leading. However, in matters of love and sex, Chacko's Western style of living is not much different from Ammu's Indian life. Clearly, Roy is modernistic in her approach to life as well as to art. Her style of writing and her language show that. But she should have nurtured the social and cultural values of India. If she attempts to cut asunder the age-old caste and creed shackles through the Ammu-Velutha meetings, one can understand her viewpoint. If she advocates the liberation of Indian woman from the clutches of a patriarchal society, it is tolerable. Even if she tries to please the West through her spicy style, language and technique, it is also not objectionable. But if a writer tries to negate the social and cultural ethos of a great nation as ours and if he/she forgets the primary objective of Indian aesthetics and moral values, then he/she is committing a blunder. And Roy falls into the trap of this blunder. She must remember that Toru Dutt — "this child of the green valley of the Ganges"[6] — was deeply rooted in her soil when she wrote *Ancient Ballads and Legends of Hindustan* (1982) and that Srojini Naidu remained perfectly 'autochthonous' in her poetry after the salutary advice of Sir Edmund Gosse that she should reveal the heart of India and her multifaceted personality. Gosse had advised 'the Nightingale of India' to make poetry out of "some sincere, penetrating analysis of native passion, of the principles of antique religion, and of the soul-stirring mysterious intimations of the East."[7] Even in our own day, we have a number of women writers in English like Kamala Markandaya, Anita Desai, Shashi Deshpande and others who continually portray the variegated pictures of India — her social, moral, religious and political ethos. They have presented Indian women along with their burning problems, and know their experience in the context of their social and cultural milieu. But Arundhti Roy rather toes the line of Shobha De and Sasthi Brata in order to earn popularity fast.

To conclude, *The God of Small Things* is Arundhati Roy's first novel, and it would be a little premature to set a high premium on it. Though she herself is an architect and a screen-writer, she does not show any concern for the 'architectonic quality' of novel building in her work. In this matter, she comes nowhere beside Hardy. Also, her locale is colourless and vague, as pointed out by Narasimhaiah. There are, no doubt, signs of skill and dexterity in her art, especially in dealing with language and imagery, but how will her 'future' be secure without a companion volume to *The God of Small Things*? She will have to prove that her imagination has not gone dry and infertile. The same question was raised by the *New Yorker* reporter when he was discussing the prospect of *The God of Small Things*. "Where is the future?"[8] asked he. And I, for one, fully subscribe to this viewpoint.

NOTES AND REFERENCES

1. Arundharti Roy, *The God of Small Things*. New Delhi : Indialnk, 1997, p. 328.
2. C.D. Narasimhaiah., "The Booker Prize : A Curse to Creativity : Arundhati Roy, *The God of Small Things* (1997)," *The Literary Criterion* (Winter 1997), p. V.
3. *Ibid.*
4. Cited from *The Hindustan Times*, Lucknow ed., 16 May 1998, p. 10.
5. *Ibid.*
6. H.A.L. Fisher, "Foreword" to *The Life and Letters of Toru Dutt* by Harihar Das. London : Oxford University Press, 1921, p. VII.
7. Sir Edmund Gosse, "Introduction," *The Bird of Time*. London : William Heinemann, 1912, p. 4.
8. *The Now Yorker*, June 1997.

17

SETTING THE SCALE STRAIGHT : SOCIO-POLITICAL CONCERNS IN ARUNDHATI ROY'S FICTION

In the galaxy of contemporary Indian English fictionists, Arundhati Roy is a shinning star. She has not written much — just one novel entitled *The God of Small Things* (1997) — to date, but she has earned a good deal of popularity as well as the coveted Booker Prize for it. The novel under review is to be marked for its socio-political concerns, its tasty and spicy prose style, its expert handling of the English language (which has been tailored to the needs on hand), its unmistakable Kerala background, and its graphic portrayal of characters (both male and female). It is but natural that it has evoked considerable response from reviewers and scholars, sometimes even mixed response from some of them, and therein lies the verve and vitality of this work. Here in this paper, I shall examine this remarkable novel from the angle of its unmistakable socio-political concerns which have endeared it to the general reading public. In my earlier paper on *The God of Small Things* published in *Points of View,*[1] I had become somewhat critical of Arundhati Roy for her western slant, for her flouting of Indian aesthetics, for her waywardness in the use of punctuation and grammar, for her deliberate distortions of the English language, for her labyrinthine story, and for her exultation in depicting some undesirable, lustful and lecherous scenes (including the Estha-Orangedrink, Lemondrink Man encounter), but in the present paper I have concentrated on her brilliant execution of some burning social and political issues of our times, and thus I have set the scale straight.

One of the dominant socio-political concerns in Arundhati's novel is the rigid caste-structure to be seen in India. This caste-oriented rigidity sometimes plays havoc with the innumerable innocent lives. The 'bigness' of 'big things' and 'big people' should be read in their generous and compassionate understanding of 'small things' and 'small people.' Unfortunately, in the present-day Indian society, this is not to be, and the inevitable consequence is tragic and claustrophobic. The weaker sections of our society — like the Paravans, the Scheduled Castes and Scheduled Tribes, the dalits and the have-nots — inescapably suffer a good deal in the process of caste-stratifications. Arundhati Roy vividly portrays the acute suffering and deep frustration of these sections in her novel. Kelan, Vellya Paapen, and Velutha are the representatives of such sections, precisely of the Untouchables. The Paravan Velutha, whom we may call the male protagonist of the novel, is looked down upon and maltreated herein almost at every stage in his life. As a small boy, when he visits the Ayemenem House in the company of his father to deliver the coconuts plucked from the trees in the compound, they come from the back entrance; as a young man, he is suspiciously treated by Comrade K.N.M. Pillai for being a card-holder of the Communist Party; and later as a mature man, he is falsely implicated in a case of attempted rape of Ammukutty (who actually loves him from the core of her heart) and is beaten badly and dragged to the police station by the Touchable Policemen where he eventually breathes his last.

Arundhati powerfully portrays the miserable condition of the Paravans (untouchables) in *The God of Small Things*. This is how the touchables like Pappachi and Mammachi treat them :

> Pappachi would not allow Paravans into the house. Nobody would. They were not allowed to touch anything that Touchables touched. Caste Hindus

> and Caste Christians. Mammachi told Estha and Rahel that she could remember a time, in her girlhood, when Paravans were expected to crawl backwards with a broom, sweeping away their footprints so that Brahmins or Syrian Christians would not defile themselves by accidentally stepping into a Paravan's footprint. In Mammachi's time, Paravans, like other Untouchables, were not allowed to walk on public roads, not allowed to cover their upper bodies, not allowed to carry umbrellas. They had to put their hands over their mouths when they spoke, to divert their polluted breath away from those whom they addressed.[2]

When the British arrived in Malabar, a number of Paravans, Pelayas and Pulayas (among whom Kelan, Velutha's grandfather, was one) converted to Christianity and joined the Anglian Church to escape the scourge of Untouchability. They came to be known as Rice-Christians because they were given some food and money by the British. But there too, they suffered humiliation and caste-distinction. They came to realize their predicament when they "were made to have separate churches, with separate services, and separate priests" (p. 75). The dawn of Independence slightly improved their condition, but the novelist sees no such improvement because they were not entitled to "any Government benefits like job reservations or bank loans at low interest rates..." (p. 74). As for Velutha, Mammachi takes pity on him and asks his father to send him to the Untouchables' School and later employs him as a skilled carpenter in her factory called Paradise Pickles and Preserves. She is also convinced that Velutha has the skills of an engineer who can mend radios, clocks and water-pumps. By nature, he is bold, fearless and adventurous. As contrasted to him, his father remains humble and servile, as he is "an Old World Paravan" (p. 76). He does not conceal the secret bonds of love between his son and Ammu, who night after night row across the river Meenachal in a little boat and meet at the haunted house, returning only at dawn. Bringing the matter to his benefactor Mammachi's notice, he tells her all what he has seen. He asks God's forgiveness for having spawned a monster. He offers to kill his son with his own bare hands (p. 78).

Subsequently, as we learn from the novel, Ammu and Velutha turn deep lovers of each other, throwing away all scruples of caste, creed and community. Ammu being a great dreamer, even in daytime, dreams of "a cheerful man with one arm" (p. 215) who leaves "no footprints in sand, no ripples in water, no image in mirrors" (p. 216). In fact, this is the fate of all the Untouchables in the dark alleys of History. Arundhati Roy successfully evokes the image of such footprintless men in her novel, and the image grows insistent as the novel progresses.[3] Velutha is simply a representative of such men, but being fiery and haughty in temper he does not sweep off his footprints with a broom, though his grandfather and father would have gladly done so. Consequently, the circumstances around him grow hostile and he is finally eliminated and his 'footprints' are totally erased by the caste-conscious society. As a Comrade, he is despised by his own party men, including comrade K.N.M. Pillai who believes that "these caste issues are very deep-rooted" (p. 278), and as an Untouchable he is not entitled to love someone of a high caste and yet survive. Baby Kochamma and Mammachi get enraged at Ammu's unwarranted behaviour and enter into a conclave and chalk out a plan of eliminating Velutha for good. The next day, Baby Kochamma reaches the Police Station and lodges a complaint against Velutha for having forced himself on her niece — "A divorcee with two children" (p. 259). On the basis of this complaint, Inspector Thomas Mathew and his touchable men barge into Velutha's house, beat him cruelly with their boots and batons, lock his arms across his back, drag him bleeding and mutilated to the police station, and throw him into the lock-up, where he eventually dies in midnight. In this way, Arundhathi has marvelously handled the theme of 'Untouchability' in her novel.

The novelist also takes up the cause of the oppressed women for a sharp focus. Though Mammachi, Baby Kochamma, and

Margaret are all sufferers in the drama of life, it is Ammukutty who suffers worst and through whom Arundhati Roy raises her banner of revolt against a male-dominated, patriarchal society. As a child, she is almost neglected by her parents who are actually an ill-mated pair (Mammachi is subjected to all kinds of ill-treatment by her scientist husband Pappachi). At that stage, she develops "a lofty sense of injustice and the mulish reckless streak that develops in Someone Small who has been bullied all their lives (*sic*) by Someone Big" (p. 182). Ammu is neither properly educated nor exposed to the proper sorts of books or people. So, she is "that sort of animal" who is brought up by "a monstrous, suspicious bully" (p. 180). When she grows up, she marries a man of her choice, a Bengali, but the marriage proves abortive. The Bengali drinks too heavily and goes morally bankrupt. He even offers his beautiful wife to his white officer to avoid a transfer in his duty. She takes no time in deciding that she should now leave her drunken husband along with her two children and return to Ayemenem to live with Mammachi and Baby Kochamma. Meanwhile, the cheerful, one-armed man starts visiting her in her dreams and she casts aside all social norms and conventions to enjoy 'the forbidden pleasures' with him at the haunted house. Now, who is this man? Answering this question herself, the novelist suggests that he is —

> The God of Loss.
> The God of Small Things.
> The God of Goose Bumps and Sudden Smiles (p. 330).

Ammu aches for this man with the whole of her biology, and gets united to him at long last, setting aside all social prescriptions and breaking 'the Love Laws' that "lay down who should be loved. And how. And how much" (p. 328). In doing so, she asserts her rights over her body; after all, it is hers. She does not bother about the purity of her future generations. That may be the botheration of Mammachi and Kochamma or of Inspector Thomas Mathew who has "a Touchable wife, Two Touchable daughters — whole Touchable generations waiting in their Touchable wombs..." (p. 259), and yet who dares to continuously tap Ammu's breasts with his baton as though he is "choosing mangoes from a basket" (p. 8), pointing out the ones he wants packed and delivered. In asserting her rights over her body, Ammu evidently becomes a liberated woman or a feminist.[4] Through her, Arundhati raises her strong protest against the age-old agonies and sufferings of the suppressed class of women. For Ammu, the traditional society turns tyrannical and revengeful, and the eventual outcome is disastrous (as it was to Velutha, her lover).

Apart from what we have observed above, there is yet another social evil — that of child-abuse and child-negligence — prevalent in our country which has been highlighted by the novelist in *The God of Small Things*. Anyone reading Chapter 4 of the novel is at first simply revulsed and shockingly disturbed by the encounter of Estha with the Orange-drink, Lemon-drink Man, but suddenly one realizes, on a second thought, that this Chapter ("Abhilash Talkies") is written with a different purpose in view[5] — to bring to the fore the question of child-abuse and child-negligence in our society. In a moment of negligence by the mother, the boy Estha saunters away to the Refreshment Counter during the film-interval where the Orangedrink, Lemondrink Man physically abuses him. This is how the perverted man behaves with the innocent boy :

> Now if you'll kindly hold this for me; the Orangedrink, Lemondrink Man said, handling Estha his penis through his soft white muslin dhoti, I'll get you your drink. Orange? Lemon? (p. 103).

The novelist does not stop there and goes a step ahead as a realist to describe the ejaculation of this bastard in the following manner :

> Then the gristly-bristly face [of the man], contorted and Estha's hand was wet and hot and sticky. It had egg white on it. White egg white. Quarter-boiled (p. 104).

Consequently, the boy develops headache and starts vomiting. What the beastly man does is highly unethical and unnatural.

Arundhati has definitely succeeded, through this episode, in raising the issue of child-abuse and child-negligence. Should I mention here that the untimely and tragic death of Sophie Mol over the river is another instance of child-negligence? If as a mother of two girls, Arundhati raises such issues she is perfectly justified.

Arundhati Roy also ponders over certain political developments in India, such as the dawn of Independence, the formation of the Congress Government at the Centre, and the spread of Communism in Kerala and West Bengal. In her view, the Indian society riven by caste considerations and religious prejudices has not improved even after Independence. This is what we gather from the following extract :

> After Independence they [Christians] found they were not entitled to any Government benefits like job reservations or bank loans at low interest rates, because, officially, on paper, they were Christians, and, therefore, casteless (p. 74).

This is certainly a dig at the Congress Government, but it is somewhat coloured and distorted. Arundhati, however, keeps her wrath and indignation reserved for the Communists and their Party owing their allegiance to an external power. Whether she has been able to evoke the Kerala locale in her novel or not,[6] she has remarkably portrayed the nature of functioning of Communism in her State through the characters of Comrade K.N.M. Pillai and Comrade E.M.S. Namboodiripad.

Comrade Pillai is introduced in the very first Chapter of the novel. His printing press — Lucky Press — was once the Ayemenem office of the Communist Party, where midnight study meetings were held and pamphlets of the party were printed and distributed. Pillai is depicted as "essentially a political man" and as "a professional omeletteer." And further : "He walked through the world like a chameleon. Never revealing himself, never appearing not to. Emerging through chaos unscathed" (p. 14). Pillai is not repentant, as he was not responsible, for what had happened to Velutha and Ammu, though he vividly recalls their tragic end. In Chapter 4, Pillai's political ambitions come out clearly and he aspires to fight the Kottayam by-elections to the Legislative Assembly. To remain in the limelight, he incites the workers of the factory (Paradise Pickless & Preserves) to demand yearly bonus, provident fund, and accident insurance, knowing fully well that the factory is running into a heavy debt. But he never comes out openly against Chacko, the factory-manager. Similarly, he is jealous of Velutha for his being the only card-holder of the Communist Party, but he does not vent his feelings in public. Pillai wants to organize the factory workers into a labour union. In short, Pillai is portrayed as a suspicious and scheming man, who always looks to his personal gains and advances in life.

Comrade Namboodiripad is worst hit by the novelist. He is owner of the History House — a five-star hotel chain — across the river which is spacious enough, with its air-tight and panelled storeroom, to feed an army for a year. This is his ancestral home, and here he is introduced to the visitors as 'Kearla's Mao Tse Tung.' In Chapter 2, the novelist tries to explain as to why Communism is so successful in Kerala, perhaps in Bengal too. The main reasons suggested by her are : (1) it has something to do with the large population of Christians in Kerala, and Marxism is a simple substitute for Christianity : "Replace God with Marx, Satan with the bourgeoisie, Heaven with a classless society, the Church with the Party, and the form and purpose of the journey remained similar" (p. 66) and (2) it has to do something with the comparatively high level of literacy in the State. The novelist, however, hastens to add that the second reason is not due to the Communist movement, and that Communism crept into Kerala insidiously. As a reformist movement, it never "overtly questioned the traditional values of a caste-ridden, extremely traditional community." According to her, the Marxists "worked from *within* the communal divides, never challenging them, never appearing not to" (p. 67). Then, she furnishes the details of the Communists winning the State Assembly Elections and E.M.S. Namboodiripad heading the Government as the Chief Minister. Suddenly, the

Communists find themselves in a piquant situation — having to govern a people and foment revolution simultaneously. Namboodiripad evolved his own theory to enforce land reforms, neutralising the police, subvert the judiciary, and to restrain the Congress Government at the Centre. Ironically enough, the peaceful part of the Peaceful Transition comes to an end even before the year is out, and the Marxists frequently resort to riots and strikes and the incidents of police brutality shake the whole of Kerala. Within the next two years, Kerala is on the brink of a civil war, and Nehru dismisses the Communist Government, announcing fresh elections. The Congress Party returns to power. But after a gap of ten years, the Communists led by E.M.S. Namboodiripad come to power again in Kerala. At that time, Kerala was reeling in the aftermath of famine and hunger. Comrade Namboodiripad implemented the Peaceful Transition soberly this time, but this also earned him "the wrath of the Chinese Communist Party" (p. 68), which accused him of providing relief to the people and thereby blunting the edge of intended revolution. Now, Peking started patronising the Naxalites, the most militant faction of the Communist Party of India (M), who had staged an armed resurrection in Naxalbari, a village in Bengal, and who had organized peasants into fighting cadres, seized land, expelled the owners and established the People's Court to try Class Enemies. In due course, the Naxalite movement spread across the country and struck terror in every human heart. In Kerala, a landlord in Palghat was tied to a lamp-post and beheaded. All this happened because Marxism upheld "the doctrine of class struggle and the dependence of all forms of consciousness upon class interests."[7] The killing of the landlord is what Mikhail Lifshitz calls the outcome of "the struggle between the bourgeoisie and the nobility."[8] The terrorist activities of the Naxalites compelled Namboodiripad to expel them from his Party, while he himself continued "the business of harnessing anger for parliamentary purposes" (p. 69). Thus, Arundhati treats Namboodiripad as a double-dealer and cunning politician, having set his eyes on power. She calls him a "Running Dog, Soviet

Stooge" (p. 69), an outrageous statement no doubt. All the same, her treatment of Communism and its governance in Kerala is comprehensive enough to enable us to form an idea about it.

To conclude, Arundhati Roy has raised certain raging social and political problems of our times in her wonderful novel, *The God of Small Things*. Her preoccupations with the socio-political concerns of modern India render her a powerful writer rooted in ground reality. Whether "literary prizes" are "nationalistic events" or not[9] — a question raised by the *New Yorker* reviewer while commenting on Madame Roy's novel — it is a matter of gratification to us all that Arundhati has highlighted some of the burning socio-political issues of our nation in her novel. Her recent active involvement in the 'Narmada Bachao Andolan' (*i.e.*, 'Save Narmada Movement') along with Medha Patekar and Sripad Dharmadhikari further consolidates this fact and displays the direction of her socio-political thinking in an unambiguous way.

NOTES AND REFERENCES

1. This paper appeared in *Points of View*, V, No. 2 (Winter, 1998), pp. 101–107.
2. Arundhati Roy, *The God Of Small Things* (New Delhi : India Ink Publishing Co. Pvt. Ltd. 1997), pp. 73-74.
   — Subsequent references to this work are given in the paper itself.
3. This image occurs at least six times in the novel — pp. 216-218 twice, 265, 289 and 290.
4. The noted feminist Simone de Beauvoir defines 'feminism' as "economic independence and liberation from orthodox tradition of society." *The Second Sex*, trans. And ed. H.M. Parshley (1955; Middlesex : Penguin Books, 986), p. 126.
5. I was reminded of it by an alert lady participant when I was delivering my lecture on Arundhati Roy's *The God of Small Things* at the Refresher Course being organized by the Department of English, Kurukshetra University, Kurukshetra (Haryana) in November 1998.
6. Prof. C.D. Narasimhaiah thinks that "...it isn't Kerala, it is Roy's fanciful picture, with remote resemblance to Kerala..." — "Editorial I — The Booker Prize : A Curse to Creativity : Arundhati Roy,

The God of Small Things (1997)," *The Literary Criterion* (Winter, 1997), p. v.

7. Mikhail Lifshitz, "Literature and the Class Struggle," *Literature and Marxism*, ed. Engel Flores (Allahabad : Indian Publishers, 1945), p. 77.
8. *Ibid.*, p. 81.
9. *See* John Updike, *The New Yorker* (June 23–30, 1997).

INDEX